EPIDICUS BY PLAUTUS

Epidicus by Plautus

An Annotated Latin Text, with a Prose Translation

by Catherine Tracy

https://www.openbookpublishers.com

© 2021 Catherine Tracy

This work is licensed under a Creative Commons Attribution-NonCommercial-NoDerivatives 4.0 International license (CC BY-NC-ND 4.0). This license allows you to share, copy, distribute and transmit the work for non-commercial purposes, providing attribution is made to the author (but not in any way that suggests that she endorses you or your use of the work). Attribution should include the following information:

Catherine Tracy, *Epidicus by Plautus: An Annotated Latin Text, with a Prose Translation*. Cambridge, UK: Open Book Publishers, 2021. https://doi.org/10.11647/OBP.0269

In order to access detailed and updated information on the license, please visit https://doi.org/10.11647/OBP.0269#copyright. Further details about CC BY-NC-ND licenses are available at http://creativecommons.org/licenses/by-nc-nd/4.0

Every effort has been made to identify and contact copyright holders and any omission or error will be corrected if notification is made to the publisher.

All external links were active at the time of publication unless otherwise stated and have been archived via the Internet Archive Wayback Machine at https://archive.org/web

Digital material and resources associated with this volume are available at https://doi.org/10.11647/OBP.0269#resources

ISBN Paperback: 978-1-80064-284-3
ISBN Hardback: 978-1-80064-285-0
ISBN Digital (PDF): 978-1-80064-286-7
ISBN Digital ebook (epub): 978-1-80064-287-4
ISBN Digital ebook (azw3): 978-1-80064-288-1
ISBN Digital ebook (xml): 978-1-80064-289-8
DOI: 10.11647/OBP.0269

Cover image: Marble figure of a comic actor. Roman, 1st–2nd century. Photo by Joanbanjo, Wikimedia, https://commons.wikimedia.org/wiki/File:Actor_borratxo,_exposici%C3%B3_la_Bellesa_del_Cos,_MARQ.JPG.

Cover design by Anna Gatti.

Contents

Acknowledgments	vii
Introduction	1
The Plot of *Epidicus*	12
Loose Ends	14
The Roman Theatre	16
Latin Text of *Epidicus* with Language Notes	19
Helpful Information for Reading the Latin Text	21
The Rhythm of Plautus	27
Trochaic Septenarii	27
Iambic Senarii	28
The Play in Latin	31
PERSONAE	33
ACTVS I	35
1.1 EPIDICVS, THESPRIO	35
1.2 STRATIPPOCLES, CHAERIBVLVS, EPIDICVS	46
ACTVS II	53
2.1 APOECIDES, PERIPHANES	53
2.2 EPIDICVS, APOECIDES, PERIPHANES	55
2.3 EPIDICVS	68
ACTVS III	71
3.1 STRATIPPOCLES, CHAERIBVLVS	71
3.2 EPIDICVS, STRATIPPOCLES, CHAERIBVLVS	73
3.3 PERIPHANES, APOECIDES, SERVOS	78
3.4 MILES, PERIPHANES	83
3.4a PERIPHANES, MILES, FIDICINA	86
ACTVS IV	91
4.1 PHILIPPA, PERIPHANES	91
4.2 ACROPOLISTIS, PERIPHANES, PHILIPPA	96
ACTVS V	101
5.1 STRATIPPOCLES, EPIDICVS, DANISTA, TELESTIS	101
5.2 PERIPHANES, APOECIDES, EPIDICVS	108
Translation of Plautus's *Epidicus*	117
About the Translation	119

The Play in English		123
Cast of Characters		125
Setting		127
ACT 1		129
1.1	Scene with Epidicus and Thesprio	129
1.2	Scene with Stratippocles, Chaeribulus, and Epidicus	135
ACT 2		139
2.1	Scene with Apoecides and Periphanes	139
2.2	Scene with Epidicus, Periphanes, and Apoecides	140
2.3	Scene with Epidicus	147
ACT 3		149
3.1	Scene with Stratippocles and Chaeribulus	149
3.2	Scene with Epidicus, Stratippocles, and Chaeribulus	150
3.3	Scene with Periphanes, Apoecides, a Slave, and the [Hired] Lyre-Player (Who Doesn't Speak in this Scene)	153
3.4	Scene with the Soldier and Periphanes (and an Unnamed, Non-Speaking Slave)	155
3.4a	Scene with Periphanes, the Soldier, and the [Hired] Lyre-Player	156
ACT 4		159
4.1	Scene with Philippa and Periphanes	159
4.2	Scene with Acropolistis, Periphanes, and Philippa	162
ACT 5		165
5.1	Scene with Stratippocles, Epidicus, the Moneylender, and Telestis	165
5.2	Scene with Periphanes, Apoecides, and Epidicus	168
Argumentum (Plot Summary)		173
Acrostic Translation of the *Argumentum*		175
Literal Translation of the *Argumentum*		177
Works Cited		179
Index		183

Acknowledgments

This project was inspired by my wonderful students at Bishop's University in Sherbrooke, Quebec (Canada), who often don't have any background in Classics but who show such enthusiasm for what is fascinating, horrifying, or just plain weird about ancient Rome. I wrote the book to encourage them to learn Latin, and to help them appreciate Plautus even if they don't know any Latin. I wish to thank the plucky students of my third-year Latin class of Fall 2020 who, pandemic notwithstanding, made their way through the Latin play with me and helped me to improve the vocabulary and grammar annotations. When they had trouble with the Latin, I knew I needed to add another footnote.

I am also exceedingly grateful to the kind and meticulous comments of Dr John Henderson, series adviser at Open Book Publishers. It was a privilege to have an expert of such high caliber to help me root out mistakes and clarify my writing.

The supportive and friendly atmosphere at Bishop's University, located on the traditional and unceded territory of the Abenaki people and the Wabenaki confederacy, gave me the time and space to work on this project, and that too was invaluable. Our small library is more than compensated for by our excellent librarians and library staff, and the inter-library loan system. My colleague and friend, Dr Rebecca Harries of the BU Drama department, has taught me a great deal over the years about the theatre. While I've always loved Plautus, I have a much better understanding of Roman drama thanks to our many delightful conversations on the practice and history of the theatre.

Thank you also to my husband, Oisín Feeley, who has always been supportive and encouraging. Finally, my love and gratitude to my daughter, Sorcha Feeley, who diligently did her remote learning during the COVID-19 pandemic without interrupting me more than a few times in any day despite how boring she found it to be learning online by herself.

Introduction

"I love the play *Epidicus* as much as I love myself," claims the wily slave Chrysalus in another of Plautus's plays (*Bacchides* 214), implying, we'd like to think, that the playwright was particularly proud of it.[1] *Epidicus* is a play that translates well and manages to be very funny despite the millennia that have passed since its original production. What makes it so appealing is the star character: the slave Epidicus. While Romans accepted the inhumanity of slavery as a fact of life (there was no ancient abolitionist movement), the plays of Plautus, and *Epidicus* in particular, show us that Roman spectators loved to see a slave outwit a stupid master, at least in the ritualized context of the *fabula palliata* (comedy set in the Greek world).[2]

The *fabulae palliatae* used stock characters that the spectators would recognize and expect to act in characteristic ways. Apuleius (second century CE) gives us a list of some of these stock characters:

> the lying pimp, the ardent lover, the wily slave, the teasing girlfriend, the wife that gets in the way, the permissive mother, the stern uncle, the helpful pal, the belligerent soldier, [...] gluttonous parasites, stingy fathers, and sassy sex workers. (Apuleius, *Florida* 16)

In other ancient lists of comic stock characters, the "father" is defined as "harsh" or "angry" or by his tendency to be tricked by his slave, the "soldier" is "boastful", and additional characters are listed as the "running slave" (usually a different character from the "wily slave"), the "dishonest procuress", the "virtuous wife", and the "shameless flatterer".[3]

Stock characters might behave according to recognizable patterns and within a limited set of plot lines, but such constraints did not hinder Plautus from creating memorable and innovative comic romps.

---

1 The line from *Bacchides* cannot be taken uncritically as Plautus's enthusiastic endorsement of *Epidicus*, however, as it was at least partly a joke (see Gunderson 2015: 228).

2 The adjective *palliata* comes from the Latin word *pallium*, referring to a cloak commonly associated with Greek male attire in which most of the actors in a *fabula palliata* were dressed. By contrast, comedy with a Roman setting, of which unfortunately only fragments survive, was called *fabula togata* (plural: *fabulae togatae*), in which at least some of the actors wore togas.

3 Plaut.us, *Captiui* 57–58; Terence, *Eunuchus* 35–40 and *Heauton Timorumenos* 37–39; Horace *Epistulae* 2.1.170–173; Ovid, *Amores* 1.15.17–18.

Reading the play today is entertaining, but it also gives us some insight into the world of mid-republican Rome (Plautus lived from about 254 BCE till 184 BCE). *Epidicus*, like all Roman comedy of the *palliata* genre, was inspired by the Greek New Comedies circulated from Athens a hundred years before. The characters have Greek names, and the action is usually supposed to take place in Athens, which does, it is true, pose a minor problem when we want to use Plautus to illustrate the world of Rome. The plays, however, were not direct translations of Greek originals. As Siobhán McElduff explains when discussing Plautus's art: "translating drama is not simply a matter of linguistic replacement (itself a complicated endeavor), but of adapting a play so that it appeals to a new audience, often one with a different set of demands and expectations" (McElduff 2013: 62). Plautus's Roman audiences enjoyed other forms of comic drama, including Atellan farces (short improvised comic skits originating in Atella, an Oscan town in Italy) and mime performances (short, low-brow comic dramas), and the exuberance of these theatrical forms doubtless influenced the spirit of the *fabulae palliatae*. It is important to understand that the *fabulae palliatae*, though strongly influenced by Greek literature, were composed for Latin-speaking Italy. The versions of the *palliata* genre that we have were adapted specifically for Roman audiences, with topical references to the city of Rome, and jokes about contemporary Roman fashions (see lines 222–235 of *Epidicus*, for example) and historical events. The Greek costumes allowed the playwrights to make jokes about Roman life that would not have been permitted by the sponsoring magistrates if the characters had been dressed in togas (Kocur 2018: 207).

Epidicus, probably one of Plautus's later plays, is a great example of Plautus adapting a basic Greek romantic plot line into an irreverent situation comedy that depicts characters (mis)behaving within a fantasy "Athens" that mixed stereotypes of Greek culture with day-to-day Roman life. Where we have evidence of the Greek source for any of Plautus's plays we see that Plautus's approach was fundamentally different to that of his Greek models, with the triumph of the underdog predominating over the Greek focus on traditional family values (Anderson 1993: 29; see also Stürner 2020).

The Greek original for *Epidicus*, if there was one, has not survived. Some scholars believe that it was based on a Greek play that made much more of the young master's love affair, and ended with his marriage to his half-sister, which would have been legal in Athens had she been a citizen, though such a marriage would not have been legal in Rome.[4] However it may have played out in the

---

4   There are two lost Greek comedies, known only by title, called *Homopatrioi* (Ὁμοπάτριοι), one by Antiphanes and the other by Menander, which may have been the model for *Epidicus* (Katsouris 1977: 321). True, Goldberg 1978 argued that we lack evidence to assume that *Epidicus* was based on a Greek script, and he found some evidence to suggest that — exceptionally — it was an original plot by Plautus. But more recent scholarship has tended to be less interested

Greek play that inspired Plautus, *Epidicus* gives us no charming love scenes, and in fact makes the young man surprisingly unappealing, so that we enjoy, rather than sympathize with, his final discomfiture when he learns that the woman he'd hoped to make into his slave- or freed-girlfriend is now out of his reach. Plautus always puts comic effect ahead of sentimentality, and in *Epidicus*, the romantic plight of the young man Stratippocles serves only to place the wily slave Epidicus in a series of situations where he must use his wits to get out of impossible situations.

What can we learn about Rome from the play *Epidicus* then? While the play gives us a ludicrously sanitized view of what it was like to be a slave, it nevertheless conveys to us the ubiquity of slavery in Rome, and it can be a useful jumping-off point for an informed reader to consider how Plautus's ancient audiences thought about slavery. The cheerful ingenuity of Epidicus can't completely hide the brutal reality of slavery: we know that the impossible situations he finds himself in are due to his abusive masters. Stratippocles, the freeborn son of the household, has the power to cause Epidicus real harm (a severe beating at the very least), so when he demands that Epidicus solve his problems for him, Epidicus has little choice but to obey. Solving the son's problems, however, means cheating his legal master Periphanes (Stratippocles's father), and if he gets found out Epidicus will suffer worse harm from him. Slave owners often kept torturers whose job was to punish slaves who angered their masters (see line 147 of this play), and we know from joking references in Plautus's comedies that slaves lived under constant threat of corporal punishment and torture.

Rome's overseas expansion during the 3rd century BCE had begun the process of turning Roman Italy from a society that owned slaves into, by the mid 2nd century BCE, what is called a "slave society", in which slavery becomes a significant element of the society's economy, and in which enslaved people have come to form a large proportion (at least 20%) of the population (Hunt 2018: 20). Men who fought in Roman wars risked enslavement if they were defeated, and if their army was victorious they helped to bring about the enslavement of the defeated soldiers as well as of the women, children, and other civilians of the captured towns and states.

Slaves in republican Rome had no right to fair treatment by their owners and no recourse when their owners abused them. There were no legal restrictions on a slave owner's right to destroy his or her slave (Dowling 2006: 12). While a small number of slaves were treated comparatively well because of their invaluable skill-sets and/or the decency of their particular owner, most lived under the very real threat of cruel punishments, such as "spikes, red-hot irons,

---

in this hypothetical source for the play, though Arnott 2001 shows how closely some elements of the play correspond to various examples of Greek New Comedy.

crosses, leg shackles, ropes, chains, prisons, restraints, leg traps, neck irons" (so listed by a slave character in another play by Plautus: *Asinaria* 548–52).

Slaves had no right to bodily autonomy, and indeed the physical and sexual abuse of slaves (male and female) was a deliberate means of subjugating them. Slaves were not only separated from their families upon enslavement but were considered no longer to have parents or ancestors (see line 340 of this play, and note 53 on page 150); they lost the right to their own names, and even if they were eventually freed, their legal name became that of their former owner. Those born into slavery likewise were deemed not to have parents in a legal sense; they might be identified as the offspring of a particular slave woman, but she had no parental rights over her children and could be sold away from them, or they could be sold away from her. When a male slave owner fathered a child by one of his female slaves, the child was automatically a slave and had no filial claim on her or his father.

In the opening scene of this play, Epidicus jokes to his fellow slave Thesprio about thieving slaves getting a hand cut off as a punishment (11–11a). Epidicus's young master (Stratippocles) threatens to have Epidicus severely beaten by the slaves his father keeps for the purpose (147) and then sent to the mill to push the treadmill if Epidicus doesn't find a way to settle Stratippocles's debt, a seemingly impossible situation for a slave, though not for the clever Epidicus (lines 121 and 145). At lines 610–626 Epidicus, who thinks that he's about to be found out and punished for his lies, expresses his fear of crucifixion, and a strong desire to run away.

The agonizing and slow form of execution known as crucifixion was reserved, in the Roman world, mainly for slaves and convicted criminals. Crucifixion involved suspending the victim on a post with or without a cross-piece, with flogging and/or disemboweling and/or impaling potentially forming part of the execution (Harley 2019: 305). Such a form of execution, even if rarely carried out, is so horrifying that we must wonder how it could be such a common subject for jokes in Roman comedy.

It is true that crucifixion never occurs within the plays, on or off stage, nor do the plays mention crucifixion as something that had been done prior to the action of the play. But crucifixion did exist as one of the methods that a real-life slave-owner had for terrorizing his or her slaves. A little over one hundred years after Plautus's time, Cicero mentions a slave owner having her slave crucified (Cicero *Pro Cluentio* 187). Cicero calls such an act "dangerous and inhuman wickedness" (*infestum scelus et immane*), but Cicero's outrage was due to the fact that the poor slave was thus prevented from bearing witness against his murderous owner, rather than due to any sympathy for the slave (the slave's testimony, had he not been crucified, would have been extracted under torture, as Roman law required). An inscription from Puteoli (a town about 200 km south of Rome) reflects the right of slave owners to have their slaves crucified, listing four sesterces as the pay for each of the labourers who were needed to carry the cross-piece (*patibulum*), for each of the floggers (*uerberatores*), and for the executioner (*carnifex*) (*AE* 1971, no. 88, II.8–10).

When, at line 78, the slave Thesprio tells Epidicus to "go get crucified", and at 513 Periphanes expresses the same wish to the hired freedwoman lyre-player, we are not meant to take the threats at face value (especially in the latter case, since the lyre-player was not a slave). No doubt these jokes found favour with the slave-owning members of the audience who probably viewed the punishment of slaves simply as a solution to the difficulties of managing their own slaves. It has been suggested, furthermore, that the joking references to crucifixion in the *fabulae palliatae* "confirm[ed] the Roman audience in its sense of superiority and power", but that the "cunning slave" is never actually crucified because his bad behaviour has all been for the benefit of the young man's love affair that the audience naturally wants to see succeed (Parker 1989: 240; 246). Another possibility is that the slave avoids the threatened punishment because his role in the comedy is to celebrate "pure anarchic fun" and to represent, for the audience, "an alternative humanity, parodic of the free citizen and released from the obligations that the demands of dignity impose on the free" (Fitzgerald 2019: 188–199). The high stakes (painful and disfiguring punishment) emphasize the slave's heroism, too.

These approaches interpret the references to slave punishment through the lens of the free spectators, but how did the slaves and former slaves in Plautus's audience respond to these jokes when crucifixion was a terrifying reality for some unfortunate slaves? Modern readers should not be deluded into thinking that the light-hearted references to such cruelty in Plautus's plays meant that no one in the ancient audiences found the idea of these punishments upsetting. Were their feelings unimportant to Plautus, or did they have a more complicated response? Applause, even from enslaved spectators, was still applause, making it unlikely that Plautus didn't care about entertaining the slaves in the audience. Jokes about abuse may have helped the slaves in the audience endure it in their own lives. It is also probable that individual slaves were able to persuade themselves that only bad slaves got punished, and that good slaves like themselves could safely laugh at the bad ones on stage (while perhaps secretly admiring the bad behaviour). Everyone could, at least, recognize how this ideology was supposed to work.

It is also likely that the torture references loomed less large for the slaves in the audience than the fact that, on stage, the wily slave magnificently dominates his master. Richlin has argued that the triumph of the wily slave on the *palliata* stage may have given voice to those who had been enslaved, and created a safe, though temporary, way for slaves and former slaves to experience the undermining of slave owners (Richlin 2020: 354–355; Richlin 2017: 26 and throughout). The slaves in Plautus's audience could thus be expected to enjoy Epidicus's triumph over his master Periphanes as a delightful though unrealistic alternative to their own less successful relationships with their masters.

Epidicus's behaviour would not, of course, have been plausible for real Roman slaves. Furthermore, since the plays produced in Rome were sponsored by magistrates from a slave-owning elite, we know the plays could not have been fundamentally subversive of slavery as an institution, however much the slaves in the audience may have enjoyed them. It is intriguing to speculate about how the slave owners in Plautus's audience reacted to the wily slave outwitting his master. Did it serve to justify their brutal control of their own slaves, or did they laugh at the helpless dupes on stage who couldn't dominate their slaves as well as they fancied they themselves did? Fitzgerald's suggestion, mentioned above, that they identified with the stage slave's ability to live without worrying about the dignity required of free citizens is certainly possible.

Epidicus references the brutality and inhumanity of slavery within a madcap and cheerful comic setting that ultimately rejoices in one (male) slave's fundamental (and fictional) power over his hapless owner, which creates a cognitive dissonance with which modern readers should attempt to engage. The plays of Plautus were, above all, fantasies. We are told that another form of comic drama in Rome (the comic *fabulae togatae*, or comedies in Roman dress) rarely included wily slaves that were cleverer than their masters (Donatus, *On the Eunuch* 57), which makes it clear that slaves outwitting their masters was a pleasure enjoyed by Roman audiences only in specific and ritualized settings.

The fantastical schemes of a clever male slave on stage, and his relationship to the lived experiences of enslaved men in the real world, give us one way to look at mid-Republican Rome. Another is to look at how Plautus depicted women, both slave and free/freed.

Epidicus shows us how vulnerable women were to mistreatment in the world of the ancient Mediterranean: the old man Periphanes had impregnated and then abandoned Philippa; years later their daughter Telestis was captured and sold as a slave; and we ought to sympathize with Acropolistis and the other sex workers who have to make their living by pleasing wealthy men, though the Roman audience generally saw them simply as desirable and rapacious (see lines 213–235 of this play).

In the plays of Plautus, women who have become sex workers greedily deplete the fortunes of the hapless men who want to buy access to their bodies, and then become clownish alcoholics when they're too old to attract customers anymore. Only women who have not yet started sex work are ever discovered to be freeborn daughters of citizens and thus worthy of marriage. Marriage in

Rome, especially among the wealthy, was about linking two families and was arranged by, or had at least to be approved by, the male head of the household (*pater familias*). The bride's chastity was an important aspect of her value as a wife, hence the unmarriageability of practicing sex workers. The misfortunes that the female characters suffer through no fault of their own may inspire a modern reader's sympathy, but in the plays self-pity is simply what women do (Dutsch 2008: 49, citing Donatus *Ad Ad*. 291.4).

The female stock characters in Plautus are divided between middle-aged (who are usually depicted as no longer desirable) and young (and thus desirable). These groups are further subdivided into the categories of freeborn citizens, free or freed non-citizens, and slaves. *Epidicus* includes examples of most of these types. Interestingly, the middle-aged freeborn woman (Philippa) is depicted as still desirable, since the old man Periphanes hopes to marry her. Philippa, in the *Epidicus*, follows the self-pitying-woman script (mentioned above), as evidenced by her opening speech and Periphanes's response:

> **Philippa:** [*weeping and wringing her hands*] If a person suffers so much that she even pities herself, then she's really pitiable. I should know: so many things are coming at me at once, breaking my heart. Trouble on top of trouble keeps me in a state of worry: poverty and fear are terrorizing me, and there's no safe place where I can pin my hopes. [*sobbing*] My daughter has been captured by the enemy, and I don't know where she may be now.
>
> **Periphanes:** [*Catching sight of Philippa*] Who is that foreign woman, coming along looking so fearful, who's moaning and pitying herself? (526–534)

It is perhaps Philippa's relative passivity and powerlessness that makes her worthy of marriage, since other middle-aged women in the plays of Plautus who exercise or attempt to exercise power over men are not depicted as desirable (see Plautus's *Casina*, for example). Passivity is a characteristic of most of the marriageable women in Plautus; in *Epidicus* the marriageable Telestis is even more passive than her mother Philippa. Passivity is not sufficient on its own to make them marriageable, however; to be worthy of marriage in Plautus a woman must be a citizen, and either a virgin (as we are to assume with Telestis), or to have had sex only with the man who eventually marries her (as we are to assume with Philippa).

The play shows us the Roman reality that freeborn young women like Telestis needed family support to protect them from capture and sexual exploitation. If her father Periphanes had not interested himself in her welfare she would have been forced into sexual slavery (by Periphanes's son Stratippocles, despite his boast at line 110 that he had not so far used force on her). Sexual abuse of slaves was both common and also an established part of the enslavement process of women and girls after the sacking of a town. As Kathy Gaca has shown, women and girls captured in war were routinely brutalized as part of the domination of the defeated people, a process known as andrapodization (from the Greek *andrapodisis* or *andrapodismos*) (Gaca 2011: 80).

This vulnerability works as an uncomplicated plot device in the plays of Plautus. Freeborn and virginal women are rescued from the sex trade just in time, while those who had already entered the sex trade before the play's action are cheerfully accepting of their permanently unmarriageable status. Acropolistis, in *Epidicus*, is viewed as primarily a sex worker, and indeed Epidicus assumes that she will be available to compensate Stratippocles by becoming his concubine after his disappointment in finding out that Telestis is his half sister (line 653). Acropolistis's lyre-playing skills do not hint at an alternate career to sex work, since professional women in the Roman world were generally assumed to be sex workers as well. Women and men who performed on the stage were deemed *infames*, which meant that they had lost *fama*, or reputation, and they held reduced civic rights. The bodies of free/freed professional women were assumed to be for sale, and if the women were slaves their bodies belonged to their masters.

Life for a sex worker in mid-republican Rome would have been precarious, but though Plautus's audience might be prompted to feel sorry for the recently enslaved Telestis and be glad when she regains her free-born status, the same cannot be said of women like Acropolistis who have already entered the sex trade. Acropolistis is depicted as relatively self-reliant, and capable of looking after herself. When Periphanes realizes she is not his daughter and is furious with her for tricking him, she responds with humorous logic, claiming that she can't be blamed for obediently doing what was asked of her (by Epidicus), and for calling Periphanes "father" in response to him calling her "daughter" (lines 584–592).

Her obedience somewhat undermines Periphanes's right to be angry with her, since it is a womanly virtue in the world of Plautus to obey. The passive obedience of Telestis is what nearly condemns her to a life of sex slavery, but it is also what makes her worthy of being rescued. Philippa's prior relationship with the young Periphanes is also marked by her passivity and compliance (see note 5 on page 12 on the question of whether or not Periphanes had in fact raped her). In Roman comedy it is not a woman's choices that fit her to a life of respectable marriage on the one hand, or infamous sex work on the other; instead it is what is allowed to happen to her that changes her status and her future prospects. It is therefore her protectors, or lack thereof, who define her status.

How might Plautus have thought about the real women in his audiences, and how would they have interpreted his plays? We know that enslaved, freed, and free women watched the plays. The prologue of Plautus's *Poenulus* includes a direct address to the audience, and refers to various different groups including "nannies / nursemaids" (*nutrices* 28) and "married women" (*matronae* 32). The *nutrices* would have been slaves or else free/freed lower-class women, while the *matronae* would have been freeborn, and probably citizens, coming from all classes.

How much did Plautus and his actors care about keeping these women entertained? Marshall has argued that "Plautus sought to take the diverse individuals in the audience and treat them as a corporate whole, perhaps at the expense of a scapegoat or two", and lists as these potential scapegoats a "reluctant spectator", a "Greek slave or tourist", or "the *praeco*" — that is, the crier or announcer whose job was to announce the play and make the audience pay attention (Marshall 2006: 77). It is evident that the female members of the audience ought to be added to Marshall's list of scapegoats, especially given that the "nannies" and "married women" mentioned above from the prologue of the *Poenulus* are told, respectively, to stay at home with the children they are in charge of, and to be sure to laugh quietly so as not to annoy their husbands. Regardless of the women's class, it seems, Roman men were always ready to laugh at jokes that told women to shut up.

Plautus's depiction of female characters on the stage is not by any means wholly misogynistic, but most of the women in Plautus are not given as full a range of human emotions as the male characters are (bearing in mind that the male characters are by no means fully fleshed out as characters themselves). This must partly have been due to the fact that the Roman comedies were meant to be set in the Greek world (usually Athens), where, as the fifth-century Athenian general Perikles had reportedly said, women achieved glory by not being talked about by men, no matter whether that talk was about their virtues or their flaws (Thucydides 2.45). Women in Rome were far freer in their movements than their Athenian counterparts, but they were not the target audience for the plays of Plautus. The female characters in Plautus were played by male actors in masks, unlike mime dramas where female actors could play starring roles, and this would have further diminished the likelihood of the actors and the playwright viewing women as their target audience.

The limited behaviours and outcomes for the female characters in Plautus must have fit within the Roman audience's ideas about women's roles, even if the reality for Roman women would have been significantly more varied. We can't know if the Roman women watching Plautus's plays viewed the stage women as relating in any way to their own real lives, but it is likely that the plays' emphasis on the fates deserved by each of the stage women had the effect of teaching them their place in Roman society.

Reading *Epidicus* also allows us to see some of the more casual aspects of life on the lower end of the Roman social scale. Students of Roman history are usually familiar with the praetorship as a step on the *cursus honorum*, that is, as one of the coveted political offices for which ambitious men of the senatorial class campaigned energetically, and they have probably learned about the retinue of lictors who accompanied the higher magistrates and symbolized their authority by carrying the *fasces* (bundles of rods with or without axe heads attached). We see in Plautus that, to the ordinary Roman public, the praetor was primarily seen as the judge who dealt with bankruptcies, fraud cases, and the like. At the beginning of the *Epidicus*, the title character uses formal legal language for comic effect (line 24), in response to which the other slave, Thesprio, makes a joke about Epidicus playing praetor and deserving a beating with his own lictors' *fasces*. This probably inspired shocked and delighted laughter amongst the lower-class members of Plautus's audience, who had reason to fear the praetor's power. If a real praetor was present in the audience (a likely possibility), his reaction to the joke would have enhanced its comic effect.

Students will also know about Rome's nearly constant warfare; in the plays of Plautus we get to see how frequently warfare and its consequences appear as background to the plots. Greek warfare, especially after Alexander the Great, tended to involve soldiers hiring themselves out as mercenaries, while Roman soldiers of Plautus's time were drafted to serve the republic. The plays juggle with both of these military practices, and soldiers in the audience would have been able to mock the Greek mercenaries while appreciating the military metaphors. In *Epidicus* the slaves deplore and joke about the cowardliness of Stratippocles's conduct in battle (lines 29–38 tell us that he threw away his weapons and ran away), and military metaphors are casually used at lines 343 and 381 to illustrate the strategic efforts of Epidicus and Stratippocles to outsmart Periphanes and win the *praeda* ("war prize", that is, the enslaved woman Stratippocles is in love with). When the unnamed soldier in the play (who is characteristically boastful and belligerent as his stock character requires him to be) meets Periphanes (whom we find out was himself a boastful soldier in his youth) we get to laugh at their self-aggrandizement and sense of entitlement in much the same way that Plautus's ancient audience must have done (lines 442–455). More importantly we see that successful soldiers, at least in the fantasies of the Roman audiences, were able to enrich themselves from their campaigns, and that the economic power of wealthy soldiers was at odds with the way the Roman audiences felt power ought to be distributed. Wealthy soldiers in Plautus usually end up being very properly outwitted by the less wealthy characters. Burton 2020 discusses the multifaceted ways in which the plays of Plautus were intended to appeal to spectators who had personal experience in Rome's wars.

At least two characters in the play show us sanitized examples of some of the direct victims of warfare: Telestis, whose capture would have condemned her to a life of sex slavery had she not been rescued, and Thesprio, whose name (meaning "man from Thesprotis"), tells us that he was probably also a war captive, since captured slaves were usually given new names, with the new slave name often being a reference to their place of origin (Strabo 7. 3.12). Lines 210–211 of the play mention the boys and young women that Stratippocles and his fellow soldiers have brought back as slaves from the war in Thebes: enslaving the conquered was a consequence of war that was uncontroversial to the Roman audiences.

The religious references in the play illustrate the pervasiveness of religion in everyday life in the ancient Mediterranean. It is, however, far from clear how Roman these references are, rather than (fictionalized) Greek. Since the play is set in Athens, or rather "Athens", we have to accept the likelihood that some of the religious references were meant to be a comic version of what the average Roman could believe was normal in the Greek world (on this see Jocelyn 2001). Characters swear by the demigods Hercules and Pollux (both naturalized Greek imports — Herakles and Polydeukes — to Roman religion) and make repeated references to personal religious rituals. When Apoecides jokes about Periphanes's ritual offerings to his dead wife's tomb (lines 173–177), does this suggest that the Roman audiences laughed at the insincerity of those carrying out personal religious rituals in Rome, or did they only find it funny because they thought they were laughing at Greek religious insincerity? The unnamed freelance lyre-player (who appears in act 4, scene 1, and who has a short speaking role in lines 496–516) has, she tells us, been hired to play her lyre for a religious ritual Periphanes was to have performed, and this points to the regular domestic rituals conducted by the male head of a Roman household (*pater familias*), though we do not know if hiring a lyre-player for the ritual would have seemed normal to the Roman audience, or if it was meant to be a comic example of an alien Greek ritual (Jocelyn 2001: 280). The Greek setting, of course, would have made jokes about religious rituals safer, since it could be plausibly denied that they were attacks on Roman ritual.

The repeated ritual imagery throughout the play, where the slave Epidicus is likened to a "sacrificial victim, sacrificer, embalmer, *auspex*, Agamemnon, and son of Vulcan" has been discussed by T. H. M. Gellar-Goad, who argues that the *Epidicus* "uses ritual imagery and religious associations to reflect power relationships between characters" (Gellar-Goad 2012: 149). The play thus shows us the ubiquity of religion in Roman life and the ways in which religious imagery could be used in popular performances as shorthand for social themes.

Finally, the play conjures up exaggerated versions of the ways that Romans might get into debt, and depicts the rascally nature of moneylenders. We see that husbands resented their wealthy wives (lines 173–180), and that the famous paternal power (*patria potestas*) — which we know from legal sources gave, at least in theory, near absolute power to a man over his sons — was something that Roman audiences liked to see flouted, at least on stage, if not in real-life Rome. It is likely that the now lost *fabulae togatae* (comedies set in Rome) forbore to depict this sort of undermining of Roman paternal power; the *togatae* seem to have had a less frivolous approach to family life (Manuwald 2010: 5). The *fabulae palliatae*, however, show us that Plautus's Roman audience enjoyed seeing the perennially outwitted father on stage in fantasy-"Athens".

The Plot of *Epidicus*

The complicated tricks the slave Epidicus uses to outwit his master are what makes the play so funny, but sorting out the various young women around whom the plot hinges requires some concentration.

The first woman is Acropolistis, who is a slave trained as a courtesan and as a lyre-player (*fidicina*). We are told in the opening dialogue of the play that Stratippocles, the son of Periphanes, fell madly in love (actually, "lust" is the more appropriate word) with Acropolistis before he left to fight with the army in the nearby state of Thebes (remember that the play is supposedly set in the Greek state of Athens, and its characters are supposed to be Greeks). He left instructions for Epidicus, a slave of his household, to somehow get hold of enough money to buy her for him. Like most young men in Roman comedy, Stratippocles is financially dependent on his father who could not approve of wasting large sums of money buying courtesans, so Stratippocles's repeated insistence that Epidicus buy Acropolistis might seem an impossible task.

Nothing, however, is impossible for such a wily slave as Epidicus, the star of the show. Epidicus convinces Stratippocles's father Periphanes that Acropolistis is the latter's illegitimate daughter. Years before, Periphanes had raped or had a fling with[5] a woman called Philippa whom he had not married (presumably

---

5   An unfortunate result of Greek and Roman predatory attitudes around sex and possessive attitudes around women means that the question of whether or not Philippa had consented to the sexual encounter with Periphanes was not considered important enough to be made clear in the Latin text. In a virgin-bride culture, any sex with a young woman of marriageable status was considered a sexual crime because it ruined her value as a family asset unless she then married the man. Wolfgang de Melo's 2011 translation of *Epidicus* uses the term "rape" (to translate *compressae* in line 5 of the *Argumentum*) and later has Periphanes say that he "forc[ed Philippa] to lie with [him]" (to translate *comprimere* at line 540b). Henry Thomas Riley, in his 1852 translation of *Epidicus*, used the rather quaint Victorian terms "seduction" and "intrigue". While the verb *perpulit* (or possibly *pepulit*, according to one of the manuscript traditions) at line 541a of the play seems to suggest force was used, it is not unambiguous in meaning. The play simply emphasizes Periphanes's selfishness in having thus compromised Philippa's marriage prospects. Rape as a plot point in a culture that valued a woman's *pudicitia* (sexual modesty and chastity) allowed the play to "increase the dramatic impact of citizen girls" without the raped woman losing her claim to *pudicitia* (Witzke 2020: 337). Philippa's potential willingness to marry Periphanes years after their sexual encounter would have seemed, to the Roman audience, like a satisfactory conclusion for her regardless of whether or not he had used force. On rape as a plot point in New Comedy see Rosivach 1998 (chapter 2); see also Omitowoju 2009 on the relative unimportance of the woman's consent in Athenian attitudes around extra-marital sex (chapter 2; see also Part 2 of her book for discussion of illicit sex in New Comedy).

he was already married to Stratippocles's mother at the time), and Philippa had borne him a daughter named Telestis. The widowed Periphanes has been planning on marrying Philippa and is now delighted to rescue his long-lost daughter (as he thinks) and to welcome her into his home. Periphanes therefore has provided the money to buy the pretend Telestis (who is really his son's girlfriend Acropolistis).

So far so good: Epidicus has got the young master what he wants, and presumably hopes that Periphanes will never discover the trick. How Stratippocles would have been able to carry on an affair with a woman living in his household as his half-sister is not addressed, but the silliness of such an arrangement is part of the fun.

As we learn in the opening dialogue of the play, however, Epidicus's efforts to get Stratippocles access to Acropolistis turn out to have been wasted, since the shallow Stratippocles has already transferred his interest to a different woman. This second woman is a recent war captive, and Stratippocles has borrowed money at an extortionate rate of interest in order to buy her and bring her back from Thebes. She's from a "good family" as we're told, and Stratippocles boasts to his friend Chaeribulus that he has so far not forced himself on her[6] (which Sharon James calls "perhaps the play's most implausible feature", given the expected behaviour of young men in Roman comedy, see James 2020: 114). His self-restraint is important for the plot, because we eventually find out that she is the real Telestis, and thus Stratippocles's half-sister. Stratippocles, who seems to have few redeeming qualities, now tells Epidicus that he'll send him to work at the mill (exhausting, miserable work used to punish disobedient slaves) unless Epidicus quickly finds a way to pay back the money Stratippocles had borrowed to buy Telestis.

The quick-thinking Epidicus comes up with another scheme; one which, as Barbiero notes, is essentially a repetition or reverse of his first trick (see chapter 5 of her forthcoming book). Epidicus tells Periphanes (Stratippocles's father) that Stratippocles has borrowed a lot of money with the plan of buying a lyre-playing courtesan (supposedly Acropolistis) so that he can set her free. Periphanes is horrified, and jumps at Epidicus's plan, which is that Periphanes should buy the woman before his son can and then sell her to a wealthy soldier so that she'll be out of Stratippocles's reach. Periphanes gives Epidicus the money to make the purchase, but Epidicus uses the money to pay off Stratippocles's debt instead. Meanwhile Epidicus hires a freedwoman (that is, a former slave) who is also a lyre-player and brings her home to play the part of Acropolistis.

Epidicus may have temporarily achieved his aim (of getting Stratippocles what he wants), but he knows that there is no way to prevent the truth from

---

6   Here the Latin is quite clear that rape is meant: Stratippocles says that he hasn't used violence nor violated her chastity (*at pudicitiae eius numquam nec uim nec uitium attuli*, line 110).

coming out once the hired lyre-player is discovered not to be Acropolistis. Indeed, when Periphanes tries to sell the false Acropolistis to a wealthy soldier who had been planning on buying the real Acropolistis, he finds out that Epidicus has tricked him. He doesn't yet realize that he was also tricked into thinking the real Acropolistis was his daughter Telestis, but that trick too is soon discovered: Philippa, Telestis's mother whom Periphanes had abandoned years ago, arrives looking for her daughter whom she knows has been made a captive. Periphanes happily tells her that he has Telestis safe in his house, but when Philippa sees Acropolistis and of course knows she is not her daughter Telestis, the truth comes out. Periphanes has now been tricked into giving up two large sums of money to buy slave women who were not who he thought they were, and he intends to punish Epidicus harshly.

Epidicus, knowing this, talks wildly of running away, but then he comes face to face with the real Telestis, whom he has so far in the play only heard about as an unnamed war captive (line 43). He recognizes her as his master's long-lost daughter and knows that Periphanes will forgive everything in his joy at being reunited with her. Stratippocles isn't pleased to find out that his newly acquired courtesan is his own half-sister, but Epidicus tells him to make do with Acropolistis. Epidicus then guilt-trips Periphanes into promising him many rewards, and the play ends with the triumphant celebration of how the clever slave won his freedom thanks to his own bad behaviour.

Loose Ends

Over a century of scholarship has reflected worries about the apparent loose ends and small holes in the plot of *Epidicus*. Some people have been bothered by the fact that we are not given the expected happy conclusion to the young master's love affair, for example. Stratippocles is left looking foolish, as the object of his desire turns out to be his half-sister and therefore out of bounds, and he does not respond with any obvious enthusiasm to Epidicus's suggestion at line 653 that he make do with Acropolistis after all. Another apparent loose end is the fact that the marriage of Periphanes and Philippa is not announced with the fanfare we might expect (though probably Periphanes asking to take Philippa's hand at line 559 implies a marriage — see Maurice 2006: 42; James 2020: 114). Periphanes's plan (line 190) to get his son Stratippocles married off and thus to clear the way for Periphanes to marry Philippa is dropped without any explanation. Epidicus's original plan (lines 364–370) to trick the pimp into playing a role in the fake purchase of the hired lyre-player is not mentioned again (we don't know if Epidicus ended up carrying out this part of his plan or not). We don't know if the Euboean soldier of line 153 is the same as the Rhodian soldier of line 300, and if they are, why Epidicus refers to them by different demonyms. Epidicus's plan to coach the hired lyre-player to convincingly play the role of Acropolistis seems not to have been carried out, since the hired lyre-player's response to getting found out suggests instead that she was lied to by Epidicus rather than coached to play a role. There is no explanation as to how Epidicus thought he could sell Acropolistis to the rich soldier of line 153 when he has already convinced Periphanes that she is his daughter Telestis. We never find out what is to happen to Acropolistis: will she become Stratippocles's concubine, or will Periphanes punish her for her part in Epidicus's tricks by sending her out of town as suggested in line 279?

Some of the loose ends might be due to abridgments of the play made by later producers, to the loss of an original prologue and/or epilogue that tidied up the loose ends, or to Plautus retaining only parts of a now lost Greek original plot. Ultimately these loose ends shouldn't matter, however. There is certainly no need, as Niall Slater put it, to interpret the *Epidicus* as "a ham-fisted re-writing of the ending of a lost Greek original" (Slater 2001: 191). Plautus's comic genius was to use the Greek plot lines as a jumping off point for the exuberant interactions between the trickster and his dupes, so we ought not to expect such a carefully constructed plot as we might find in Greek comedy. Plautus, Malcolm Willcock rightly wrote, "is more concerned with vivid comic scenes than with the antecedents of the plot, or for that matter the future of the characters (Willcock 1995: 28).

The play should be evaluated on its own terms, as a Roman comedy. The supposed problems may simply be due to a mistaken assumption by modern critics that the plays of Plautus are fundamentally love stories. The Greek New Comedies on which Roman comedy was based were, as Sharon James notes, "a marriage-minded genre", but in the plays of Plautus a concluding marriage for the young man (*adulescens*) and the freeborn young woman (*uirgo*) is not the primary goal (James 2020: 109). James argues that Plautus in fact had a "constitutional lack of interest in setting up citizen marriages, families, and social harmony", and his plays were not focused on marriage as the happy ending, even when the plot ended with a marriage (James 2020: 119).

If, instead of focusing on the happy conclusion of the freeborn man's love affairs in *Epidicus*, we realize that the play is about the trickster Epidicus's impressive ability to outwit his masters, then the plot's loose ends become unimportant. "The very weakness of Epidicus's plans" emphasizes his brilliance in nevertheless achieving his ends (Maurice 2006: 43). Especially when seen in performance, the *Epidicus's* complicated plot and madcap approach to the various tricks of the title character are unlikely to cause any real confusion, or prevent readers or spectators from thoroughly enjoying the play.

The Roman Theatre

What would a performance of a Plautus play have been like for late-third- / early-second-century BCE Romans? For moral and political reasons, the Roman senate refused to allow the building of any permanent theatres in the city of Rome until the middle of the first century BCE. As a consequence, every time plays were produced for one of the religious festivals a temporary wooden stage was built, and possibly seating as well. References in Plautus's plays make it fairly clear that in his day most of his audiences were usually or always seated — this was half a century before the senate attempted to ban the spectators from sitting (Sear 2006: 55).[7] For the original performances of Plautus's plays either a stage and seating was built for each dramatic festival, or a stage was built in front of pre-existing seating, such as the steps of the temple for the deity in whose honour the festival was being held. The seating area would not have been very large: an estimate for the seating area at the Temple of Magna Mater where Plautus's *Pseudolus* was staged in 191 BCE suggests that the audience might have been between 1300–1600 (Goldberg 1998: 14). The comparatively intimate space for Roman plays (as opposed to the much larger spaces of Greek theatres) would have allowed the actors, such as the speaker of the prologue, the hungry hanger-on (*parasitus*, or "parasite"), or the wily slave, to create a rapport with the audience (Moore 1998: 33).

Unlike Greek theatrical productions, which used both the lower orchestra level and the raised stage, the plays of Plautus were staged on a single level, intended to represent a street with one or more houses (Vitruvius 5.6.2). The characters could go in and out of doors that led into the "houses", or they could move on and off stage from the right and left. The set for *Epidicus* had the house of Periphanes on the spectators' left and the house of Chaeribulus on their right; the exit at stage left (to the spectators' right)) represented the direction of the forum, while the other exit (stage right) indicated the direction of the harbour (Duckworth-Wheeler 1940: 97).

The troop of actors was called a *grex*, a Latin word also used to mean a "flock" or "herd" of animals. Amy Richlin draws a picture of how a troop of actors might have looked in the middle of the third century BCE, touring central Italy mostly on foot (Richlin 2017: 3–4). She suggests a group of eleven men and boys, most of them not native Latin speakers. Five of them are slaves, in Richlin's scenario, owned by their fellow actors and trained from an early age to perform on stage; several of those who aren't slaves are former slaves

---

7   There was a brief attempt in the middle of the second century BCE by the senate to require spectators to stand during dramatic performances. Sitting down was deemed an immoral luxury and was associated with Athenian democratic principles (Athenians sat at their political assemblies, which seemed, to the oligarchic Roman senatorial class, to explain their dangerously democratic approach to government — see Cicero *Pro Flacco* 16).

(freedmen). The social status of actors was low, and they lived precarious lives (Richlin pictures them as "hardly ever get[ting] enough to eat" - 3). In Plautus's play the *Cistellaria*, the *grex* speaks the final lines in unison, promising that the actors who performed badly would be flogged, while those who had performed well would get a drink (*qui deliquit uapulabit, qui non deliquit bibet* — 785). In Plautus's *Casina* the speaker of the prologue promises that the boy playing the part of the young girl Casina will be available for paid sex after the play (lines 84–86). Even if these were just jokes they suggest that the enslaved actors, at least, could face violence and exploitation in their jobs.

The status of the playwrights was also low, and their financial situation precarious despite the money they could make selling their plays for performances. An ancient tradition (Gellius, *Noctes Atticae* 3.3.14) tells us that Plautus lost his savings and hired himself out to work at a mill, writing three of his plays during this period of grueling labour. Richlin argues that, though such backstories for ancient authors must be treated with skepticism, having to resort to physical labour to make ends meet is plausible for a playwright of Plautus's independent status who had no patron to support him through periods of financial disaster (Richlin 2017: 5–6).

By Plautus's time there may have been twenty-five to thirty days per year dedicated to theatrical performances in Rome (Marshall 2006: 19). Plays were put on as part of the many state-sponsored religious festivals, and, as far as we know, anyone could attend them free of charge. Slaves probably had to stand at the back, but men and women could sit together and, though no doubt rich theatre-goers tended to be able to get the best seats by sending slaves ahead to reserve spaces for them, segregated seating for the senatorial class was not yet official in Rome (Sear 2006: 2).[8]

Given that the class of the wealthiest Romans paid for the performances, and that it is only because members of the elite valued Plautus that any of his plays survive to this day, it is not unreasonable to assume that the plays were composed for the elite, rather than for the less privileged members of the audience (see especially McCarthy 2000 on this). Nevertheless, the enjoyment of the audience as a whole was important to the success of the performance, which means that the plays were performed with an awareness of how they might be received by rich and poor, slave owners and slaves, men and women.

---

8   It may have been that case that, even before seats were officially reserved for senators in 194 BCE, no one would have dared to sit in front of the senators (Jocelyn 2001: 263 n.4).

Latin Text of *Epidicus* with Language Notes

From the Latin text of W. M. Lindsay, with vocabulary and grammar help by Catherine Tracy

[**Note**: for the acrostic *argumentum* (plot summary) that was added to the play perhaps around 150 CE, see page 173]

Helpful Information for Reading the Latin Text

Students who read the play in Latin will see that there are a few ways in which this text differs from the Latin introduced in most beginners' textbooks. This is partly because, between the time of Plautus and the time of Cicero and Caesar, the spelling of some Latin words changed, and partly because poetic Latin retained some variant forms after they had disappeared from Latin prose. The Latin of Plautus's day is called "Early Latin", as opposed to the later "Classical Latin" that most Latin textbooks teach. The following points will enable readers of the Latin text of *Epidicus* to take in their stride most of the quirks of Plautus's Latin as they appear in this play.

1. **The letter "*u*":** When writing, the Romans did not distinguish between the vowel "*u*" and the semivowel that was later written as "*v*" (which was pronounced like our "w"), and the Latin text of the play used in this volume (which is Lindsay's widely used edition from 1903) therefore uses the letter "*u*" for both the vowel and the semivowel. When written in upper case both the vowel and the semivowel are written like a capital "*V*".

    For example, in the word *"iuuenis"* (line 5 of the play), the first "*u*" is a vowel, while the second is a semivowel, and it would consequently be spelled *"iuvenis"* in most Latin textbooks (like its English derivative "juvenile"). The reason introductory Latin textbooks distinguish between the two is because it is believed to help beginners learn how to pronounce Latin correctly. Those whose Latin skills have reached the point where they can read this play should have no real trouble distinguishing the vowel "*u*" from the semivowel "*u*".

2. **Avoidance of *"uu"*:** Early Latin tended to avoid placing the vowel "*u*" immediately after another "*u*". For this reason we find that *"seruus"* (nominative singular) and *"seruum"* (accusative singular) in Plautus are usually spelled *"seruos"* and *"seruom"*, respectively. Similarly we see the Early Latin spellings *"aequom"*, *"confluont"*, *"emortuom"*, *"saluos"*, *"suom"*, *"tuom"*, *"uolt"*, *"uoltu"*, etc. (instead of the Classical

Latin spellings of these words: *"aequum"*, *"confluunt"*, *"emortuum"*, *"saluus"*, *"suum"*, *"tuum"*, *"uult"*, *"uultu"*).

3. **"Quo-/qu-" where you might expect "cu-"**: the conjunction that was later spelled *"cum"* is spelled *"quom"* in Early Latin (though the same is not true for the preposition *"cum"*, which is so spelled in both Early and Classical Latin). In this Latin text we also see *"quoius/quoiius"*, *"quoi"*, *"quor/qur"*, and *"utquomque"* (instead of the Classical Latin *"cuius"*, *"cui"*, *"cur"*, and *"utcumque"*).

4. **"Qui" where you might expect "quo", "qua" or "quibus"**: the singular and plural ablative forms of the relative and interrogative pronouns, and of the interrogative adjective (which are normally *"quo"*, *"qua"*, and *"quibus"*) can be instead written as *"qui"* in Plautus. Similarly in this play we see *"quicum"* (instead of the more standard *"quacum"*) and *"aliqui"* (instead of *"aliquo"*).

5. **The spelling "-ei-" where you might expect "-ī-"**: some words that, in Classical Latin, came to be spelled with a long *"i"* were spelled instead with *"ei"* in Early Latin; in this play we see *"preimum"*, *"quei"*, *"sei"*, *"seic"*, *"sein"*, and *"uestei"* (instead of the Classical Latin *"primum"*, *"qui"*, *"si"* *"sic"*, *"si+ne"*, and *"uesti"*).

6. **The spelling of prepositional compounds**: where a preposition has become the prefix of a word, this Latin text preserves the original spelling, so that we see *"inmortales"*, *"adligabit"*, and *"adcurentur"* (instead of the Classical Latin *"immortales"*, *"alligabit"*, and *"accurentur"*.)

7. **"Aps", "ap-" where you might expect "a", "ab-"**: the preposition *"a"* (short for *"ab"*) before the word *"te"* was usually *"aps"* in the time of Plautus. Prepositional compounds that in Classical Latin would begin with *"abs-"* in Early Latin are spelled *"aps-"*; thus we see *"apscedat"*, *"apsentem"*, *"apsoluam"*, *"apstulit"*, and *"apsurde"*, etc. (instead of the Classical Latin *"abscedat"*, *"absentem"*, *"absoluam"*, *"abstulit"*, and *"absurde"*).

8. **Superlative adjectives/adverbs ending in *"-umus"* instead of *"-imus"*, etc.**: in Early Latin the superlative forms of adjectives and adverbs were often spelled with a *"-u-"* for the penultimate vowel instead of the *"-i-"* that was standard in Classical Latin. Hence in this play we see the forms *"festiuissumus"*, *"maxumae"*, *"meritissumo"*, *"optuma"*, *"planissume"*, *"proxumum"*, etc. (instead of the Classical Latin spellings *"festiuissimus"*, *"maximae"*, *"meritissimo"*, *"optima"*, *"planissime"*, *"proximum"*).

9. **The syllable *"uo-"* where you might expect *"ue-"*:** some words that in Classical Latin include the syllable *"ue-"* (such as *"uertere"*) were written instead with the syllable *"uo-"* (like *"uortere"*). Hence in this play we find the forms *"uorsutior"*, *"uortitur"*, and *"uotuit"* (instead of the Classical Latin *"uertitur"*, *"uersutior"*, and *"uetuit"*).

10. ***"Illic"*, *"istoc"*, etc.:** students will be familiar with the *"-c"* that ends half of the Classical Latin forms of the demonstrative pronoun/adjective *"hic"*, *"haec"*, *"hoc"*. This final *"-c"* (originally it was *"-ce"*) could also be added, in Early Latin, to forms of *"ille"* and *"iste"*, so we get *"illic"*, *"illoc"*, *"istac"*, *"istaec"*, *"istanc"*, *"istoc"*, *"istuc"*, etc. (instead of the Classical Latin *"ille"*, *"illo"*, *"istā"*, *"ista"*, *"istam"*, *"isto"*, *"istud"*).

11. **Variant verb forms:**

    a. **Future in *"-so"*:** in this play we see the alternate future forms *"faxo"* (from *"facio"*) and *"adempsit"* (instead of *adimet*, from the verb *"adimo"*). *"Faxo"* does not, however, simply substitute for *"faciam"* (which Plautus uses in its essential future sense), but tends to function as a statement of the speaker's certainty, so should be translated as "I promise" or "definitely".

    b. **Future in *"-asso"*, *"-assis"*, etc.:** in clauses introduced by *si, nisi, nei* (*ni*), *ubi*, or *siue*, Plautus used an older form of the future tense of some first-conjugation verbs by adding *"-asso"*, *"-assis"*, *"assit"*, etc. to the stem; hence we find *"commostrasso"*, *"comparassit"* and *"orassis"* (instead of the Classical Latin *"commonstrabo"*, *"comparabit"*, and *"orabis"*).[1]

    c. **Future in *"-ibo"*, *"-ibis"*, etc.:** the future tense signifier *"-bi-"* which in Classical Latin is used only for the first and second conjugations and in the verb *"eo"*, can also appear in Early Latin in verbs of the fourth conjugation, so that in this play we see *"reperibitur"*, *"saeuibunt"*, and *"scibit"* (instead of the Classical Latin *"reperietur*, *"saeuient"*, and *"sciet"*).

    d. **Imperfect in *"-ibam"*, etc.:** The imperfect active forms of fourth-conjugation verbs sometimes have no *"-e-"* before the tense signifier *"-ba-"*; thus in this play we see the form *"exaudibam"* (instead of the more standard *"exaudiebam"*).

    e. **Singular imperatives *"face"* and *"duce"*:** whereas in Classical Latin the singular imperatives of the verbs *"dico"*, *"duco"*, *"facio"*,

---

1   There is some scholarly uncertainty as to the mood and tense of these forms (see Duckworth-Wheeler 1940: 178–179).

and *"fero"* are *"dic"*, *"duc"*, *"fac"*, and *"fer"*, respectively, in Early Latin the forms *"dice"*, *"duce"*, and *"face"* (but not *"fere"*) could be used. In this play we see *"duce"* and *"dice"* once each, and *"face"* twice, but also *"fac"* several times.

f. **"*Euenat*" and "*euenant*" instead of "*eueniat*" and "*eueniant*":** the present subjunctive third-person singular and plural of the verb *"euenio"* appears in Early Latin as *"euenat"* and *"evenant"*.

g. **Present passive infinitive in "*-ier*":** Plautus sometimes used an older form of the present passive infinitive, which ended in *"-er"*, so that in this play we see *"percontarier"* and *"praestolarier"* (instead of the Classical Latin *"percontari"* and *"praestolari"*).

h. **Perfect system forms of "*sum*" in perfect passive tenses:** perfect passive forms of verbs that in Classical Latin use *"sum"*, *"eram"*, or *"ero"* (indicative) or *"sim"*, *"essem"* (subjunctive) sometimes use instead the perfect system forms *"fui"*, *"fueram"*, *"fuero"* (indicative) and *"fuerim"*, *"fuissem"* (subjunctive). Thus in this play we see *"fuero elocutus"* and *"induta fuerit"* (instead of the Classical Latin *"ero elocutus"* and *"induta sit"*).

i. **Present subjunctive of "*sum*":** alternative forms to the Classical Latin *"sim"*, *"sis"*, *"sit"*, and *"sint"* often appear in Early Latin as *"siem"*, *"sies"*, *"siet"*, and *"sient"* (in this play only *"sies"* and *"siet"* appear).

12. **Contractions:** the final *"-s"* of words normally ending in *"-us"* or *"-is"* was pronounced weakly enough that it did not affect the scansion of the line the way a normal consonant would, and in this version of the Latin text the weak final *"-s"* is not written. Hence we get *"minu'"*, *"dici'"*, *"rebu'"*, and *"priu'"*, etc. (contracted from *"minus"*, *"dicis"*, *"rebus"*, and *"prius"*).

For the same reason, a word ending in *"-us"* followed by the word *"es"* or *"est"*, is written without the final *"-s"* of the first word and the initial *"e-"* of *"es/est"* when the meter requires it. Hence we get *"captiost"*, *"mercatust"*, *"timidu's"*, and *"ueritust"*, etc. (instead of *"captio est"*, *"mercatus est"*, *"timidus es"*, and *"ueritus est"*).

The initial *"e-"* of *"es/est"* when it follows a word ending in *"-m"* or in a vowel was either not pronounced or pronounced very lightly, and thus Lindsay's text does not write that final *"-e"*. Hence we see *"corruptumst"*, *"ergost"*, *"tu's"*, and *"ubist"*, etc. (contracted from *"corruptum est"*, *"ergo est"*, *"tu es"*, and *"ubi est"*).

When metrically necessary, the interrogatory suffix *"-ne/-n"* is often shortened to *"-n"* even when not followed by a word beginning with a vowel, such as *"nouistin"* (instead of *"nouistine"*), *"meministin"* (instead of *"meministine"*), *"perpetuen"* (instead of *"perpetuene"*), and *"men"* (instead of *"mene"*). A final "s" disappears before the suffix *"-ne"* (usually shorted to *"-n"*), so that we get *"ain"*, *"audin"*, *"patierin"*, *"potin"*, *"satine"*, *"scin"*, *"uiden"*, etc. (instead of *"aisne"*, *"audisne"*, *"patierisne"*, *"potisne"*, *"satisne"*, *"scisne"*, and *"uidesne"*).

13. **"Med" instead of "me"**: Plautus at least sometimes used the Early Latin ablative/accusative forms of the personal pronouns (*med* and *ted*); in this play we find *"med"* instead of *"me"* twice, though he used *"me"* more commonly.

14. **"-ii-" for the semivowel "-i-"**: we see the forms *"eiius"*, *"huiius"*, and *"quoiius"* (instead of the later spellings *"eius"*, *"huius"* and *"quoius/cuius"*).

15. **Poetic forms *"mī"* and *"nīl"***: Plautus used the forms *"mī"* and *"nīl"* (for *"mihi"* and *"nihil"*) when the rhythm of the line required it.

16. **Other common variant forms:** Plautus preferred to use the variant form *"lubet"* and its cognates (such as *"lubens"* and *"lubentius"*), instead of the later spelling of these words with *"lib-"*. We also find the spelling *"sacruficas"*, *"periclum"*, and *"caussa"* (which in Classical Latin would be *"sacrificas"*, *"periculum"*, and *"causa"*).

The Rhythm of Plautus

The actors in Plautus's plays often broke into song, in a variety of very complicated meters ("meter" refers to the rhythmic structure of the line) that continued the play's action rather than, like the choral interludes in Greek drama, being a break from the action. Furthermore, much of the dialogue was sung or spoken with accompaniment on one or more musical instruments (usually a woodwind instrument called a *tibia* and some sort of percussion); these sections of sung or chanted dialogue are commonly called in English "recitative", like the "spoken" parts of an opera that are sung to accompanying music but that are not self-contained arias or songs. Songs and recitative made up nearly two-thirds of the lines in Plautus's plays, while the remaining third, written in a meter called iambic senarii, was spoken without music (Duckworth 1952/1971: 363).

Those who want to experience *Epidicus* in at least some of its metrical complexity are encouraged to consult a book on Latin meter (*The Meters of Greek and Latin Poetry* by Halporn *et al.* is a good place to start[2]). Beginners who have learned the basic rules of elision and vowel length should practice reading the two most common meters of Plautus: **trochaic septenarii** (which was generally recited or chanted to the music of the *tibia*), and the spoken passages in the **iambic senarius** meter.

Trochaic Septenarii

A line of trochaic septenarii is theoretically made up of seven trochees plus an additional anceps (either long or short) syllable at the end. A basic trochee is a long syllable followed by a short syllable (— ∪), but in a line of Latin trochaic septenarii the short syllable in the first six trochees can be either long or short. An anceps syllable is usually represented by X, so that a trochee, where the so-called short syllable is actually an anceps, would be symbolized like this: — X.

Furthermore, since the important thing about syllable length in Latin meter is literally how long it took to pronounce, two short syllables can replace a long

---

[2] Any good Latin grammar, such as Bennett's *New Latin Grammar* or Allen & Greenough's *New Latin Grammar for Schools and Colleges*, will provide a helpfully simplified explanation of Latin meter.

syllable, allowing a so-called trochee to potentially be replaced by a spondee (— —), a dactyl (— ∪ ∪), an anapaest (∪ ∪ —), a tribrach (∪ ∪ ∪), or a proceleusmatic (∪ ∪ ∪ ∪). That so many variations are possible may sound anarchic, but with enough practice it is possible to get a sense of the unifying rhythm that makes each line of trochaic septenarii distinct from the other meters in the play. Plautus used meter changes to differentiate between different characters and different aspects of his plays, so getting a feel for the rhythm will add to an appreciation of the play.

Almost the whole of scene 2 in Act 1 (lines 104–163) is written in trochaic septenarii. We can visualize the scansion of lines 104–105 as follows:

```
—∪∪   |  —∪    |   —∪     |   — —   ||   —∪     |   — —    |   —∪       |  x
rem tibi | sᵤₘ elo- |  -cutus  |  omnem  ||  Chaeri-  |  -bulₑ at- |  -quₑ admo-  | -dum

— —    |  — —    |   —∪        |   — —    ||   —∪       |   — —    |   —∪      |  x
mₑorum  |  maero- |  -rᵤₘ atquₑ a- |  -morum  ||  summₐₘ e-  |  -dicta- |  -ui ti-  | -bi
```

- The letters printed in subscript are elided, which means they were either barely pronounced, or not pronounced at all.

- A natural pause in the line, where a diaeresis (a word and the metrical foot ending in the same place) coincides with a pause in the sense of the line, is represented by this symbol: ‖ and usually appears after the fourth foot. This diaeresis is one of the distinct aspects of a line of trochaic septenarii.

- In line 105, the "e" and the "o" of "meorum" are pronounced together as a long syllable (this is called synizesis).

- The final syllable of a line of verse can be either long or short regardless of the meter, since a reader or actor would pause at the ends of lines, thereby effectually lengthening a short final syllable.

The following lines of *Epidicus* are in trochaic septenarii: 1–2; 23; 44–45; 50–51; 86; 88; 90; 91; 93; 95; 97; 99–163; 190–305; 333; 547–733.

Iambic Senarii

A line of iambic senarii is theoretically made up of six iambs. A basic iamb is a short syllable followed by a long: ∪ —, but the "short" syllable of the iamb in Roman comedy is an anceps (can be either long or short) in all but the last foot; in fact, the anceps is more often long than short in Plautus's iambic senarii. To further complicate matters, any of the first four iambs in the line can be replaced with a dactyl (a long followed by two shorts: — ∪ ∪) or with an anapaest (two shorts followed by a long: ∪ ∪ —). Since a long syllable can be replaced by two short syllables (except for the final syllable in a line of iambic senarii), one of Plautus's iambs can potentially look like this: ⏑ ⏑ ⏑ ⏑.

We can visualize the scansion of lines 310–311, both in the iambic senarius meter, as follows:

```
— ⏑⏑      |  — ⏑⏑     |  — ‖ —     |   — —     |   — —      |  ⏑ x
quod pol e- |  -go metu- |   -o si    |   senex   |   resci-   |  -uerit

  — —      |  ⏑⏑ —     |  — ‖ ⏑⏑    |   ⏑ —     |   — —      |  ⏑ x
 nₑulmos   |  parasi-   |  -tos faci- | -at quₐₑus- | -quₑatton- |  -deant
```

- The prominent caesurae are here marked with the same notation as for the diaeresis in the trochaic septenarii above: ‖.

  A caesura is the ending of a word in the middle of a foot; in Plautus a line of iambic senarii usually has a prominent caesura (where a pause in the sense of the line coincides with a caesura) in the third or fourth foot.

The following lines of *Epidicus* are in iambic senarii: all of the *Argumentum*; 24; 46–47; 177; 306–319; 382–525.

A dedicated student of Plautine meter will eventually need to learn the more complicated choral meters to fully experience the play, but beginners can start slow, and there is no need to feel discouraged if you can't scan a particular line. Aim instead to acquire a sense of the rhythm by scanning the less complicated lines. Timothy Moore's article on introducing students to the music of Roman comedy provides useful suggestions to instructors as to how best to approach teaching scansion in Plautus (Moore 2013).

A word of encouragement: Latin poets took occasional liberties with the strict rules of meter (see section 367: "Special Peculiarities" in Bennett's *New Latin Grammar* and Moore 2013: 229–230), which can make scansion more complicated. Furthermore, the plays of Plautus have not come down to us without numerous copying errors creeping in, and though experts attempt to fix these errors (and the faulty meter of a line can be a hint that an error has crept in), sometimes it can be quite challenging to work out the meter of a line. If you find you can't scan a line properly, move on and try another.

The Play in Latin

PERSONAE

ACROPOLISTIS: FIDICINA (a lyre-player and female slave who was Stratippocles's girlfriend till just before the action of the play begins; she is first mentioned by Epidicus in Act 1, scene 1 as the *"fidicina"* that Stratippocles ordered Epidicus to buy for him)

APOECIDES: SENEX (an old man, friend of Periphanes, first appearing in Act 2, scene 1)

CHAERIBVLVS: ADVLESCENS (a freeborn young man, friend of Stratippocles, first appearing in Act 1, scene 2)

DANISTA (the moneylender from whom Stratippocles borrowed in order to buy Telestis; he first appears in Act 5, scene 1)

EPIDICVS: SERVOS (a male slave of Periphanes's household who is the con-man hero of the play)

FIDICINA (a freedwoman and professional musician who appears in Act 3, scene 4a)

MILES (a wealthy and boastful soldier, first appearing in Act 3, scene 4)

PERIPHANES: SENEX (an old man, father of Stratippocles, first appearing in Act 2, scene 1)

PHILIPPA: MVLIER (a poor middle-aged woman, mother of Telestis; she first appears in Act 4, scene 1)

SERVOS (unnamed male slave belonging to Periphanes's household who appears in Act 3, scene 3)

STRATIPPOCLES: ADVLESCENS (a freeborn young man, son of Periphanes, who is first mentioned in Act 1, scene 1, and first appears in Act 1, scene 2)

TELESTIS: VIRGO (a freeborn young woman, illegitimate daughter of Philippa and Periphanes; Stratippocles, not knowing she is his half-sister, buys her as a war captive; she first appears in Act 5, scene 1)

THESPRIO: SERVOS (a male slave of Periphanes's household who appears in Act 1, scene 1

ACTVS I

1.1 EPIDICVS, THESPRIO

Scene summary: Thesprio, a slave in the Athenian household of Periphanes, returns from Thebes where Periphanes's son Stratippocles has been serving as a soldier. He encounters Epidicus, another of Periphanes's slaves, and the two begin a comic routine, each insulting the other. We find out that Stratippocles has abandoned his weapons in battle (showing us that he is a cowardly soldier), and that he has borrowed a large sum of money with which he has bought a young woman who was taken captive when the Athenian army had captured Thebes. Epidicus is horrified because, before Stratippocles had left for the war, his young master had been in love with a different young slave woman, a lyre-player called Acropolistis. Stratippocles had insisted that Epidicus find a way to buy Acropolistis for him while he was away in Thebes, and the clever, scheming Epidicus had done so by tricking Periphanes into buying her, after making him believe that Acropolistis was actually his long-lost illegitimate daughter Telestis. The scene ends with Epidicus desperately trying to think of some way to get out of the inevitable punishment he'll get from Periphanes when his trick is found out.

Epidicus: Heus,[1] adulescens! **Thesprio:** quis properantem me reprehendit pallio?
Epidicus: familiaris. **Thesprio:** fateor,[2] nam odio es[3] nimium familiariter.[4]
Epidicus: respice uero, Thesprio. **Thesprio:** oh, Epidicumne ego conspicor?[5]

---

1 *heus*: "hey!" (used to try to get someone's attention).
2 *fateor, fateri, fassus sum*: "admit", "confess".
3 *odio es* (*odio* is dative of purpose): "you are an object of hatred".
4 *familiaris... familiariter*: this is a play on words: *familiaris* means "fellow slave", while *familiariter* means "on friendly terms".
5 *conspicor, conspicari, conspicatus sum*: "catch sight of", "see".

Epidicus: sati'[6] recte oculis uteris.[7]   5

Thesprio: salue. **Epidicus:** di dent quae uelis.

uenire saluom gaudeo.[8] **Thesprio:** quid ceterum? **Epidicus:** quod eo adsolet:[9]

cena tibi dabitur. **Thesprio:** spondeo — **Epidicus:** quid? **Thesprio:** me accepturum,[10] si dabis.

Epidicus: quid

tu agis?[11] ut uales?[12] **Thesprio:** ex-   9a

emplum adesse[13] — **Epidicus:** intellego. eugae![14]   9b

corpulentior uidere atque habitior.[15] **Thesprio:** huic gratia.[16]   10

Epidicus: quam[17] quidem te iam diu

perdidisse[18] oportuit.[19]   11a

Thesprio: minu'[20] iam furtificus[21] sum quam antehac. **Epidicus:** quid ita?[22] **Thesprio:** rapio propalam.[23]

Epidicus: di inmortales[24] te infelicent,[25] ut tu es gradibus grandibus![26]

nam ut[27] apud portum te conspexi, curriculo[28] occepi[29] sequi:

---

6 *sati'* = *satis*: "enough", "sufficiently".
7 *uteris* (second-person singular present deponent indicative) < *utor, uti, usus sum* (+ ablative).
8 *uenire saluom gaudeo*: "I am glad that you've come home safe and sound" (a formulaic greeting).
9 *quod eo adsolet*: "what's usual with that [greeting]" (*eo* is an adverb here, meaning "there", "in that place").
10 *spondeo me accepturum* [*esse*] is an indirect statement.
11 *quid tu agis*: "what's up with you?" "how are you doing?"
12 *ut*: "how".
13 *exemplum adesse*: "the very model of good health is before [you]" (the introductory verb is missing from this indirect statement, or else Epidicus's *intellego* is meant to complete it. I have followed Duckworth-Wheeler in moving *intellego* from Thesprio's line to Epidicus').
14 *eugae* = *euge* (exclamation of approval or joy): "good", "well done".
15 *habitior* (a comparative adjective < *habeo*): "better kept", "in better condition."
16 *huic gratia*: "thanks to this" ("this" refers to his left hand).
17 *quam* (fem. acc. sing. of the relative pronoun; the antecedent is *huic* in line 10).
18 *perdo, perdere, perdidi, perditus*: "ruin", "lose".
19 *oportuit* (impersonal verb); translate here as "you ought".
20 *minu'* = *minus*.
21 *furtificus, -a, -um*: "thievish", with the implication of furtive sneakiness.
22 *quid ita?*: "why so?"
23 *propalam* (adverb): "openly", "publicly".
24 *inmortales* = *immortales*.
25 *infelico, -are*: "grant bad luck".
26 *gradibus grandibus* < *gradus, -us* (m.): "step", "stride" and *grandis, -e* (adjective): "huge", "enormous" (they are datives of reference); translate the phrase: "what enormous steps you're taking".
27 *ut*: "when".
28 *curriculo* (adverb): "by running", "at full speed".
29 *occipio, occipere, occepi / occoepi, occeptum*: "begin".

uix adipiscendi³⁰ potestas modo fuit. **Thesprio:** scurra³¹ es. **Epidicus:** 15
scio

te esse equidem hominem militarem. **Thesprio:** audacter³² quamuis³³
dicito.³⁴

Epidicus: quid agis? perpetuen³⁵ ualuisti? **Thesprio:** uarie.³⁶ **Epidicus:**
qui uarie ualent,

capreaginum³⁷ hominum non placet³⁸ mihi neque pantherinum
genus.

Thesprio: quid tibi uis dicam nisi quod est? **Epidicus:** ut illae res *?³⁹
Thesprio: probe.⁴⁰

Epidicus: quid erilis⁴¹ noster filius? **Thesprio:** ualet pugilice atque 20
athletice.⁴²

Epidicus: uoluptabilem mihi nuntium tuo aduentu adportas,
Thesprio.

sed ubist⁴³ is? **Thesprio:** aduenit simul.⁴⁴ **Epidicus:** ubi is ergost?⁴⁵ nisi
si in uidulo⁴⁶

aut si in mellina⁴⁷ attulisti. **Thesprio:** di te perdant! **Epidicus:** te
uolo —

percontari:⁴⁸ operam da, opera reddetur tibi.⁴⁹

Thesprio: ius 25

---

30 *adipiscendi* (gerund) < *adipiscor, adipisci, adeptus*: "overtake", "catch up".
31 *scurra, -ae* (m.): a fashionable man of the town; an idler.
32 *audacter* (adverb): "boldly".
33 *quamuis* (adverb): "as much as you want".
34 *dicito* (second-person singular future imperative active) < *dico, dicere*.
35 *perpetuen* = *perpetue* + *ne* (adverb): "continually".
36 *uarie* (adverb): "so-so" (*uarie* could also mean "spotted" or "striped", hence Epidicus's reference to (presumably spotted) goats and leopards. His joke refers to slaves being "striped" due to having been severely beaten.
37 *capreaginus, -a, -um*: "goatlike", "goaty" (modifies *genus*).
38 While *placet* is singular, its subject is nevertheless *qui uarie ualent*.
39 *ut illae res** (some word(s) missing): "how did it go?".
40 *probe*: "fine".
41 *erilis, -e* (adjective): "relating to the *erus* (master)".
42 *pugilice atque athletice*: "like a boxer and like an athlete".
43 *ubist* = *ubi est*.
44 *simul* (adverb): "right now", "at the same time".
45 *ergost* = *ergo est*.
46 *uidulus, -i* (m.): "suitcase".
47 *mellina, -ae* (f.): a bag made of the skin of a marten or badger (*meles*).
48 *percontari* is a complementary infinitive after *uolo*; *te* is the direct object of *percontari*.
49 *operam da, opera reddetur tibi*: literally "pay attention, [and] attention will be paid to you". This seems to have been a formulaic phrase used in the law courts, which is why Thesprio jokes about *ius* in the next line.

dicis. **Epidicus:** me decet.⁵⁰ **Thesprio:** iam tu autem 25a
nobis praeturam geris?⁵¹ **Epidicus:** quem⁵² 25b
dices⁵³ digniorem esse hominem hodie Athenis⁵⁴ alterum?
Thesprio: at unum a praetura tua,
Epidice, abest.⁵⁵ **Epidicus:** quidnam?⁵⁶ **Thesprio:** scies: 27a
lictores⁵⁷ duo, duo ulmei⁵⁸ 27b
fasces uirgarum.⁵⁹ **Epidicus:** uae tibi!
sed quid ais? **Thesprio:** quid rogas? **Epidicus:** ubi arma sunt
Stratippocli?⁶⁰
Thesprio: pol⁶¹ illa ad hostis⁶² transfugerunt.⁶³ **Epidicus:** armane?⁶⁴ 30
Thesprio: atque quidem cito.⁶⁵
Epidicus: serione⁶⁶ dici'⁶⁷ tu? 30a
Thesprio: serio, inquam: hostes habent. 31
Epidicus: edepol⁶⁸ facinus inprobum.⁶⁹ **Thesprio:** at iam ante⁷⁰ alii
fecerunt idem.⁷¹
erit illi illa res honori.⁷² **Epidicus:** qui? **Thesprio:** quia ante aliis fuit.⁷³

---

50 Epidicus says *me decet* probably because *ius dicis* sounds a bit like the name *Epidicus* (it's the sort of terrible joke that an audience will enjoy because it's so terrible).
51 *nobis praeturam geris*: "you're acting the praetor for us".
52 *quem... hominem... alterum*: "what other man".
53 *dices* introduces indirect discourse with the infinitive *esse*. The accusative subject of *esse* is *quem... hominem... alterum*.
54 *Athenis* (locative).
55 The subject of *abest* is *unum*, in line 27.
56 *quidnam* (from *quisnam, quidnam*, a more emphatic version of *quis, quid*).
57 Lictors were officials whose job was to walk in front of magistrates to give them status and authority. Lictors carried bundles of sticks (sometimes including a double axe head) called *fasces*, which symbolized the magistrate's authority to scourge and even execute citizens. The urban praetor had two lictors, while the ruling consul had twelve. The modern term "fascism" comes from the Roman *fasces*.
58 *ulmeus, -a, -um*: "[made of] elm wood".
59 *uirga, -ae* (f.): "sticks," "rods".
60 *Stratippocli* (dative) < *Stratippocles, -is*.
61 *pol*: "by Pollux" (see note 8 on page 131 for the use of the swear words *pol* and *edepol*).
62 *hostīs* (accusative plural).
63 *transfugio, -ere, -fugi, –* : "go over to the enemy", "desert".
64 *armane* = *arma* + *ne* (making the sentence into a question).
65 *cito* (adverb): "quickly", "speedily".
66 *serio* (adverb): "seriously".
67 *dici'* = *dicis*.
68 *edepol*: "by Pollux".
69 *facinus inprobum* = *facinus improbum* (accusative of exclamation): "what a shameful deed!", "what a crime!"
70 *iam ante*: "before now".
71 *idem*: "the same thing".
72 *honori* (dative of purpose); *erit illi illa res honori* "that affair will end up honourably for him".
73 *quia ante aliis fuit*: "because it has ended up honourably for others before him". This may be a disparaging reference to the fugitives from the Battle of Cannae who were thought to have

Mulciber,[74] credo, arma fecit quae habuit Stratippocles:
trauolauerunt[75] ad hostis.[76] **Epidicus:** tum ille prognatus[77] Theti[78]   35
sine[79] perdat:[80] alia adportabunt[81] ei Neri[82] filiae.
id modo uidendum est, ut[83] materies[84] suppetat[85] scutariis,[86]
si in singulis[87] stipendiis[88] is ad hostis[89] exuuias[90] dabit.
Thesprio: supersede[91] istis rebu'[92] iam. **Epidicus:** tu ipse ubi lubet[93]
finem face.[94]
Thesprio: desiste percontarier.[95] **Epidicus:** loquere[96] ipse: ubist[97]   40
Stratippocles?
Thesprio: est caussa qua caussa[98] simul mecum ire ueritust.[99]
Epidicus: quidnam[100] id est?

---

been honoured undeservedly for their defeat (see Duckworth-Wheeler 1940: 125).

74 *Mulciber, Mulciberis* (m.): another name for Vulcan, the Roman blacksmith god, and god of fire generally.
75 *trauolauerunt = transuolauerunt < transuolo, -are, -aui, -atus*: "fly across".
76 *hostīs* (accusative plural).
77 *prognatus, -a, -um*: "sprung from", "descended from" (followed by the ablative; the word was archaic even in Plautus's time, and is here intended to parody the language of tragedy or epic — see de Melo 2013: 340).
78 *Theti*: alternative ablative form of *Thetis, Thetidis* (f.), the name of a sea goddess, mother of the Greek hero Achilles.
79 *sine* (second-person singular present imperative active) < *sino, sinere, siui, situm*: "allow", "permit".
80 *sine perdat*: "let [that son of Thetis] lose [them]."
81 *adportabunt = apportabunt*.
82 *Neri* (alternative genitive singular form of *Nereus*, a sea god and father of Thetis).
83 *uidendum est* introduces the *ut* clause (construction found only in Plautus).
84 *materies, -ei* (f.): "wood", "material" [for making shields].
85 *suppeto, -ere, -iui, -itus* (+ dative): "be at hand", "be equal to", "be sufficient for", "agree with".
86 *scutarius, -i* (m.): "shield-maker" (the *scutarii* probably refer to the divine helpers of Vulcan).
87 *singuli, -ae, -a*: "each", "every".
88 *stipendium, -i* (n.): "military campaign".
89 *ad hostis*: "to the enemy" (we would expect *hostibus*, dative of indirect object).
90 *exuuiae, -arum* (f.): "spoils", "booty".
91 *supersedeo, -sedere, -sedi, -sessus*: "be superior to", "refrain from" + ablative.
92 *rebu' = rebus*.
93 *lubet = libet*: "it is pleasing"; *ubi lubet*: "whenever you want".
94 *face = fac < facio, -ere, feci, factum*.
95 *percontarier = percontari*.
96 *loquere* (second-person singular present imperative deponent) < *loquor, loqui, locutus sum*.
97 *ubist = ubi est*.
98 *est caussa quā caussā = est causa quā causā*: "there is a reason [that he's not here] and it's because...".
99 *ueritust = ueritus est* (perfect passive participle masculine nominative singular) < *uereor, uereri, ueritus sum*.
100 *quidnam* (from *quisnam, quidnam*, a more emphatic version of *quis, quid*).

Thesprio: patrem uidere se neuolt[101] etiamnunc. **Epidicus:** quapropter?[102] **Thesprio:** scies.
quia forma lepida et liberali[103] captiuam adulescentulam[104]
de praeda[105] mercatust.[106] **Epidicus:** quid ego ex te audio? **Thesprio:** hoc quod fabulor.[107]
Epidicus: qur[108] eam emit? **Thesprio:** animi[109] caussa.[110] **Epidicus:**   45
quot illic[111] homo animos habet?
nam certo,[112] priu' quam[113] hinc[114] ad legionem abiit domo,
ipse mandauit[115] mihi ab lenone[116] ut fidicina,[117]
quam amabat, emeretur sibi. id[118] ei impetratum[119] reddidi.[120]
Thesprio: utquomque[121] in alto[122] uentust,[123] Epidice, exim[124] uelum[125] uortitur.[126]
Epidicus: uae misero mihi, male perdidit me! **Thesprio:** quid istuc?[127]   50
quidnam | est?

---

101 *neuolt = non uult.*
102 *quapropter*: "why?" "for what reason?".
103 *formā lepidā et liberali* (ablative of description).
104 *adulescentula, -ae* (f.): "young woman", "teenaged girl".
105 *de praeda*: "from the spoils/booty [he acquired from the campaign]".
106 *mercatust = mercatus est < mercor, -ari, -atus sum*: "buy".
107 *hoc quod fabulor*: "what I'm telling you."
108 *qur = cur.*
109 *animus, -i* (m.): (in this context) "pleasure", "whim".
110 *caussa = causa.*
111 *illic = ille.*
112 *certo*: "certainly".
113 *priu' quam = prius quam*: "before".
114 *hinc*: "from this place", "from here", "hence".
115 *mandauit mihi [...] ut fidicina emeretur sibi* (indirect command): "he ordered me to buy a lyre-player".
116 *leno, -onis* (m.): "pimp", "brothel keeper".
117 *fidicina, -ae* (f.): a woman trained in playing the lyre, who was usually a slave or freedwoman and who was assumed, like all female performers, to be a sex worker.
118 *id* (refers to the act of buying the *fidicina*).
119 *impetro, -are, -aui, -atum*: "achieve", "bring to pass".
120 *reddo, -ere, reddidi, redditus*: (in this context) "render", "cause [something] to be". The phrase *id ei impetratum reddidi* should be translated "I made it happen for him" or "I did what he asked."
121 *utquomque = utcumque*: "however", "whichever way".
122 *altum, -i* (n.): "the sea".
123 *uentust = uentus est; uentus, -i* (m.): "wind".
124 *exim* (adverb): "so", "in that way".
125 *uelum, -i* (n.): "sail".
126 *uortitur = uertitur < uerto, -ere, uerti, uersum*: "turn", "direct".
127 *quid istuc*: "what are you talking about".

Epidicus: quid[128] istanc[129] quam emit, quanti[130] eam emit? **Thesprio:** uili.[131] **Epidicus:** haud istuc te rogo.[132]

Thesprio: quid igitur? **Epidicus:** quot[133] minis?[134]

Thesprio: tot: quadraginta[135] minis. 52a

id adeo[136] argentum[137] ab danista[138] apud Thebas[139] sumpsit[140] faenore[141]

in dies minasque argenti singulas nummis.[142] **Epidicus:** papae![143]

Thesprio: et is danista aduenit una[144] cum eo, qui argentum petit. 55

Epidicus: di inmortales! ut ego interii[145] basilice![146] **Thesprio:** quid iam? aut quid est,

Epidice? **Epidicus:** perdidit[147] me. **Thesprio:** quis? **Epidicus:** ille qui arma perdidit.

Thesprio: nam quid ita? **Epidicus:** quia cottidie ipse ad me ab legione epistulas

mittebat — sed taceam optumum est,

plus scire satiust[148] quam loqui seruom hominem;[149] ea sapientia est. 60

Thesprio: nescio edepol quid [tu] timidu's,[150] trepidas,[151] Epidice, ita uoltu[152] tuo

---

128 *quid*: "anyway".
129 *istanc = istam* (here intensifying *quam*): "that girl whom [he bought]".
130 *quanti* (genitive of indefinite price): "for how much [money]".
131 *uilis, -e* (adjective): "[for a] cheap [price]".
132 *haud istuc te rogo*: "that's not what I'm asking you."
133 *quot*: "how many" is answered by Thesprio with *tot*: "this many" (no doubt illustrating the number with his fingers).
134 *minis* (ablative of price) < *mina, -ae* (f.): a Greek unit of money equivalent to 430g of silver.
135 *quadraginta* (indeclinable): "forty".
136 *adeo*: "precisely", "exactly".
137 *id adeo argentum*: "this exact amount of money".
138 *danista, -ae* (m.): "moneylender".
139 *apud Thebas*: "in Thebes".
140 *sumo, -ere, sumpsi, sumptum*: "obtain", "get".
141 *faenus, faenoris* (n.): "interest", "usury".
142 *nummus, -i* (m.): "coin" (possibly a *sestertius*, a small silver coin, theoretically equal to 2.5 grams of silver); *in dies minasque argenti singulas nummis*: "at the rate of a *sestertius* a day for each silver *mina*" (this is an extortionate rate of interest).
143 *papae*: an expression of surprise, or, as in this case, of horror.
144 *unā*: "at the same time", "along with him".
145 *intereo, interire, interiui / interii, interitus*: "perish", "die", "be ruined".
146 *basilice* (adverb): "royally, "completely".
147 *perdo, perdere, perdidi, perditus*: "ruin", "lose" (note that the same word is used in different ways here and at the end of this line, but the pun is difficult to replicate in English).
148 *satiust = satius est; satius =* comparative form of *satis*: "better".
149 *plus scire satiust quam loqui seruom hominem*: "it is enough for a slave to know more than he says [aloud]"; *seruom = seruum; hominem* is in apposition to *seruom*.
150 *timidu's = timidus es.*
151 *trepido, -are, -aui, -atum*: "tremble", "be in a state of anxiety".
152 *uoltu = uultu* from *uultus, -us* (m.): "face", "expression". The manuscript tradition has *uoltum tuom*, which Lindsay retains, but the emendation to *uoltu tuo* makes more sense.

uideor uidere commeruisse¹⁵³ hic me apsente¹⁵⁴ in te aliquid mali.¹⁵⁵
Epidicus: potin¹⁵⁶ ut molestus ne sies?¹⁵⁷ **Thesprio:** abeo. **Epidicus:** asta,¹⁵⁸ abire¹⁵⁹ hinc non sinam.¹⁶⁰

Thesprio: quid nunc me retines? **Epidicus:** amatne istam quam emit de praeda? **Thesprio:** rogas?
deperit.¹⁶¹

Epidicus: deagetur¹⁶²corium¹⁶³ de tergo meo.   65

Thesprio: plusque amat quam te umquam amauit. **Epidicus:** Iuppiter te perduit!¹⁶⁴

Thesprio: mitte¹⁶⁵ nunciam,¹⁶⁶

nam ille me uotuit¹⁶⁷ domum ue-   67a

-nire, ad Chaeribulum¹⁶⁸ iussit¹⁶⁹

huc in proxumum;¹⁷⁰   68a

ibi manere iussit, eo¹⁷¹ uenturust¹⁷² ipsus.¹⁷³ **Epidicus:** quid ita?¹⁷⁴

Thesprio: dicam:

quia patrem priu'¹⁷⁵ conuenire se non uolt¹⁷⁶ neque conspicari,¹⁷⁷   70

---

153 *commeruisse* (supply *te* as the accusative subject of *commeruisse*): "that you have gotten involved in" (+ accusative).
154 *apsente = absente; me apsente* is an ablative absolute.
155 *aliquid mali* (genitive of the whole): "something bad".
156 *potin = potisne* [*es*].
157 *potin ut molestus ne sies*: "can you not be annoying?", "can't you stop bothering me?" (*sies = sis*).
158 *asto, astare, astiti, -*: "wait", "stay", "stand near".
159 *abire* (supply *te* as the accusative subject of *abire*, introduced by *sinam*).
160 *sinam* (first-person singular future active indicative) < *sino, sinere, siui, situm*: "allow".
161 *depereo, -ire, -ii/iui, -itum* (conjugated like *eo, ire*): "die", "be destroyed"; translate here: "fall desperately in love".
162 *deago, -ere, degi, -*: "remove"
163 *corium, -ii* (n.): "skin", "hide".
164 *perduit = perdat* < *perdo, perdere, perdidi, perditum*: "destroy", "ruin".
165 *mitto, -ere, misi, missum*: here translate as "let go".
166 *nunciam = nunc + iam* (emphatic form of *nunc*).
167 *uotuit = uetuit* < *ueto, uetare, uetui, uetitus*: "forbid".
168 Chaeribulus, another young man, is the friend and neighbour of Stratippocles (the young master).
169 For *iussit* reuse *me... uenire* in order to complete the sense of the verb; similarly you need to supply *me* as object of *iussit* in line 69.
170 *proxumum = proximum*, here translate as "next door [house]".
171 *eo*: "there", "to that place".
172 *uenturust = uenturus est*.
173 *ipsus = ipse*.
174 *quid ita*: "why so?"
175 *priu' = prius*; translate with *quam* in line 71; *priu' ... quam*: "before"; "until".
176 *uolt = uult* < *uolo, uelle, uolui, -*.
177 *conspicor, conspicari, conspicatus sum*: "catch sight of", "see".

quam id argentum, quod debetur pro illa,[178] dinumerauerit.[179]

Epidicus: eu[180] edepol res turbulentas![181] **Thesprio:** mitte me ut eam[182] nunciam.[183]

Epidicus: haecine[184] ubi scibit[185] senex, puppis[186] pereunda est[187] probe.[188]

Thesprio: quid[189] istuc ad me attinet, 75

quo tu intereas[190] modo?

Epidicus: quia perire solus nolo, te cupio perire mecum, beneuolens cum beneuolente. **Thesprio:** abi in malam rem maxumam[191] a me

cum istac[192] condicione.[193] **Epidicus:** i sane,[194] — siquidem[195] festinas magis.[196]

Thesprio: numquam hominem quemquam[197] conueni unde[198] 80 abierim[199] lubentius.[200] —

Epidicus: illic[201] hinc abiit. solus nunc es.[202] quo in loco haec res[203] sit uides

---

178 *illa* = the slave girl Stratippocles has just bought on credit.
179 *dinumero, dinumerare, dinumeraui, dinumeratus*: "pay out".
180 *eu*: an exclamation, often of joy, but here of lamentation.
181 *res turbulentas* (accusative of exclamation): "what a terrible situation!".
182 *eam* < *eo, ire, iui/ii, itum*: "go".
183 *nunciam* = *nunc* + *iam*.
184 *haecine* = *haec*: "these things"; the suffix *-ne*, while identical in form to the interrogative suffix *-ne*, here functions as a firm statement or affirmation.
185 *scibit* = *sciet* < *scio, scire, sciui, scitum*.
186 *puppis, puppis* (f.): "ship".
187 *pereunda est* (gerundive, passive periphrastic) < *pereo, perire, periui / perii, peritus*: "die", "be ruined"; here translate as "sink" or "be shipwrecked".
188 *probe*: "thoroughly".
189 *quid istuc ad me attinet*: "why does that concern me?", "what's it to me?".
190 *intereo, interire, interii, interitum*: "be ruined", "die".
191 *malam rem maxumam* is a euphemistic way of referring to the *malam crucem* (the cross on which a slave who was given the most extreme penalty would be crucified).
192 *istac* = *istā* (feminine ablative singular of *iste, ista, istud*).
193 *condicio, -onis* (f.): "option", "proposal".
194 *sane*: "certainly", "however" (used here to add force to the imperative *i*).
195 *siquidem*: "if indeed", "since".
196 *festinas magis*: "you're in such a hurry".
197 *quemquam* < *quisquam, cuiusquam*: "anyone", "any [man])".
198 *unde*: here translate as "from whom".
199 *abierim* (first-person singular perfect subjunctive active) < *abeo, -ire, -iui / -ii, -itum*: "go away".
200 *lubentius* = *libentius*: "cheerfully".
201 *illic* = *ille*.
202 Epidicus is talking to himself in this speech, hence the use of the second-person singular and the vocative *Epidice*.
203 *res, rei* (f.): "matter", "situation".

Epidice: nisi quid tibi[204] in tete[205] auxili[206] est, apsumptus es.[207]
tantae in te impendent[208] ruinae:[209] nisi suffulcis[210] firmiter,
non potes supsistere:[211] itaque in te inruont[212] montes mali.[213]
neque[214] ego nunc 85
quo modo[215]
me expeditum[216] ex impedito[217] faciam, consilium placet. 86
ego miser
perpuli[218]
meis dolis senem[219] ut censeret suam[220] sese emere filiam: 88
is suo
filio
fidicinam[221] emit, quam ipse[222] amat, quam abiens mandauit[223] mihi. 90
si sibi nunc alteram 90a
ab legione adduxit animi caussa,[224] corium[225] perdidi.
nam ubi senex
senserit[226] 92a
sibi data esse uerba,[227] uirgis dorsum dispoliet meum.[228] —

---

204 *tibi* (dative of reference).
205 *tete* = *te* + *te* (the suffix -*te* adds emphasis to the pronoun).
206 *auxili* (genitive of the whole after *quid*): "[any] help".
207 *apsumptus* = *absumptus* < *absumo, -ere, -sumpsi, -sumptus*: "annihilate", "ruin".
208 *impendeo, -ere*: "hang over".
209 *ruina, -ae* (f.): "catastrophe", "disaster".
210 *suffulcio, suffulcire, suffulsi, suffultus*: "prop up" (supply *te* as a direct object).
211 *supsistere* = *subsistere* < *subsisto, -ere, –stiti, –*: "remain standing".
212 *inruont* = *irruont* (third-person plural present indicative active) < *irruo, -ere, -ui, -utum*: "run headlong into", "topple down on", "crash down on".
213 *mali* (genitive) < *malum, -i* (n.): "evil", "trouble", "bad luck".
214 *neque* (translate with *consilium placet*): "a plan doesn't seem good", "there is no good plan".
215 *quo modo*: "how", "in what way".
216 *expeditum* (perfect passive participle; agrees with *me*) < *expedio, expedire, expediui, expeditus*: "disengage," "set free".
217 *impedito* (perfect passive participle) < *impedio, impedio, impedire, impediui, impeditus*: "encumber", "trap". Here it modifies a missing ablative *me*; translate *quo modo me expeditum ex impedito faciam*: "how I can free myself from this predicament".
218 *perpello, perpellere, perpuli, perpulsus*: "compel", "prevail upon".
219 *senem* "old man" refers to the old master Periphanes.
220 *suam... filiam* is the direct object of *emere*; *sese* is the accusative subject of *emere*.
221 This is the *fidicina* he mentioned in line 47.
222 *ipse* here refers to the young master Stratippocles.
223 After *mandauit* supply *ut emerem*.
224 *caussa* = *causa*.
225 *corium, -ii* (n.): "skin", "hide".
226 *sentio, sentire, sensi, sensum*: "realize".
227 *sibi data esse uerba*: "that he has been tricked / lied to".
228 *dispolio, -are, -aui, -atum*: "strip for flogging"; *uirgis dorsum dispoliet meum*: "he'll strip my back for a flogging with rods / cudgels".

at enim tu
praecaue.[229]   94a
at enim — bat enim![230] nihil est istuc.[231] plane hoc corruptumst[232]   95
caput.
nequam[233] homo es,
Epidice.   96a
qui[234] lubidost[235] male loqui? — quia tute te<te>[236] deseris.[237] —
quid faciam?
men[238] rogas?   98a
tuquidem[239] antehac aliis solebas dare consilia mutua.[240]
aliquid[241] aliqua[242] reperiundumst.[243] sed ego cesso[244] ire obuiam[245]   100
adulescenti, ut quid negoti[246] sit sciam? atque ipse illic[247] est.
tristis est. cum Chaeribulo incedit aequali[248] suo.
huc concedam,[249] orationem unde[250] horum placide[251] persequar.[252]

---

229 *praecaueo, praecauere, praecaui, praecautum*: "beware".
230 *bat*: a comic word to rhyme with *at*, similar to the Yiddish-origin "shm-reduplication" we see in English phrases like "fancy-shmancy".
231 *nihil est istuc*: "it's no use".
232 *corruptumst = corruptum est* (the subject is *caput*).
233 *nequam* (indeclinable): "worthless".
234 *qui* (an old ablative form): "how", "why".
235 *lubidost = lubido est = libido est*: "is it a pleasure [for me]", "is there a desire [in me]".
236 The suffix -*te* adds emphasis to the pronoun.
237 *desero, -ere, -serui, -sertus*: "abandon", "give up [on]".
238 *men = me + ne*.
239 *tuquidem = tu quidem*.
240 *mutuus, -a, -um*: "mutual", "reciprocal". This is difficult to translate here, but the idea seems to be that Epidicus used to give advice to others in the expectation of getting advice from them in return.
241 *aliquid*: "some [scheme]", some [solution]".
242 *aliqua*: "somehow".
243 *reperiundumst = reperiendum est*.
244 *cesso, -are, -aui, -atum* (intransitive): "hold back from", "delay" (+ infinitive).
245 *obuiam* (adverb): "in the way", "to meet" (+ dative).
246 *negoti = negotii* (genitive of the whole after *quid*): "[what sort] of trouble / situation".
247 *illic = ille*.
248 *aequalis, -e*: "peer", "friend of the same age".
249 *concedam* (future indicative) < *concedo, -ere, -cessi, -cessum*: "withdraw", "move back".
250 *unde*: "from which place", "where".
251 *placide* (adverb): "quietly".
252 *persequor, -sequi, -cutus sum* (present subjunctive, either hortatory or purpose clause after a missing *ut*): "follow" (in the sense of "hear"), "note down".

1.2 STRATIPPOCLES, CHAERIBVLVS, EPIDICVS

Scene summary: With Epicus eavesdropping on the conversation, Stratippocles arrives with his friend Chaeribulus and complains to him about the debt he's incurred for his new slave girl. He gets angry at Chaeribulus for not being able to give him the money he needs, and then says he'll send the slave Epidicus to work at the mill if he doesn't find a way to pay his debt for him. Epidicus makes his presence known, and attempts to make Stratippocles aware of how much Epidicus has already risked on his behalf in buying Acropolistis for him with his father's money. Stratippocles feels no remorse, however, and just demands that Epidicus find a way to pay off his current debt and get rid of Acropolistis (whom Periphanes thinks is his daughter Telestis). Epidicus says that he knows of a rich soldier from Euboea who will buy Acropolistis and promises to find some way to pay off Stratippocles's debt. Stratippocles, Chaeribulus, and Epidicus all go into Chaeribulus's house.

Stratippocles: Rem tibi sum elocutus[1] omnem, Chaeribule, atque admodum[2]

meorum maerorum[3] atque amorum summam[4] edictaui[5] tibi.   105

Chaeribulus: praeter[6] aetatem et uirtutem stultus es, Stratippocles.

idne pudet te, quia captiuam genere prognatam[7] bono

in[8] praeda es mercatus?[9] quis erit uitio[10] qui id uortat tibi?

Stratippocles: qui[11] inuident omnis[12] inimicos mihi illoc[13] facto repperi;[14]

at pudicitiae eiius[15] numquam nec uim nec uitium[16] attuli.[17]   110

---

1   *eloquor, eloqui, elocutus sum*: "tell in detail" (+ dative of person told).
2   *admodum* (adverb): "fully", "thoroughly".
3   *maeror, maeroris* (m.): "sadness", "misery". "woe".
4   *summa, -ae* (f.): "main point", "sum total".
5   *edicto, -are, -aui, -atum*: "tell", "lay out" (+ dative of person told).
6   *praeter*: "contrary to" (+ accusative).
7   *prognatus, -a, -um*: "descended from".
8   *in*: "amongst" (+ ablative *praedā*).
9   *mercor, -ari, -atus sum*: "buy".
10 *uitio qui id uortat tibi*: "who would blame you for it".
11 *qui*: "those who".
12 *omnīs = omnēs* (masculine accusative plural).
13 *illoc = illo*.
14 *reperio, reperire, repperi, repertum*: "find".
15 *eiius = eius*.
16 *uitium, -ii* (n.): "crime", "violation".
17 *affero, afferre, attuli, allatum* (or *adfero, adferre, adtuli, adlatum*): "bring", "deliver", "use" (+ accusative).

Chaeribulus: iam istoc[18] probior[19] [es] meo quidem animo, quom[20] in amore temperes.[21]

Stratippocles: nihil agit qui diffidentem[22] uerbis solatur[23] suis;

is est amicus, qui[24] in re dubia re iuuat, ubi rest[25] opus.

Chaeribulus: quid tibi me uis facere? **Stratippocles:** argenti[26] dare quadraginta[27] minas,[28]

quod danistae[29] detur, unde ego illud sumpsi[30] faenore.[31]   115

Chaeribulus: si hercle[32] haberem <pollicerer>.[33] **Stratippocles:** nam quid te igitur retulit

beneficum esse oratione,[34] si ad rem[35] auxilium emortuom[36] est?

Chaeribulus: quin[37] edepol[38] egomet[39] clamore[40] differor,[41] difflagitor.[42]

Stratippocles: malim[43] istius modi[44] mihi amicos furno[45] mersos[46] quam foro.[47]

---

18 *istoc = isto*: "by that very fact".
19 *probior* (masc. nom. sing. comparative): "[you are] more honourable" (supply *es*) < *probus, -a, -um*.
20 *quom = cum*.
21 *tempero, -are, -aui, -atus*: "control oneself".
22 *diffido, -ere, diffisus sum*: "lack confidence", "despair".
23 *solor, -ari, -atus sum*: "console", "comfort".
24 *qui in re dubia re iuuat ubi re est opus*: "who, in difficult circumstances, gives actual help when there's a need for it."
25 *rest = re est*.
26 *argentum, -i* (n.): "silver", "money".
27 *quadraginta* (indeclinable): "forty".
28 *mina, -ae* (f.): a Greek unit of money equivalent to 430g of silver.
29 *danista, -ae* (m.): "moneylender".
30 *sumo, -ere, sumpsi, sumptum*: "obtain", "get".
31 *faenus, -oris* (n.): "interest"; "usury".
32 *hercle*: "by Hercules!" (see note 21 on page 136 for the use of *hercle* and *mehercle*).
33 *pollicerer* (apodosis of a present contrary-to-fact conditional sentence, with *si haberem* being the protasis): first-person singular imperfect subjunctive deponent < *polliceor, polliceri, pollicitus sum*: "offer", "promise".
34 *nam quid te igitur retulit te beneficum esse oratione*: "so what was the use of you being generous in your speech".
35 *rem*: "the matter at hand".
36 *emortuom = emortuum < emortuus, -a, -um*: "dead" (modifies *auxilium*).
37 *quin*: "but", "really".
38 *edepol*: "by Pollux" (a mild oath).
39 *egomet = ego + -met*: "I, myself".
40 *clamore*: (in this instance) "verbal harassment by debt collectors".
41 *differo, differre, distuli, dilatum*: "disturb".
42 *difflagito, difflagitare, difflagitaui, difflagitatus*: "dun", "harass for debt repayment".
43 *malo, malle, malui, –*: "prefer". Lindsay's text gives this line as: *malim istiusmodi mi amicos forno occensos quam foro*, but Duckworth-Wheeler's emendations make more sense here.
44 *modus, -i* (m.): "type", "kind" (*istius modi* is a genitive of quality after *amicos*).
45 *furnus, -i* (m.): "oven".
46 *mergo, mergere, mersi, mersum*: "plunge", "immerse" (supply *esse*, with *amicos* as the accusative subject of the passive infinitive *mersum esse*).
47 *forum, -i* (n.): "forum" (where bankruptcies were dealt with before the praetor); the alliteration of *furno* and *foro* explains why Stratippocles takes such an extreme view of his

sed operam[48] Epidici nunc me[49] emere pretio pretioso[50] uelim.   120
quem[51] quidem ego hominem inrigatum[52] plagis[53] pistori[54] dabo,
nisi hodie priu'[55] comparassit[56] mihi quadraginta minas
quam argenti fuero elocutus[57] ei postremam syllabam.[58]
Epidicus: salua res est: bene promittit, spero, seruabit fidem.[59]
sine meo sumptu[60] paratae iam sunt scapulis[61] symbolae.[62]   125
adgrediar[63] hominem. aduenientem peregre[64] erum[65] suom[66]
Stratippoclem[67]
impertit[68] salute seruos[69] Epidicus? **Stratippocles:** ubi is est?
Epidicus: adest.
saluom huc aduenisse[70] — **Stratippocles:** tam[71] tibi istuc[72] credo
quam mihi.
Epidicus: benene usque ualuisti? **Stratippocles:** a morbo[73] ualui, ab
animo aeger fui.

---

indebted friends.
48 *opera, -ae* (f.): "service", "help".
49 *me* should perhaps be *mi/mihi* (see Duckworth-Wheeler 1940: 177).
50 *pretio pretioso* (ablative of price): "for a large amount of money".
51 *quem* (connecting relative, modifying *hominem*): translate "that [man]".
52 *inrigatum = irrigatum; irrigo, -are, -aui, -atum*: "beat soundly".
53 *plaga, -ae* (f.): "blow", "whiplash".
54 *pistor, -is* (m.): "miller". Flour mills were powered by treadmills turned by animals or humans. It was exhausting work, and being sent to work at a mill was a dreaded punishment. Lucius, a man turned into a donkey in Apuleius's *Metamorphoses* (9.11–12), describes what it was like for him to be made to work the treadmill.
55 *priu' = prius; priu'* should be translated with *quam* in the next line; *priu'... quam*: "before".
56 *nisi... comparassit*: "[unless] he gets hold of".
57 *fuero elocutus = ero elocutus*: "I'll tell (someone in the dative) in detail". Perfect passive forms that normally use *sum, eram*, or *ero* (indicative) or *sim, essem* (subjunctive) sometimes instead use *fui, fueram, fuero* (indicative) and *fuerim, fuissem* (subjunctive) — see Bennett 102, notes 36, 37, http://www.thelatinlibrary.com/bennett.html#NtA_36
58 *argenti... postremam syllabam*: "the last syllable of the [amount] of money".
59 *spero, seruabit fidem*: "he'll keep his word, I hope".
60 *sumptus, -us* (m.): "expense", "charge".
61 *scapula, -ae* (f.): "shoulder", "back".
62 *symbola, -ae* (f.): the monetary contribution owed by participants in a group banquet, paid for by the subscribers; here translate as "contributions", "donations".
63 *adgrediar = aggrediar < aggredior, aggredi, aggressus sum*: "approach".
64 *peregre* (adverb): "from abroad".
65 *erus, -i* (m.): "master".
66 *suom = suum*.
67 *Stratippoclem* (accusative singular).
68 *impertit salute*: "greets".
69 *seruos = seruus*.
70 *saluom huc aduenisse* (supply *gaudeo*; a formulaic greeting to someone who has returned from abroad, see line 7): "I'm happy to see you're safely back again".
71 *tam... quam*: "as much... as".
72 *istuc*: "as far as that goes".
73 *a morbo... ab animo*: "as far as illness goes... in my mind...".

Epidicus: quod ad me attinuit,[74] ego curaui: quod mandasti[75] <tu> 130
mihi,
impetratum est;[76] empta ancillast,[77] quod tute[78] ad me litteras
missiculabas.[79] **Stratippocles:** perdidisti omnem operam. **Epidicus:**
nam qui[80] perdidi?
Stratippocles: quia meo neque cara est cordi neque placet.[81]
Epidicus: quid retulit[82]
mihi tanto opere[83] te mandare et mittere ad me epistulas?
Stratippocles: illam amabam olim, nunc iam alia cura impendet[84] 135
pectori.
Epidicus: hercle miserum est ingratum esse homini id quod facias
bene.[85]
ego quod bene feci male feci, quia amor mutauit locum.[86]
Stratippocles: desipiebam[87] mentis[88] quom illa scripta mittebam tibi.
Epidicus: men[89] piacularem[90] oportet fieri ob stultitiam tuam,
ut meum tergum tuae stultitiae subdas[91] succidaneum?[92] 140
Stratippocles: quid[93] istic[94] uerba facimus? huic homini opust[95]
quadraginta minis
celeriter calidis,[96] danistae quas resoluat,[97] et cito.

---

74 *attineo, -ere, -ui, -attentum*: "concern", "pertain to".
75 *mandasti = mandauisti < mando, -are, -aui, -atum*: "order", "entrust".
76 *impetro, -are, -aui, -atus*: "achieve", "get", "obtain".
77 *ancillast = ancilla est < ancilla, -ae* (f.): "female slave", "slave girl".
78 The suffix *-te* adds emphasis to the pronoun.
79 *missiculo, -are, -aui, -atum*: "send often", "keep sending".
80 *qui*: "how".
81 *cara est... placet* (*ancilla* is the subject of both verbs).
82 *quid retulit*: "what was the use" (completed by the accusative-infinitive construction).
83 *tanto opere*: "so much".
84 *impendeo, -ere*: "hang over".
85 *miserum est ingratum esse homini id quod facias bene*: "it's upsetting when a favour you do for someone is unappreciated".
86 *amor mutauit locum*: "you've switched loves" (literally "your love changed place").
87 *desipio, -ere, -ui, –*: "be foolish", "be out of one's right mind".
88 *mentis* (genitive of respect).
89 *men = me + ne*.
90 *piacularis, -e*: "sacrificial victim".
91 *subdo, -ere, -didi, -ditum*: "substitute".
92 *succidaneus, -a, -um* (a rare word referring to another type of sacrificial victim): "substitute victim".
93 *quid*: "why".
94 *istic* (adverb): "now", "here", "there".
95 *opust = opus est*.
96 *calidis*: "red hot" (apparently implying that the *minae* need to be quick in coming).
97 *resoluo, -ere, -solui, -solutum* (subjunctive in a relative clause of purpose): "pay".

Epidicus: dic modo: unde auferre[98] me uis? quo a tarpezita[99] peto?
Stratippocles: unde lubet.[100] nam ni ante solem occasum[101] e lo<culis adferes>[102]

meam domum ne inbitas:[103] tu te in pistrinum[104] <conferas.>[105]   145
Epidicus: facile tu istuc[106] sine periclo[107] et cura, corde[108] libero fabulare;[109] noui[110] ego nostros:[111] mihi dolet[112] quom[113] ego uapulo.[114]
Stratippocles: quid tu nunc? patierin[115] ut ego me interimam?[116]
Epidicus: ne feceris.[117]

ego istuc[118] accedam[119] periclum[120] potius[121] atque audaciam.[122]
Stratippocles: nunc places, nunc ego te laudo. **Epidicus:** patiar ego   150
istuc quod lubet.[123]

Stratippocles: quid illa fiet fidicina igitur?[124] **Epidicus:** aliqua res reperibitur,[125]

aliqua ope exsoluam,[126] extricabor[127] aliqua. **Stratippocles:** plenus consili's.[128]

---

98 *aufero, -ferre, apstuli, ablatum*: "get", "take".
99 *tarpezita = trapezita, -ae* (m.): "moneylender".
100 *lubet = libet*: "it is pleasing"; *unde lubet*: "[borrow it] from wherever you want".
101 *occido, -ere, -cidi, -casum*: "set", "sink".
102 *ni ante solem occasum e lo<culis adferes>*: "unless you bring it from some stash before the sun has set".
103 *inbitas = ineas < ineo, -ire, -iui/ii, -itum*: "go into", "enter".
104 *pistrinum, -i* (n.): "flour mill" (where slaves or animals were made to push a treadmill for grinding grain into flour).
105 *se confero, conferre, contuli, collatum*: "take oneself"; "go".
106 *istuc*: "about that".
107 *periclo = periculo < periculum, i* (n.): "danger", "risk".
108 *cor, cordis* (n.): "heart".
109 *fabulare = fabularis < fabulor, -ari, -atus sum*: "speak".
110 *nosco, -ere, noui, notum*: "get to know", "know", "recognize".
111 *nostros* (substantive adjective): "our [fellow slaves]", "our [floggers]" (referring to the slaves whom Stratippocles would order to beat Epidicus).
112 *mihi dolet*: "I feel pain".
113 *quom = cum*.
114 *uapulo, -are, -aui, -atum*: "be beaten", "get a beating".
115 *patierin = patierisne < patior, pati, passus sum*: "allow".
116 *interimo, -ere, interimi, interemptum*: "kill".
117 *ne feceris* (prohibitive subjunctive): "don't do [it]".
118 *istuc* (modifies *periclum*) = *istud*.
119 *accedo, -ere, -essi, -essum*: "approach", "face up to".
120 *periclum = periculum*.
121 *potius*: "rather [than let you kill yourself]".
122 *audacia, -ae* (f.): "daring plan".
123 *patiar ego istuc quod lubet*: "I'll endure whatever you want [me to]".
124 *quid illa fiet fidicina igitur*: "so what will be done with the lyre-player?"
125 *reperibitur = reperietur*.
126 *exsoluo, -ere, -i, -utum*: "solve", "deliver", "free", "discharge" (supply *te* as the direct object of *exsoluam* and *extricabor*.
127 *extricor, -ari, -atus sum*: "disentangle", "free", "release".
128 *consili's = consili es; consilium, -i/-ii* (n.): "scheming".

noui ego te. **Epidicus:** est Euboicus[129] miles locuples,[130] multo auro potens,[131]

qui ubi tibi[132] istam[133] emptam esse scibit[134] atque hanc adductam[135] alteram,[136]

continuo[137] te orabit ultro[138] ut illam[139] tramittas[140] sibi.   155

sed ubi illa est quam tu adduxisti[141] tecum? **Stratippocles:** iam[142] faxo[143] hic[144] erit.

Chaeribulus: quid hic nunc agimus?[145] **Stratippocles:** eamus intro huc ad te,[146] ut hunc hodie diem

luculente[147] habeamus. — [148] **Epidicus:** ite intro, ego de re argentaria[149]

iam senatum[150] conuocabo in corde consiliarium,[151]

quoi[152] potissumum[153] indicatur[154] bellum, unde argentum auferam.   160

Epidice, uide quid agas, ita res subito haec obiectast[155] tibi;

non enim nunc tibi dormitandi neque cunctandi[156] copia[157] est.

---

129 *Euboicus, -a, -um*: "Euboean", "from (or serving as a soldier on) the island of Euboea".
130 *locuples, -pletis*: "wealthy".
131 *multio auro potens*: "with a lot of buying power".
132 *tibi* (dative of reference): "for you", "on your behalf".
133 *istam* (refers to the *fidicina*, the first girl Stratippocles was in love with).
134 *scibit = sciet < scio, scire, sciui, scitum*: "know".
135 *adductam* (supply *esse*): "[that the other girl] has been brought [as well]".
136 *hanc... alteram* (refers to the second girl whom Stratippocles has just brought home).
137 *continuo* (adverb): "immediately".
138 *ultro* (adverb): "voluntarily", "on his own initiative".
139 *illam* (refers to the *fidicina*).
140 *tramitto, -ere, –misi, -missum*: "send over", "hand over".
141 *adduco, -ere, adduxi, adductum*: "bring".
142 *iam*: "already"; translate here: "soon".
143 *faxo* (alternative form of the first-person singular future indicative active of *facio, -ere*): "I'll make [it happen]", "I promise", "definitely".
144 *hic*: "here".
145 *quid hic nunc agimus*: "what should we do now?" (despite the indicative mood this works best as a deliberative question).
146 *ad te*: "to your house".
147 *luculente* (adverb): "excellently", "well", "agreeably".
148 *habeamus*: "spend", "pass", "keep" [this day].
149 *de re argentaria*: "regarding the money situation".
150 Epidicus uses the metaphor of the senate to refer to his own internal deliberations as to what course he should take.
151 *consiliarius, -a, -um* (modifies *senatum*): "advice-giving".
152 *quoi = cui* (dative because of the compound verb *indicatur*): "[against] whom".
153 *potissumum = potissimum* (adverb): "especially".
154 *indico, -ere, indixi, indictum*: "publicly declare".
155 *obiectast = obiecta est < obicio/obiicio, -ere, obieci, obiectum*: "throw at", "assign" (+ dative).
156 *dormitandi... cunctandi* (gerunds): "dozing... delaying".
157 *copia, -ae* (f.): "opportunity".

adeundum.¹⁵⁸ senem oppugnare¹⁵⁹ certumst¹⁶⁰ consilium mihi.¹⁶¹
ibo intro atque adulescenti dicam nostro erili¹⁶² filio,
ne hinc foras¹⁶³ exambulet¹⁶⁴ neue¹⁶⁵ obuiam¹⁶⁶ ueniat seni. —   165

---

158 *adeundum* (gerundive; supply *est*): "it must be done!".
159 *oppugno, -are, -aui, -atum*: "fight against", "make an attack on".
160 *certumst* = *certum est*.
161 *senem oppugnare certumst consilium mihi*: "my plan is settled: I'll make an attack on the old man".
162 *erilis, -e*: "relating to the *erus* (master)".
163 *foras* (adverb): "out of doors".
164 *exambulo, -are, -aui, -atum*: "stroll out", "walk out".
165 *neue*: "and so that... not".
166 *obuiam* (adverb): "into the presence of" (+ dative).

ACTVS II

2.1 APOECIDES, PERIPHANES

Scene summary: The two old men, Periphanes and his friend Apoecides, come out of Periphanes's house (which is next door to Chaeribulus's). Their conversation tells us that the widowed Periphanes is planning on marrying a woman (whom, we later find out, is called Philippa), the mother of his illegitimate daughter Telestis, but he's worried about how his son Stratippocles will react.

Apoecides: Plerique[1] homines, quos quom[2] nil[3] refert[4] pudet,
ubi pudendum est[5] ibi eos deserit[6] pudor,   166a
quom usust[7] ut pudeat.[8]
is[9] adeo[10] tu's.[11] quid est quod[12] pudendum siet,[13]
genere gnatam[14] bono[15] pauperem[16] domum
ducere te uxorem?[17]   170

---

1 *plerusque, pleraque, plerumque*: "many", "most".
2 *quom = cum*.
3 *nil = nihil*.
4 *quos quom nihil refert pudet*: "who feel shame about something that doesn't [actually] matter".
5 *pudendum est* (impersonal use of the gerundive in passive periphrastic): "[when] they ought to feel shame".
6 *desero, -ere, -serui, -sertum*: "abandon".
7 *usust = usus est* (impersonal; *= opus est*): "there is need".
8 *ut pudeat* (impersonal verb in a substantive clause after *usus est*; see Bennett 295.6, http://www.thelatinlibrary.com/bennett.html#sect295): "that there should be shame"; translate here: "that he should feel shame".
9 *is*: translate here: "this sort of man".
10 *adeo*: "precisely", "exactly".
11 *tu's = tu es*.
12 *quid est quod*: "what is there that".
13 *siet = sit*.
14 *gnatam = natam < nata, -ae* (f.): "daughter".
15 *genere bono* (ablative of separation, see Bennett 215): "from a good family".
16 *pauper, pauperis*: "poor", "poverty-stricken".
17 *domum ducere... uxorem*: (literally) "to lead a wife home"; translate here: "marry".

praesertim[18] eam, qua ex[19] tibi commemores[20] hanc quae domist[21]
filiam prognatam.[22] 171–2
Periphanes: reuereor filium.[23] **Apoecides:** at pol[24] ego te credidi[25]
uxorem, quam tu extulisti,[26] pudore exsequi,[27]
quoiius[28] quotiens sepulcrum uides, sacruficas[29] 175
ilico[30] Orco[31] hostiis,[32] neque adeo iniuria,[33]
quia licitumst[34] eam tibi uiuendo[35] uincere. **Periphanes:** oh![36]
Hercules[37] ego fui, dum illa mecum fuit;
neque sexta aerumna[38] acerbior Herculi[39] quam[40] illa mihi obiectast.[41]
Apoecides: pulchra edepol[42] dos[43] pecuniast.[44] **Periphanes:** quae 180
quidem pol non maritast.[45]

---

18 *praesertim*: "especially".
19 *qua ex = ex qua*: "from whom".
20 *commemoro, -are, -aui, -atus* (subjunctive because it is a subordinate clause within the indirect discourse of lines 169–170, see Bennett 314): "mention", "say".
21 *domist = domi est* (locative).
22 *hanc... filiam prognatam* (supply *esse*; indirect discourse after *commemores*): "that this daughter... was born".
23 *reuereor filium*: "I have respect for my son", "I'm afraid my son [won't like it]".
24 *pol*: "by Pollux".
25 *te credidi... exsequi* (indirect discourse).
26 *ecfero/effero, ecferre/efferre, extuli, elatus*: "carry out for burial", "bury".
27 *pudore exsequi*: literally "to follow with decency"; translate here: "to show respect to" (+ accusative).
28 *quoiius = cuius*.
29 *sacruficas = sacrificas < sacrifico, -are, -aui, -atum*: "sacrifice", "offer a sacrifice".
30 *ilico*: "on the spot", "immediately".
31 *Orcus, -i* (m.): Orcus, god of death and the underworld.
32 *hostia, -ae* (f.): "sacrificial victim", "animal sacrifice".
33 *neque adeo inuria*: "and rightly too".
34 *licitumst = licitum est < licet, licuit, licitum est* (impersonal): "it was lawful", "it was permitted" (+ dative of the person to whom it was permitted, in this case *tibi*).
35 *uiuendo* (gerund; ablative of means).
36 *oh* (exclamation of surprise, either happy or unhappy): here translate as "ugh!".
37 *Hercules, -is* (m.): "Hercules", or perhaps here "a Hercules".
38 *aerumna, -ae* (f.): "distress", "hardship", "labour", "task"; the Sixth Labour of Hercules, according to common Roman versions, was that of the belt of Amazon Hippolyta (Duckworth-Wheeler 1940: 218).
39 *Herculi* (dative).
40 *quam illa mihi obiectast*: "than that [labour that] was assigned to me".
41 *obiectast = obiecta est* (*sexta aerumna* is the subject of *obiectast*): "thrown (at); translate here: "assigned (to)".
42 *edepol*: "by Pollux".
43 *dos, dotis* (f): "dowry".
44 *pecuniast = pecunia est*.
45 *quae quidem pol non maritast*: "yes, by Pollux – at least, it would be if it came without marriage" (*maritast = marita est*).

2.2 EPIDICVS, APOECIDES, PERIPHANES

Scene summary: Epidicus comes out and sees the old men before they see him. He overhears Periphanes planning a marriage for Stratippocles and worrying about a rumour that Stratippocles has been devoting himself to a young lyre-playing slave-woman (we know she is Acropolistis). Epidicus hits on a scheme to cheat Periphanes out of the money needed to repay Stratippocles's debt. He pretends he's been searching for them all over town to tell them the news that the legion has arrived home from the war in Thebes, and that he has overheard two women who say that Stratippocles was planning on borrowing the money to buy, and then manumit, his lyre-playing girlfriend. Periphanes is very upset at his son for ruining his credit and wasting money like this, and gladly takes Epidicus's advice, which is to arrange a marriage for Stratippocles to some unnamed woman, and to buy Acropolistis himself but arrange for her to be sent out of the city and out of Stratippocles's reach. Epidicus persuades Periphanes not to involve himself personally in the purchase of the slave woman (ostensibly to ensure that Stratippocles won't find out that his own father has bought her), and promises him that he'll recoup the money and even make a profit by selling her on to a wealthy Rhodian soldier (perhaps the same soldier as the Euboean one Epidicus mentioned act 1, scene 2). Periphanes agrees to send his friend Apoecides with Epidicus to carry out the purchase.

Epidicus: St![1]

tacete, habete animum bonum.[2]

liquido[3] exeo foras[4] auspicio, aui[5] sinistera;[6]   183–4

acutum cultrum habeo, senis[7] qui[8] exenterem[9] marsuppium.[10]   185

sed eccum[11] ipsum ante[12] aedis[13] conspicor[14] <cum> Apoecide

---

1 *st*: "sh", "shush" (command to be silent).
2 *animum bonum*: "good courage".
3 *liquidus, -a, -um*: "clear".
4 *foras* (adverb): "outside".
5 *auis, -is* (f.): "bird".
6 *sinistera = sinistra* (ablative feminine singular, modifying *aui*) < *sinister, -tra, -trum*: "left". (Birds seen flying by on the left were usually considered to be a favourable omen).
7 *senex, senis* (m.): "old man".
8 *qui = quo* (ablative of means).
9 *exentero, -are, -aui, -atus*: "disembowel"; (in the context of a purse or store of money) "empty". Epidicus's imagery here suggests that Periphanes and his *marsuppium* are going to be cut open like an animal sacrifice in Roman religious ritual.
10 *marsuppium, -ii* (n.): "purse", "moneybag".
11 *eccum = ecce + hunc*: "look, there he is!".
12 *ante* (preposition + accusative): "in front of".
13 *aedis/aedes, -is* (f.): "building", "house" (often used in the plural, as here).
14 *conspicor, -ari, -atus sum*: "notice", "see".

qualis[15] uolo uetulos[16] duo.

iam ego me conuortam[17] in hirudinem[18] atque eorum exsugebo[19] sanguinem,

senati[20] qui columen[21] cluent.[22]

Apoecides:[23] continuo[24] ut maritus[25] fiat. **Periphanes:** laudo consilium tuom.[26] 190

nam ego illum audiui in amorem[27] haerere[28] apud nescioquam[29] fidicinam,

id[30] ego excrucior.[31] **Epidicus:** di hercle omnes me adiuuant, augent, amant:

ipsi hiquidem[32] mihi dant uiam, quo pacto[33] ab se[34] argentum auferam.

age nunciam[35] orna[36] te, Epidice, et palliolum[37] in collum[38] conice[39]

itaque adsimulato[40] quasi[41] per urbem totam hominem quaesiueris.[42] 195

---

15 *qualis* (masc. plural accusative): "of the kind".
16 *uetulus, -a, -um*: "elderly". There may be a pun here that continues Epidicus's sacrificial imagery, since *uetulos* sounds like *uitulos* ("calves"), animals used in religious sacrifice (see Gellar-Goad 2012 and Barrios-Lech 2014).
17 *conuorto/conuerto, -ere, -ti, -sum*: "turn [oneself] into".
18 *hirudo, -inis* (f.): "leech".
19 *exsugeo, -ere* (variant form of *ex(s)ugo, -ere, exsuxi, exsuctum*): "suck out".
20 *senati = senatūs* (genitive singular of *senatus, -ūs*).
21 *columen, -inis* (n.): "pillar" (here in the sense of "most valuable member").
22 *cluo, -ere, -, -* : "be calling"; "be said to be".
23 There may be some lines missing here, in which Apoecides probably tried to persuade Periphanes that if he married off his son Stratippocles it would leave Periphanes free to remarry.
24 *continuo* (adverb): "immediately".
25 *maritus, -a, -um*: "married".
26 *tuom = tuum*.
27 *in amorem = in amore*.
28 *haereo, -ere, haesi, haesum*: "hang around (someone)", "keep near/close to (someone)".
29 *nescioquam = nescio quam*.
30 *id* (accusative of inner object): "[I'm upset about] it".
31 *excrucio, -are, -aui, -atum*: literally "crucify", but here "torture", "upset".
32 *hiquidem = hi quidem*.
33 *pactum, pacti* (n.): "manner", "way".
34 *se* (refers to the old men).
35 *nunciam = nunc + iam* (emphatic form of *nunc*).
36 *orno, -are, -aui, -atum*: "dress up", "equip"; translate here: "get ready".
37 *palliolum, -i* (n.): "little pallium", "little Greek cloak", "hood".
38 *collum, -i* (n.): "neck".
39 *conicio, -ere, conieci, coniectum*: "throw over" (Epidicus gathers up the loose folds of his *palliolum*, and throws them around his neck or over his shoulder in order to look the part of a slave running to carry out an errand for his master).
40 *adsimulato* (second-person singular future imperative active) < *adsimulo, -are, -aui, -atum*: "act the part", "pretend".
41 *quasi* (adverb): "as though" (followed by the subjunctive mood).
42 *quaesiueris* (second-person singular perfect active subjunctive) < *quaero, -ere, quaesiui, quaesitum*: "seek", "look for".

age, si quid agis.[43] di inmortales![44] utinam conueniam[45] domi[46]
Periphanem, per omnem urbem quem sum defessus[47] quaerere:[48]
per medicinas,[49] per tostrinas,[50] in gymnasio atque in foro,
per myropolia[51] et lanienas[52] circumque argentarias.[53]
rogitando sum raucus[54] factus, paene in cursu concidi.[55]   200
Periphanes: Epidice! **Epidicus:** Epidicum quis est qui reuocat?
Periphanes: ego sum, Periphanes.
Apoecides: et ego Apoecides sum. **Epidicus:** et egoquidem[56] sum
Epidicus. sed, ere,[57] optuma[58]
uos uideo opportunitate[59] ambo aduenire. **Periphanes:** quid rei est?[60]
Epidicus: mane, <mane>, sine[61] respirem quaeso.[62] **Periphanes:**
immo[63] adquiesce.[64] **Epidicus:** animo malest.[65]
Apoecides: recipe anhelitum.[66] **Periphanes:** clementer,[67] requiesce.   205
Epidicus: animum aduortite.[68]
a legione omnes remissi sunt domum[69] Thebis.[70] **Apoecides:** <quis hoc>
scit factum? **Epidicus:** ego ita dico factum esse. **Periphanes:** scin[71] tu
istuc?[72] **Epidicus:** scio.

---

43 *age, si quid agis*: "act, if you're going to act", "if you're going to do anything, do it".
44 *inmortales = immortales*.
45 *conuenio, -ire, -ueni, -uentum*: "meet", "meet with".
46 *domi* (locative case).
47 *defetiscor, -isci, defessus sum*: "become exhausted", "be worn out".
48 *quaerere* (this infinitive is used where later Latin would use a gerund).
49 *medicinus, -a, um; medicinas* modifies a missing *tabernas*: "doctor's [offices]".
50 *tostrinas = tonstrinas < tonstrinus, -a, -um*: "barber [shops]", "hairdressers' [establishments]"
51 *myropolium, -ii* (n.): "perfumer's shop".
52 *laniena, lanienae* (f): "butcher's shop".
53 *argentarius, -a, -um*: "bankers [counters]".
54 *raucus, -a, -um*: "hoarse".
55 *concido, -ere, concidi, concisum*: "faint", "collapse".
56 *egoquidem = ego quidem*.
57 *erus, -i* (m.): "master".
58 *optumā = optimā*.
59 *optumā opportunitate* (ablative of time when).
60 *quid rei est*: "what's the matter?".
61 *sino, -ere, siui, situm*: "allow", "let" (+ subjunctive).
62 *quaeso*: "please".
63 *immo*: "by all means", "indeed"; "on the contrary", "by no means".
64 *adquiesco / acquiesco, -ere, -eui, -etum*: "rest", "take a break".
65 *animo malest* (= *animo male est*): "I'm feeling faint".
66 *anhelitus, -ūs* (m.): "breath", "breathing".
67 *clementer* (adverb): "calmly", "gradually".
68 *animum aduortite*: "pay attention".
69 *domum* (accusative of place to which; no need for a preposition with *domus*): "home[ward]".
70 *Thebis* (ablative of place from which): "from Thebes".
71 *scin = scisne*.
72 *istuc = istud*.

Periphanes: qui[73] tu scis? **Epidicus:** quia ego ire uidi milites plenis[74] uiis;[75]

arma referunt et iumenta[76] ducunt. **Periphanes:** nimi'[77] factum bene!

Epidicus: tum captiuorum quid[78] ducunt secum! pueros, uirgines,   210
binos,[79] ternos,[80] alius quinque; fit concursus[81] per uias,
filios suos quisque[82] uisunt.[83] **Periphanes:** hercle rem gestam bene![84]
Epidicus: tum meretricum[85] numerus tantus quantum in urbe omni fuit
obuiam[86] ornatae[87] occurrebant suis quaequae[88] amatoribus,
eos captabant.[89] id adeo[90] qui[91] maxume animum aduorterim?[92]   215
pleraeque[93] eae sub uestimentis secum habebant retia.[94]
quom[95] ad portam[96] uenio, atque ego illam illi uideo[97] praestolarier[98]
et cum ea tibicinae[99] ibant quattuor. **Periphanes:** quicum,[100] Epidice?

---

73 *qui*: "how".
74 *plenus, -a, -um*: "full", "crowded".
75 *plenis uiis* (ablative of the way by which; see Bennett 218.9, http://www.thelatinlibrary.com/bennett.html#sect218).
76 *iumentum, -i* (n.): "mule", "pack animal".
77 *nimi'* = *nimis*: "very".
78 *captiuorum quid*: "what about the prisoners".
79 *binos* (< *binus, -a, -um*): "in twos".
80 *ternos* (< *ternus, -a, -um*): "in threes".
81 *concursus, -ūs* (m.): "collision", "traffic jam".
82 *quisque* (although *quisque* is singular, it should be taken as the plural subject of *uisunt*).
83 *uiso, uisere, uisi, uisum*: "go to see", "look at".
84 *rem gestam bene* (*rem gestam* is an accusative of exclamation): "things have gone well!".
85 *meretrix, meretricis* (f.): "courtesan", "prostitute", "[hired] girlfriend".
86 *obuiam* (adverb): "into the presence of", "to meet" (+ dative).
87 *orno, -are, -aui, -atum*: "dress up", adorn".
88 *quaequae* = *quaeque*: "each" < *quique, quaeque, quidque/quicque/quodque*.
89 *captabant*: "they were on the hunt for", "they were going to make [them] their prisoners" < *capto, -are, -aui, -atum*.
90 *adeo*: "precisely", "exactly".
91 *qui*: "how?".
92 *animum aduorterim*: "[how] did I notice?".
93 *plerusque, pleraque, plerumque*: "many", "most".
94 *retia, -ae* (f.): "net" (nets were used in hunting, and some Roman women, or perhaps just Roman sex workers, wore net tunics underneath their outer garments).
95 *quom* = *cum*.
96 *porta, -ae* (f.): "gate", "city gate".
97 *uideo* (historical present).
98 *praestolarier* = *praestolari* < *praestolor, -ari, -atus sum*: "wait for" (+ dative of person waited for).
99 *tibicina, -ae* (f.): "female player of a tibia (a reed instrument originally made from the shin bone of an animal)".
100 *quicum* = *quācum* (feminine ablative singular of the interrogative pronoun).

Epidicus: cum illa quam tuo'[101] gnatus[102] annos multos deamat,[103] deperit,[104]

ubi[105] fidemque[106] remque[107] seque teque properat perdere;[108]   220

ea praestolabatur[109] illum apud portam. **Periphanes:** uiden[110] ueneficam?[111]

Epidicus: sed uestita,[112] aurata,[113] ornata[114] ut[115] lepide,[116] ut concinne,[117] ut noue![118]

Periphanes: quid erat induta?[119] an regillam[120] induculam[121] an mendiculam?[122]

Epidicus: impluuiatam,[123] ut istae faciunt uestimentis nomina.

Periphanes: utin[124] impluuium[125] induta fuerit?[126] **Epidicus:** quid   225 istuc[127] tam mirabile est?

---

101 *tuo' = tuos = tuus.*
102 *gnatus = natus < natus, -i* (m.): "son".
103 *deamo, -are, -aui, -atum:* "adore".
104 *depereo, -ire, -ii/iui, -itum* (conjugated like *eo, ire*): "die", "be destroyed"; translate here: "fall desperately in love".
105 *ubi = in qua:* "in whom", "because of whom".
106 *fidem:* "credit".
107 *rem:* "fortune".
108 *ubi = in qua:* "in whom", "because of whom".
109 *praestolabatur < praestolor, -ari, -atus sum:* "wait for" (+ dative of person waited for).
110 *uiden = uidesne.*
111 *uenefica, -ae* (f.): "poisoner"; translate here: "witch".
112 *uestio, -ire, -iui, -itum:* "be dressed up".
113 *auro, -are, -aui, -atum:* "gild", "adorn with gold jewelry".
114 *ornata < orno, -are, -aui, -atum:* "dress up", adorn".
115 *ut:* "how" (exclamatory).
116 *lepide* (adverb): "charmingly" *< lepidus, -a, -um.*
117 *concinne* (adverb): "neatly", "elegantly" *< concinnus, -a, -um.*
118 *noue* (adverb) *< nouus, -a, -um:* "freshly", "unusually"; translate here: "wearing the latest fashion".
119 *induo, -ere, -ui, -utum:* "clothe", "dress oneself in" (+ accusative *quid*).
120 *regillam:* "royal", "regal", "queenly" (a rare word probably invented by Plautus *< regius, -a, -um*).
121 *induculam:* possibly meaning "lingerie", "underwear" (also probably invented by Plautus *< induo*).
122 *mendiculam:* "beggarly", "meager" (also probably invented by Plautus *< mendicus, -a, -um*; opposite of *regillam*).
123 *impluuiatam:* "the Skylight", "Rain-shoot" (either another comic invention of Plautus, or a name for a style or colour of garment *< impluuium, -i,* see below).
124 *utin = ut(i) + -ne.*
125 *impluuium, -ii* (n.): "skylight" (the *impluuium* was the square opening in the roof of a Roman house's main room; the word was also used to refer to the shallow trough in the floor underneath that collected the rain water, also called the *compluuium*). The joke is that Periphanes foolishly interprets Epidicus's description of the woman's *impluuiatam* dress (whatever *impluuiatam* meant, see note 123 above) as referring to the woman actually wearing the *impluuium* of a house.
126 *induta fuerit = induta sit* (perfect passive subjunctive) *< induo, -ere, indui, indutum.*
127 *istuc = istud.*

quasi[128] non fundis[129] exornatae[130] multae incedant[131] per uias.
at tributus[132] quom[133] imperatus est, negant[134] pendi[135] potis;[136]
illis quibu'[137] tributus maior penditur, pendi potest.[138]
quid istae quae[139] uestei[140] quotannis[141] nomina inueniunt noua?
tunicam rallam,[142] tunicam spissam,[143] linteolum caesicium,   230
indusiatam, patagiatam, caltulam aut crocotulam,
supparum aut — subnimium, ricam, basilicum[144] aut exoticum,[145]
cumatile aut plumatile, carinum aut cerinum — gerrae[146] maxumae![147]
cani[148] quoque etiam ademptumst[149] nomen. **Periphanes:** qui?[150]
Epidicus: uocant Laconicum.[151]
haec uocabula[152] auctiones[153] subigunt[154] ut faciant uiros.   235

---

128 *quasi* (adverb): "as though" (followed by the subjunctive mood).
129 *fundus, -i* (m.): "estate".
130 *exorno, -are, -aui, -atum* (similar to *orno, -are*, see above).
131 *incedo, -ere, -incessi, incessum*: "walk", "march along".
132 *tributus, -us* (m.) = *tributum, -i* (n.): "tax payment".
133 *quom* = *cum*.
134 *negant* (the subject of *negant* is the male clients of the prostitutes, not the women themselves).
135 *pendo, -ere, pependi, pensum*: "pay".
136 *potis* = *potis esse* = *posse*.
137 *quibu'* = *quibus*.
138 *illis quibus tributus maior penditur, pendi potest*: "they can pay the bigger tax, the one they pay over to those women, though".
139 *quid, estae quae...*: "what is it with those women who...".
140 *uestei* = *uesti* < *uestis, -is* (f.): "clothing".
141 *quotannis* (*quot* + *annus, -i*): "every year", "over the years".
142 *rallam* (word found only in Plautus, so the following definition is based on educated guesswork): "thin". The words that follow are also found only in Plautus, and their definitions are similarly guessed at, though there is little doubt about most of them: *linteolum*: "made of linen"; *caesicium*: "blue"; *indusiatam*: "under[-tunic]"; *patagiatam*: "with an embroidered edge"; *caltulam*: "short under-tunic"; *crocotulam*: "saffron-yellow"; *supparum* (a word of Oscan origin): "linen robe"; *subnimium* (a joke word based on the former word sounding like the Latin *sub* + *parum*) "slightly-too-much"; *ricam*: "veil"; *cumatile*: "sea-coloured"; *plumatile*: "feather-patterned"; *carinum*: "nut-brown"; *cerinum*: "wax-dyed" (Duckworth-Wheeler 1940: 244–247).
143 *spissus, -a, -um*: "thick".
144 *basilicus, -a, -um*: "royal", "regal".
145 *exoticus, -a, -um*: "foreign".
146 *gerrae, -arum* (f. pl.): "nonsense".
147 *maxumae* = *maximae*.
148 *cani* (dative singular) < *canis, -is* (m./f.): "dog".
149 *ademptumst* = *ademptum est* < *adimo, -ere, ademi, ademptum*: "take" (+ dative of person/thing from whom it is taken).
150 *qui*: "in what way", "what do you mean".
151 *Laconicus, -a, -um*: "Spartan" (apparently "Spartan" could refer both to a well-known dog breed from the Greek state of Sparta, and a fabric or style of clothing from Sparta).
152 *uocabulum, -i* (n.): "name".
153 *auctio, auctionis* (f.): "auction", "public sale".
154 *subigo, -ere, -subegi, subactum*: "compel", "force".

Apoecides: quin[155] tu ut[156] occepisti[157] loquere?[158] **Epidicus:** occepere[159] aliae mulieres

duae sic post[160] me fabulari[161] inter sese[162] — ego abscessi[163] sciens[164]

paullum[165] ab illis, dissimulabam[166] earum operam[167] sermoni dare;

nec satis exaudibam,[168] nec sermonis[169] fallebar[170] tamen,

quae loquerentur. **Periphanes:** id lubidost[171] scire. **Epidicus:** ibi[172]   240
illarum altera

dixit illi quicum[173] ipsa ibat — **Periphanes:** quid? **Epidicus:** tace ergo, ut audias —

postquam illam sunt conspicatae,[174] quam tuo'[175] gnatus deperit:[176]

"quam[177] facile et quam fortunate euenit[178] illi, opsecro,[179]

mulieri quam liberare uolt[180] amator!" "quisnam[181] is est?"

inquit[182] altera illi. ibi[183] illa nominat Stratippoclem   245

Periphanei[184] filium. **Periphanes:** perii[185] hercle! quid ego ex te audio?

---

155 *quin*: "but".
156 *ut*: "as" (+ indicative).
157 *occipio, -ere, occepi, occeptum*: "begin".
158 *loquere = loqueris* (second-person singular future indicative deponent) < *loquor, loqui, locutus sum*.
159 *occepere* (third-person plural perfect active indicative) < *occipio, -ere, occepi, occeptum*: "begin".
160 *post*: "behind".
161 *fabulor, -ari, -atus sum*: "talk", "chat".
162 *sese = se*.
163 *abscedo, -ere, abscessi, abscessum*: "withdraw", "step back".
164 *sciens* < *scio, scire, sciui, scitum*: "knowingly", "intentionally".
165 *paullum = paulum*: "a little [bit]", "a little way".
166 *dissimulo, -are, -aui, -atum*: "pretend... not".
167 *operam dare*: "pay attention to", "to listen to" (+ dative).
168 *exaudibam = exaudiebam* < *exaudio, -ire, -iui/ii, -itum*: "hear clearly", "understand".
169 *nec sermonis fallebar*: "their conversation wasn't hidden from me", "I didn't miss their conversation" (*sermonis* is genitive "of respect" after *fallebar* < *fallo, -ere, fefelli, falsus*: "deceive", "disappoint" used in the middle voice sense here).
170 *fallo, -ere, fefelli, falsus*: "deceive", "disappoint".
171 *lubidost = libido est*.
172 *ibi*: "then".
173 *quicum = quācum*: "with whom".
174 *conspicor, -ari, -atus sum*: "catch sight of" (+ accusative).
175 *tuo' = tuos = tuus*.
176 *deperit* < *depereo, -ire, -ii/iui, -itum* (conjugated like *eo, ire*): "die", "be destroyed", "fall desperately in love".
177 *quam... quam*: "how... how" (+ adverbs).
178 *euĕnit* (present tense).
179 *opsecro*: "please", "for goodness' sake".
180 *uolt = uult* < *uolo, uelle, uolui, —*.
181 *quisnam* < *quisnam, quidnam* (a more emphatic version of *quis, quid*).
182 *inquit*: "says".
183 *ibi*: "then".
184 *Periphanei* (genitive of *Periphanes*).
185 *pereo, perire, periui / perii, peritum*: "die", "be ruined", "be lost".

Epidicus: hoc quod actumst.[186] egomet[187] postquam id illas audiui loqui,[188]
coepi[189] rusum[190] uorsum[191] ad illas pauxillatim[192] accedere,[193]
quasi retruderet[194] hominum me uis[195] inuitum. **Periphanes:** intellego.
Epidicus: ibi[196] illa interrogauit illam: "qui[197] scis? quis id dixit tibi?"   250
"quin[198] hodie adlatae[199] tabellae sunt ad eam a Stratippocle,
eum[200] argentum sumpsisse[201] apud Thebas ab danista faenore,
id paratum et sese ob eam rem[202] id ferre." **Periphanes:** certo ego occidi![203]
Epidicus: haec sic aibat:[204] se audiuisse ex eapse[205] atque epistula.
Periphanes: quid ego faciam? nunc consilium a te expetesso,[206]   255
Apoecides.
Apoecides: reperiamus[207] aliquid[208] calidi,[209] conducibilis[210] consili.[211]

---

186 *actumst = actum est < ago, -ere, egi, actum; hoc quod actumst*: "what was done", "what happened".
187 *egomet = ego + -met*: "I, myself".
188 *loqui < loquor; illas* is the accusative subject of this infinitive, and *id* is its direct object.
189 *coepi rursum uorsum ad illas pausillatim accedere*: "I began to get gradually closer to them by slowing down", "I began to slow down little by little so as to let them get closer".
190 *rusum = rursum*: "back", "again".
191 *uorsum = uersum*: "towards".
192 *pauxillatim = paulatim*: "little by little", "gradually".
193 *accedo, -ere, accessi, accessum*: "approach", "go near".
194 *retrudo, -ere, –trusi, -trusum*: "thrust back", "force back".
195 *uis, uis* (f.): "strength", "force"; *hominum... uis*: "force of people", "crowd".
196 *ibi*: "then".
197 *qui = quo*: "how".
198 *quin*: "but".
199 *affero, afferre, attuli, allatum* (or *adfero, adferre, adtuli, adlatum*): "bring", "deliver", "use" (+ accusative).
200 *eum... sese* (Plautus is inconsistent with his pronouns here: *eum* is the accusative subject of the infinitive *sumpsisse*, and refers to Stratippocles, as does the reflexive *sese* (accusative subject of *ferre*) in the next line.
201 *eum argentum sumpsisse apud Thebas ab danista faenore* (see line 53).
202 *ob eam rem*: "for this/that reason", "for this/that purpose".
203 *occido, -ere, occidi, occasus*: "fall down", "be ruined".
204 *aibat = aiebat*: "[she] claimed".
205 *eapse = ea ipsa*.
206 *expetesso, -ere, –, –* : "want", "long for".
207 *reperiamus < reperio, reperire, repperi, repertum*: "find".
208 *aliquid*: "some sort of" (+ genitive).
209 *calidus, -a, -um*: literally "hot", but here translate as "quick", "speedy".
210 *conducibilis, -e*: "wise", "advisable".
211 *consilium, -ii* (n.): "plan", "suggestion".

nam ille quidem aut iam²¹² hic²¹³ aderit,²¹⁴ credo hercle, aut iam²¹⁵
adest. **Epidicus:** si aequom²¹⁶ siet²¹⁷
me plus sapere²¹⁸ quam uos, dederim uobis consilium catum²¹⁹
quod laudetis, ut ego opino,²²⁰ uterque — **Periphanes:** ergo ubi id²²¹
est, Epidice?
Epidicus: atque ad eam rem²²² conducibile. **Apoecides:** quid²²³ istuc²²⁴   260
dubitas dicere?
Epidicus: uos priores²²⁵ esse oportet, nos posterius²²⁶ dicere,
qui plus sapitis. **Periphanes:** heia uero!²²⁷ age dice. **Epidicus:** at
deridebitis.²²⁸
Apoecides: non edepol faciemus. **Epidicus:** immo²²⁹ si placebit utitor,²³⁰
consilium si non placebit, reperitote²³¹ rectius.²³²
mihi istic²³³ nec seritur²³⁴ nec metitur,²³⁵ nisi ea quae tu uis uolo.   265
Periphanes: gratiam habeo;²³⁶ fac participes²³⁷ nos tuae sapientiae.
Epidicus: continuo²³⁸ arbitretur²³⁹ uxor tuo gnato atque ut fidicinam

---

212 *iam*: "soon".
213 *hic*: "here".
214 *adsum, adesse, adfui, adfuturus*: "be present".
215 *iam*: "already".
216 *aequom = aequum*: "right", "fair".
217 *siet = sit*.
218 *sapio, -ere, sapiui, –* : "to be sensible", "to be wise".
219 *catus, -a, -um*: "clever", "prudent", "wise".
220 *opino = opinor < opinor, -ari, -atus sum*: "suppose", "think".
221 *id* refers to *consilium*.
222 *ad eam rem*: "for this very situation".
223 *quid*: "why".
224 *istuc = istud*.
225 *prior, prius*: "first".
226 *posterius* (adverb): "afterwards", "second".
227 *heia uero* (expresses amused doubt): "ha!", "yeah, right".
228 *derideo, -ere, derisi, derisum*: "laugh [at]", "make fun [of]".
229 *immo*: "OK then", "indeed".
230 *utitor* (second-person singular future active imperative of *utor*; normally *utor* takes the ablative, but here it takes the accusative direct object *consilium*).
231 *reperitote* (second-person plural future active imperative) < *reperio, -ire, repperi, repertum*: "find".
232 *rectius* (comparative adjective neuter accusative singular) < *rectus, -a, -um*: "a better one", "a better [plan]".
233 *istic* (adverb): "in this matter".
234 *sero, -ere, seui, satum* (impersonal use): "sow", "plant", "beget", "conceive".
235 *meto, -ere, messui, messum* (impersonal use): "reap", "harvest"; *mihi istic nec seritur nec metitur* appears to be proverbial, meaning "I've got no stake here", "I'm not personally involved".
236 *gratiam habeo*: "thank you".
237 *particeps, participis* (m.): "sharer", "partaker".
238 *continuo* (adverb): "immediately".
239 *arbitro, -are, -aui, -atum* (subjunctive after a missing *fac ut*): "select" (the verb is normally deponent in Classical Latin, but active in Plautus).

illam quam is uolt liberare, quae illum corrumpit[240] tibi,

ulciscare[241] atque ita curetur, usque ad mortem[242] ut seruiat.[243]

Apoecides: fieri oportet. **Periphanes:** facere cupio quiduis[244] dum[245] id   270
fiat modo. **Epidicus:** em![246]

nunc occasiost[247] faciundi, priu' quam[248] in urbem aduenerit,

sicut[249] cras hic aderit, hodie non uenit. **Periphanes:** qui[250] scis?
Epidicus: scio.

quia mihi alius dixit qui illinc[251] uenit mane[252] hic adfore.[253]

Periphanes: quin tu eloquere,[254] quid faciemus? **Epidicus:** sic
faciundum censeo,[255]

quasi[256] tu cupias liberare fidicinam animi gratia[257]   275

quasique ames uehementer tu illam. **Periphanes:** quam ad rem istuc
refert?[258] **Epidicus:** rogas?

ut enim praestines[259] argento, priu' quam[260] ueniat filius,

atque ut[261] eam te[262] in libertatem[263] dicas emere — **Periphanes:**
intellego.

---

240 *corrumpo, -ere, corrupi, corruptum*: "ruin", "corrupt".
241 *ulciscare* (second-person singular present subjunctive passive) < *ulciscor, -ari, ultus sum*: "punish", "take revenge on".
242 *usque ad mortem*: "till [her] dying day", "for the rest of [her] life".
243 *seruio, -ire, seruiui, seruitum*: "be a slave".
244 *quiduis*: "anything you like".
245 *dum*: "so long as".
246 *em*: "there!"; translate here: "OK, look".
247 *occasiost = occasio est*: "there's an opportunity to" (+ genitive gerundive).
248 *priu' quam = prius quam*: "before".
249 *sicut*: "as", "since".
250 *qui = quo*: "how".
251 *illinc*: "from there".
252 *mane* (adverb): "in the morning".
253 *adfore = adfuturum esse*.
254 *eloquere = eloqueris* (second-person singular present deponent indicative): "you are explaining", "you are stating".
255 *censeo, -ere, censui, censum*: "think", "recommend".
256 *quasi* (adverb): "as though" (followed by the subjunctive mood).
257 *animi gratia*: "for you own sake".
258 *quam ad rem istuc refert*: "how will that help".
259 *praestino, -are, -aui, -atum*: "buy", "purchase".
260 *priu' quam = prius quam*.
261 *ut... dicas* (substantive clause of purpose): "[arrange it] so that you [can] say".
262 *te...dicas emere* (indirect discourse): "you [can] say that you bought...".
263 *in libertatem*: "in order to free her".

Epidicus: ubi erit empta,²⁶⁴ ut²⁶⁵ aliquo²⁶⁶ ex urbe amoueas;²⁶⁷ nisi quid²⁶⁸ tuast²⁶⁹ secu'²⁷⁰ sententia. **Periphanes:** immo²⁷¹ docte!²⁷² **Epidicus:** quid tu autem, Apoecides?   280

Apoecides: quid ego²⁷³ iam nisi te commentum²⁷⁴ nimis²⁷⁵ astute²⁷⁶ intellego?²⁷⁷

Epidicus: iam igitur amota ei²⁷⁸ fuerit²⁷⁹ omnis consultatio²⁸⁰ nuptiarum,²⁸¹ ne grauetur²⁸² quod uelis.²⁸³ **Periphanes:** uiue²⁸⁴ sapis²⁸⁵ et placet. **Epidicus:** tum tu igitur calide²⁸⁶ quidquid acturu's²⁸⁷ age. **Periphanes:** rem²⁸⁸ hercle loquere.²⁸⁹ **Epidicus:** et repperi²⁹⁰ haec te   285
qui²⁹¹ apscedat²⁹² suspicio.²⁹³

---

264 *emo, -ere, emi, emptum*: "buy".
265 *ut... amoueas* (substantive clause of purpose): "[arrange it] so that you remove".
266 *aliquo*: "[to] somewhere".
267 *amoueo, -ere, -amoui, amotum*: "remove".
268 *quid*: "with respect to anything"; translate here: "in any way".
269 *tuast = tua est*.
270 *secu' = secus* (adverb): "otherwise", "contrary", "different".
271 *immo*: "by all means", "indeed"; "on the contrary", "by no means".
272 *docte*: "very clever[ly done]".
273 *quid ego = quid ego dicam*.
274 *commentum = commentum esse < comminiscor, -i, commentus sum*: "devise", "invent a story".
275 *nimis*: "too much", "exceedingly" (both meanings are implied here in a play on words, since Apoecides thinks he's praising Epidicus for such an excellent deception against Stratippocles, but the audience knows that Epidicus is actually deceiving the old men).
276 *astute < astutus, -a, -um*: "clever", "sly".
277 *intellego, -ere, -exi, ectum*: "understand"; translate here: "realize".
278 *ei* (dative after compound verb *amouere*, referring to Stratippocles): "[from] him".
279 *amota ... fuerit* (future perfect; see note 57 in Act 1, scene 2).
280 *consultatio, -onis* (f.): "hesitation", "deliberation".
281 *nuptiae, -arum* (f. pl.): "marriage ", "wedding".
282 *grauor, -ari, -atus sum*: "be annoyed at", "be upset at".
283 *uelis* (subjunctive by attraction to the mood of *grauetur*; see Bennett 324.1, http://www.thelatinlibrary.com/bennett.html#sect324).
284 *uiue* (adverb) < *uius, -a, -um*: "very".
285 *sapis < sapio, -ere, sapiui, –* : "to be sensible", "to be wise".
286 *calide* (adverb) < *calidus, -a, -um*; "quickly".
287 *acturu's = acturus es* (active periphrastic, with a meaning similar to *ages*).
288 *rem*: translate here as "truth", "reality".
289 *loquere = loqueris* (present indicative).
290 *repperi*: "I have found [out]".
291 *qui = quo*: "how".
292 *apscedat = abscedat < abscedo, -ere, -abscessi, abscessum*: "go away"; translate here: "be diverted from".
293 *suspicio, -onis* (f.): "suspicion", "mistrust".

Periphanes: sine[294] me scire. **Epidicus:** scibis,[295] audi. **Apoecides:** sapit hic pleno pectore.[296]

Epidicus: opus est[297] homine qui illo[298] argentum deferat[299] pro fidicina; nam te nolo neque opu'[300] factost.[301] **Periphanes:** quid[302] iam?

Epidicus: ne te censeat[303]

fili[304] caussa[305] facere — **Periphanes:** docte! **Epidicus:** quo illum ab illa prohibeas:

ne qua[306] ob[307] eam suspicionem difficultas euenat.[308]   290

Periphanes: quem hominem inueniemus ad eam rem utilem?

Epidicus: hic[309] erit optumus;[310]

hic poterit cauere[311] recte, iura qui et leges tenet.[312]

Periphanes: Epidico habeas gratiam.[313] **Epidicus:** sed ego istuc[314] faciam sedulo:[315]

ego illum conueniam[316] atque adducam huc ad te, quoiiast,[317] fidicinam[318] atque argentum ego cum hoc[319] feram. **Periphanes:** quanti[320] emi[321]   295

potest minimo? **Epidicus:** illane?

---

294 *sine < sino, -ere, siui, situm*: "allow", "let".
295 *scibis = scies, < scio, scire, sciui, scitum*: "know".
296 *pleno pectore* (ablative of manner): literally: "with full heart/mind"; translate here: "through and through"; the *pectus* was where wisdom was thought to be located in the body, rather than, as we might believe, the brain.
297 *opus est* (impersonal): "there is need for", "we need" (+ ablative of thing/person needed).
298 *illo*: "to that place".
299 *defero, deferre, detuli, delatum*: "deliver", "bring", "get".
300 *opu' = opus*.
301 *neque opus factost = neque opus facto est*: "and there is no need [for you] to do it.
302 *quid*: "why".
303 *censeat* (the subject is the pimp from whom Periphanes would be buying the lyre-player).
304 *fili = filii*.
305 *caussa = causa*.
306 *qua*: "in any way".
307 *ob*: "because of" (+ accusative).
308 *euenat = eueniat < euenio, -ire, -eni, - entum*: "arise", "come about", "turn out".
309 *hic*: "this man" (referring to Apoecides).
310 *optumus = optimus*.
311 *caueo, -ere, caui, cautum*: "be careful".
312 *teneo, -ere, tenui, tentum*: "hold", "grasp"; translate here: "understand".
313 *habeas gratiam*: "you should thank" (+ dative of person thanked).
314 *istuc = istud*.
315 *sedulo* (adverb): "industriously", "carefully", "zealously".
316 *conuenio, -ire, -eni, -entum*: "meet", "go to meet".
317 *quoiiast = quoiia/quoia est = cuia est* (from the archaic adjective *quoiius/quoius/cuius, -a, -um*, related to the genitive singular of *qui, quae, quod*): "whose [property] she is".
318 The manuscript tradition, followed by Linday's text, has *fidicina*, but the emendation to *fidicinam* works better.
319 *hoc* (refers to Apoecides).
320 *quanti... minimo* (genitive of indefinite price and ablative of indefinite price, respectively): "for how little", "what is the least amount for which".
321 *emi* (present passive infinitive) *< emo, -ere, emi, emptum*: "buy".

ad quadraginta[322] fortasse[323] eam posse emi minimo[324] minis.[325]
uerum si plus dederis referam, nihil in ea re captiost.[326]
atque id non decem occupatum[327] tibi erit argentum dies.[328]
Periphanes: quidum?[329] **Epidicus:** quia enim mulierem alius illam adulescens deperit,[330]
auro opulentus, magnus miles Rhodius,[331] raptor hostium,   300
gloriosus:[332] hic emet illam de te et dabit aurum lubens.[333]
face[334] modo, est lucrum[335] hic tibi amplum.[336] **Periphanes:** deos quidem oro. **Epidicus:** impetras.[337]
Apoecides: quin[338] tu is[339] intro atque huic argentum promis?[340] ego uisam[341] ad forum.
Epidice, eo[342] ueni. **Epidicus:** ne abitas[343] priu'[344] quam ego ad te uenero.
Apoecides: usque[345] opperiar.[346] — **Periphanes:** sequere tu intro. — **Epidicus:** i numera,[347]
nil[348] ego te moror.[349]   305

---

322 *quadraginta* (indeclinable): "forty".
323 *fortasse*: "it's possible that" (+ accusative-infinitive construction).
324 *minimo* (adverb): "at the lowest".
325 *minis* (ablative of price) < *mina, -ae* (f.): a Greek unit of money equivalent to 430g of silver.
326 *captiost* = *captio est*; *captio, -onis* (f.): "trickery", "deceit".
327 *occupo, -are, -aui, -atum*: "invest", "lay out [money]", "use".
328 *non decem... dies* (accusative of duration of time): "not [even] for ten days".
329 *quidum* = *qui dum*: "how does it happen that...?", "what makes you say that?", "how so?".
330 *deperit* < *depereo, -ire, -ii/iui, -itum*: "he is madly in love with" (+ accusative).
331 It is unclear whether or not this *miles Rhodius* is the same as the *miles Euboicus* of line 153; Duckworth believes not, and that the *miles Rhodius* is invented by Epidicus (Duckworth-Wheeler 1940: 273).
332 *gloriosus, -a, -um*: "boastful", "self-glorifying" (soldiers in Plautus always have this characteristic, see his play entitled *Miles Gloriosus*).
333 *lubens* = *libens*: "willingly".
334 *face* = *fac*.
335 *lucrum, -i* (n.): "profit".
336 *amplus, -a, -um*: "big", "substantial".
337 *impetro, -are, -aui, atum*: "achieve", "get", "obtain".
338 *quin*: "why... not?", "why don't you...?".
339 *is* < *eo, ire, iui/ii, itum*.
340 *promo, -ere prompsi/promsi, promptum*: "bring out".
341 *uiso, -ere, uisi, uisum*: "go to", "visit" (+ *ad*).
342 *eo*: "to that place".
343 *abeo, -ire, -iui/-ii, -itum*: "go away".
344 *priu'* = *prius*.
345 *usque*: "constantly", "the whole time".
346 *opperior, -iri, -itus sum*: "wait", "wait for".
347 *numero, -are, -aui, -atum*: "count out" (referring to the money).
348 *nil* = *nihil*; here translate as: "not at all".
349 *moror, -ari, moratus sum*: "delay".

2.3 EPIDICVS

Scene summary: While the two old men are indoors getting the money, Epidicus rejoices at how well he's fooling them. He says that, in the place of Acropolistis, whom he's supposed to be buying, he'll hire a different lyre-player. This new lyre-player was to have been hired to play the lyre for a religious sacrifice Periphanes had planned to do, but now Epidicus will coach her to play the part of Acropolistis.

Epidicus: nullum esse opinor[1] ego agrum in agro Attico
aeque[2] feracem[3] quam hic est noster Periphanes:
quin[4] ex occluso[5] atque opsignato[6] armario[7]
decutio[8] argenti tantum quantum mihi lubet.[9]
quod pol ego metuo si senex resciuerit[10]   310
ne ulmos[11] parasitos[12] faciat quae[13] usque[14] attondeant.[15]
sed me una turbat[16] res ratioque,[17] Apoecidi
quam[18] ostendam fidicinam aliquam conducticiam.[19]
atque id quoque habeo: mane[20] me iussit senex
conducere[21] aliquam fidicinam sibi huc domum,   315
dum rem diuinam[22] faceret, cantaret[23] sibi;

---

1 *opinor, opinari, opinatus sum*: "suppose", "imagine".
2 *aeque* (adverb): "equally", "to the same extent".
3 *ferax, feracis*: "fruitful", "fertile".
4 *quin*: "really".
5 *occludo, -ere, -occlusi, occludum*: "closed up", "locked up".
6 *opsignato = obsignato < obsigno, -are, -aui, -atum*: "seal", "seal up".
7 *armarium, -ii* (n.): "chest", "cupboard".
8 *decutio, decutere, decussi, decussus*: "shake out", "dislodge".
9 *lubet = libet*.
10 *resciuerit* (perfect subjunctive) < *rescisco, -ere, -resciui, -rescitum*: "learn", "find out".
11 *ulmus, -i* (f.): "elm [rod]".
12 *parasitus, -i* (m.): "[human] parasite", "hanger-on" (a *parasitus* referred to someone who would hang around wealthy friends in the hopes of getting a meal; the elm rods would be made into "parasites" in the sense that they would never be far from Epidicus's hide, i.e. Epidicus would be given a severe beating).
13 *quae* (relative pronoun, the antecedent of which is *ulmos*).
14 *usque* (adverb): "continuously", "without interruption".
15 *attondeo, -ere, attondi, attonsum*: "clip", "shear"; translate here: "thrash".
16 *turbo, -are, -aui, -atum*: "disturb", "concern".
17 *ratio, -onis* (f.): "matter", "consideration".
18 *quam* (adverb): "how".
19 *conducticius, -a, -um*: "hired", "rented".
20 *mane* (adverb): "in the morning", "this morning".
21 *conduco, -ere, -xi, -ctum*: "bring", "hire".
22 *rem diuinam*: "religious activity", "sacrifice".
23 *canto, -are, -aui, -atum*: "play [music]" (supplying *ut* will help make better sense of the subjunctive).

ea conducetur atque ei praemonstrabitur[24]
quo pacto fiat subdola[25] aduorsus[26] senem.
ibo intro, argentum accipiam ab damnoso[27] sene. —

---

24 *ei praemonstrabitur*: "it will be taught to her beforehand" < *praemonstro, -are, -aui, -atum*: "show beforehand", "direct [in advance]", "guide [in advance]".
25 *subdolus, -a, -um*: "sly", "deceitful".
26 *aduorsus = aduersus* (preposition + accusative): "toward", "against".
27 *damnosus, -a, -um*: "wasteful" (Epidicus calls the old man "wasteful" presumably because he ought to be smart enough not to be cheated by Epidicus).

ACTVS III

3.1 STRATIPPOCLES, CHAERIBVLVS

Scene summary: While Epidicus is in Periphanes's house getting the money to purchase the supposed Acropolistis, Stratippocles and Chaeribulus come on stage. Stratippocles expresses his worry that Epidicus won't be able to find a way to pay off his debt, and loses his temper with Chaeribulus for being unable to help.

    Stratippocles: Expectando[1] exedor[2] miser atque exenteror[3]   320
    quo modo mi[4] Epidici blanda dicta euenant.[5]
    nimi'[6] diu maceror:[7] sitne quid necne sit[8]
    scire cupio. **Chaeribulus:** per[9] illam tibi copiam[10]
    copiam parare[11] aliam licet: sciui equidem in principio ili-
    co[12] nullam tibi esse in illo[13] copiam. **Stratippocles:** interii[14] hercle   325
    ego!
    Chaeribulus: apsurde[15] faci'[16] qui angas[17] te animi;[18] si hercle ego
    illum semel prendero,[19]

---

1   *expecto, -are, -aui, -atum:* "wait".
2   *exedo, -ere, -edi, -esum:* "eat up", "consume".
3   *exentero, -are, -aui, -atum:* "disembowel"; here translate as "torture".
4   *mi = mihi.*
5   *euenant = eueniant < euenio, -ire, -eni, - entum:* "arise", "come about", "turn out".
6   *nimi' = nimis.*
7   *macero, -are, -aui, -atum:* "make wet", "soak"; translate here: "wear down", "worry".
8   *sitne qui necne sit:* "if it's going to happen or not".
9   *per:* "as for", "as far as [that assistance] is concerned".
10 *copia, -ae* (f.): "resources", "wealth", "assistance".
11 *paro, -are, -aui, -atum:* "prepare"; translate here: "obtain".
12 *ilico* (adverb): "immediately".
13 *illo* (referring to Epidicus).
14 *interii < intereo, interire, interiui / interii, interitus:* "perish", "die"; "be ruined".
15 *apsurde = absurde* (adverb *< absurdus, -a, -um*): "absurdly".
16 *faci' = facis.*
17 *ango, -ere, anxi, anctum:* "choke", "cause pain to".
18 *animi* (genitive of respect).
19 *prehendo/prendo, -ere, prehendi/prendi, prehensum/prensum:* "lay hold of", "catch".

numquam inridere[20] nos illum inultum[21] sinam seruom hominem. 327–8
Stratippocles: quid[22] illum ferre uis qui, tibi[23] quoi[24] diuitiae domi[25] maxumae sunt,
is[26] nummum[27] nullum habes nec sodali[28] tuo in te copiast.[29] 330
Chaeribulus: si hercle habeam pollicear[30] lubens,[31] uerum aliquid aliqua aliquo modo
alicunde[32] ab aliqui[33] aliqua tibi spes est fore[34] mecum fortunam.[35]
Stratippocles: uae tibi, muricide[36] homo! **Chaeribulus:** qui[37] tibi lubet[38] mihi male loqui?
Stratippocles: quipp'[39] tu mi[40] aliquid aliquo modo alicunde ab aliquibus[41] blatis[42]
quod nusquamst,[43] neque ego id immitto[44] in auris[45] meas, 335
nec mihi plus adiumenti[46] ades[47] quam ille qui numquam etiam natust.[48]

---

20 *inrideo, -ere, -isi, -isum*: "laugh at", "make fun of".
21 *inultus, -a, -um*: "unpunished".
22 *quid*: "what".
23 *tibi* is dative by attraction to *quoi*; translate as a nominative.
24 *quoi = cui*.
25 *domi* (locative).
26 *is* (repeating the subject *qui* in line 329): here translate as "you, who...".
27 *nummus, -i* (m.): "coin".
28 *sodalis, -is* (m.): "companion", "friend", "mate".
29 *copiast = copia est*.
30 *polliceor, polliceri, pollicitus sum*: "offer", "promise".
31 *lubens = libens*: "willingly".
32 *alicunde* (adverb): "from some source or other", "from somewhere".
33 *aliqui = aliquo*.
34 *fore = futuram esse*: "that there will be".
35 *uerum aliquid aliqua aliquo modo / alicunde ab aliqui aliqua tibi spes est fore mecum fortunam*: "but there's some hope of something somehow in some way from some source from someone — that there'll be good luck for you and me".
36 *muricidus, -a, -um* (a rare word, the meaning of which isn't entirely clear): "stupid", "cowardly".
37 *qui*: "why".
38 *lubet = libet*.
39 *quipp' = quippe*: "obviously".
40 *mi = mihi*.
41 *aliquibus = aliquis*.
42 *blatio, -ire, –, – :* "babble", "blather".
43 *nusquamst = nusquam est*: "[which] is nowhere", "[which] doesn't exist anywhere".
44 *immitto, -ere, -misi, -missum*: "admit", "let in".
45 *aurīs = aures < auris, -is* (f.): "ear".
46 *adiumentum, -i* (n.): "help", "support"; *adiumenti* is a genitive of the whole after *plus* (translate *nec mihi plus adiumenti ades quam ille qui numquam etian natust*: "you're standing by me but [you're] no more help than someone who was never born").
47 *adsum, adesse, affui, affuturus*: "be near", "be at hand", "stand by".
48 *natust = natus est < nascor, nasci, natus est*: "be born".

3.2 EPIDICVS, STRATIPPOCLES, CHAERIBVLVS

Scene summary: Epidicus joins the two young men and tells Stratippocles that he's tricked Periphanes into giving him fifty *minae*, supposedly to buy Acropolistis. He says that he plans on tricking the pimp, who had sold him Acropolistis two days earlier, into telling Periphanes that he's now just sold a lyre-player to Epidicus for the fifty *minae*. Epidicus gives the money to Stratippocles and explains the two deceptions he's played on Periphanes (firstly tricking him into thinking Acropolistis is his daughter Telestis so that he buys her, and secondly tricking him into giving him the purchase price for Acropolistis which will instead be used to pay Stratippocles's debt). Epidicus tells Stratippocles that Periphanes is arranging to get him married, and Stratippocles says he'll never agree to get married while his (new) girlfriend is alive. Epidicus tells Stratippocles that he'll hire a different lyre-player to pretend to be Acropolistis.

Epidicus: fecisti iam officium tuom,[1] me meum nunc facere oportet.
per[2] hanc curam quieto[3] tibi licet esse — hoc quidem iam periit:[4]
ni quid tibi hinc in spem referas,[5] oppido[6] hoc[7] pollinctum est;[8]
crede modo mihi: sic ego ago, sic egerunt nostri.[9]   340
pro di inmortales,[10] mihi hunc diem dedistis luculentum![11]
ut[12] facilem atque impetrabilem![13] sed ego hinc migrare[14] cesso,[15]

---

1   *tuom = tuum.*
2   *per*: "through", "by means of".
3   *quietus, -a, -um*: "calm".
4   *hoc quidem iam periit* (Epidicus says this without Periphanes or the young men hearing): "indeed, he's lost this [the money] already".
5   *niquid tibi hinc in spem referas*: "don't go hoping otherwise".
6   *opiddo* (adverb): "very much", "completely".
7   *hoc* (again refers to the money Epidicus has been given by Periphanes).
8   *pollingo, -ere, pollinxi, pollinctum*: "wash a corpse", "prepare a body for burial".
9   *nostri*: "our people", "my ancestors" (given that slaves were considered, by slave-owners, no longer to have parents or ancestors, this may be Epidicus's resistance to the deracination (uprooting from native family) of slaves; more frivolously, Epidicus may also be referring to how the class of slaves has always behaved, or may be making a reference, as a comic *seruos callidus*, about how *serui callidi* in the tradition of Roman Comedy have always behaved — see Barbiero's forthcoming book: chapter 5).
10 *inmortales = immortales.*
11 *luculentus, -a, -um*: "bright", "brilliant".
12 *ut*: "how".
13 *impetrabilis, -e*: "pleasing", "successful".
14 *migro, -are, -aui, -atum*: "depart", "get going".
15 *cesso, -are, -aui, -atum*: "be remiss", "delay", "cease from".

ut importem[16] in coloniam[17] hunc <meo> auspicio[18] commeatum.[19]
mihi cesso quom[20] sto. sed quid hoc? ante aedis[21] duo sodales[22]
erum et Chaeribulum conspicor.[23] quid hic agitis? accipe hoc sis.[24]   345
Stratippocles: quantum[25] hic inest? **Epidicus:** quantum sat[26] est et
plus satis:[27] superfit.[28]
decem minis[29] plus attuli[30] quam tu danistae debes.
dum[31] tibi ego placeam atque opsequar[32] meum tergum flocci facio.[33]
Stratippocles: nam quid[34] ita? **Epidicus:** quia ego tuom[35] patrem
faciam parenticidam.[36]
Stratippocles: quid istuc est uerbi?[37] **Epidicus:** nil moror[38] uetera[39]   350
et uolgata[40] uerba.
"peratum ductare" †at† ego follitum ductitabo.[41]

---

16 *importo, -are, -aui, -atum*: "bring", "carry".
17 *colonia, -ae* (f.): "settlement" (*coloniae* were towns established by the Romans, often in newly-conquered territory so that the *colonia*'s new population of former Roman citizens could be counted on to defend Roman interests in the area; Epidicus's reference to bringing supplies to the *colonia* is a military metaphor, implying that his efforts to cheat the old man for the young man's benefit are the equivalent of a military stratagem).
18 *meo auspicio*: "under my own auspices" (the Romans took the auspices, or readings of what the gods wanted them to do, before important actions such as military maneuvers or, in this case, bringing stolen money to Stratippocles).
19 *commeatus, -i* (m.): "provisions", "supplies" (this is an army metaphor).
20 *quom = cum*.
21 *aedīs < aedis/es, -is* (f.): "building", "house" (often used in the plural, as here).
22 *sodalis, -is* (m.): "companion", "friend", "mate".
23 *conspicor, conspicari, conspicatus sum*: "catch sight of", "see".
24 *sis = si uis*: "please", "if you please".
25 *quantus, -a, um*: "how much", "as much as".
26 *sat = satis* (adverb): "enough".
27 *plus satis = plus quam satis*.
28 *superfio, superfieri, superfactus sum*: "be left over", "be more than enough".
29 *decem minis* (ablative of degree of difference; see Bennett 223).
30 *affero, afferre, attuli, allatum* (or *adfero, adferre, adtuli, adlatum*): "bring", "deliver", "use" (+ accusative).
31 *dum*: "provided that".
32 *opsequar = obsequar < obsequor, -i, obsectus sum*: "humour", "submit to" (+ dative).
33 *flocci facere*: "to make no account of", "not to care a straw for" (+ accusative).
34 *quid*: "why".
35 *tuom = tuum*.
36 *parenticida, -ae* (f.): "parricide", "murderer of one's parent" (Plautus probably invented this word).
37 *quid istuc est uerbi*: "what sort of word is that".
38 *nil moror*: "I don't care about"
39 *uetus, -eris* (adjective): "old-fashioned", "ancient".
40 *uolgatus, -a, -um*: "commonly used".
41 *"peratum ductare" †at† ego follitum ductitabo* (the obeli, or daggers, appear on either side of the word "*at*" here because the Latin text is corrupt, and it's not obvious how to emend this rather confusing line, which refers in some way to *pera, -ae* (f.): "bag", "wallet" and to *follis, -is* (m.): "moneybag". The line relates to *parenticidam* in line 349 in that a person convicted of having

nam leno[42] omne argentum apstulit[43] pro fidicina (ego resolui,[44]
manibus his[45] denumeraui[46]) pater suam natam quam[47] esse credit;
nunc iterum ut fallatur[48] pater tibique auxilium apparetur[49]
inueni;[50] nam ita suasi[51] seni atque hanc habui orationem   355
ut quom[52] rediisses,[53] ne tibi eiius[54] copia[55] esset. **Stratippocles:** eugae![56]
Epidicus: ea iam domist[57] pro[58] filia. **Stratippocles:** <iam> teneo.[59]
Epidicus: nunc auctorem[60]
dedit mi[61] ad hanc rem Apoecidem, is apud forum manet[62] me
†quasiquae amaret† caueat.[63] **Stratippocles:** hau[64] male. **Epidicus:**
iam ipse | cautor[65] captusst.[66]
ipse in meo collo tuo'[67] pater cruminam[68] collocauit;[69]   360
is adornat,[70] adueniens[71] domi extemplo[72] ut maritus[73] fias.

---

killed his parent was traditionally punished by being sewn into a sack, possibly along with various animals, and drowned).
42   *leno, -onis* (m.): "pimp", "brothel keeper".
43   *apstulit = abstulit < aufero, auferre, abstuli, ablatum*: "take away".
44   *resoluo, -ere, resolui, resolutum*: "release"; translate here: "pay".
45   *manibus his* (ablative of means).
46   *denumero, -are, -aui, -atum*: "pay in full", "pay down".
47   *quam* (accusative of respect): "for [her], whom", "the one that".
48   *fallo, -ere, fefelli, falsum*: "deceive", "cheat".
49   *apparo, -are, -aui, -atum*: "prepare", "provide".
50   *inuenire + ut* (+ subjunctive): "to devise a plan to".
51   *suadeo, -ere, suasi, suasum*: "persuade" (+ dative of person persuaded).
52   *quom = cum*.
53   *rediisse < redeo, -ire, -ii, -itum*: "return", "come back".
54   *eiius = eius*.
55   *eiius copia*: "access to her".
56   *eugae* (exclamation): "good", "well done".
57   *domist = domi est*.
58   *pro*: "in place of".
59   *teneo, -ere, tenui, tentum*: "hold", "grasp"; translate here: "understand".
60   *auctor, -oris* (m.): translate here "adviser" (describing *Apoecidem*).
61   *mi = mihi*.
62   *maneo -ere, mansi, mansum*: "remain", "stay"; translate here: "wait for".
63   †*quasiquae amaret*† *caueat* (the text is corrupt, as evidenced by the *obeli*, or daggers, surrounding "*quasique amaret*"; translate as "supposedly to keep an eye on things").
64   *hau = haud*: "not".
65   *cautor, -oris* (m.): "cautious/wary person".
66   *captust = captus est*.
67   *tuo' = tuos = tuus*.
68   *crumina, -ae* (f.): "pouch", "purse", "small moneybag".
69   *colloco, -are, -aui, -atum*: "put", "[put in] place".
70   *adorno, -are, -aui, -atum*: "get ready", "prepare".
71   *adueniens* agrees with the subject of *fias*.
72   *extemplo*: "immediately".
73   *maritus, -a, -um*: "married".

Stratippocles: uno persuadebit modo,[74] si illam quae adducta est mecum

mihi adempsit[75] Orcus.[76] **Epidicus:** nunc ego hanc astutiam[77] institui.[78]

deueniam[79] ad lenonem domum[80] egomet[81] solus, eum ego docebo,

si quid[82] ad eum adueniam,[83] ut sibi esse datum[84] argentum dicat   365

pro fidicina, argenti minas[85] se habere quinquaginta.[86]

(quippe[87] ego qui nudiustertius[88] meis manibus denumeraui[89]

pro illa tua amica quam pater suam filiam esse retur):[90]

ibi[91] leno sceleratum[92] caput suom[93] inprudens[94] alligabit,[95]

quasi pro illa argentum acceperit quae tecum adducta nunc est.   370

Stratippocles: uorsutior[96] es quam rota[97] figularis. **Epidicus:** iam ego parabo[98]

aliquam dolosam[99] fidicinam, nummo[100] conducta quae sit,[101]

---

74 *uno persuadebit modo*: "In [only] one way will [my father] persuade [me]".
75 *adempsit* (old form of the future tense) < *adimo, -ere, ademi, ademptum*: "take" (+ dative of person/thing from whom it is taken).
76 *Orcus, -i* (m.): Orcus, god of death and the underworld.
77 *astutia, -ae* (f.): "trick", "stratagem".
78 *instituo, -ere, -ui, -utum*: "set up", "prepare".
79 *deuenio, -ire, -ueni, -uentum*: "come to", "reach".
80 *ad lenonem domum*: "to the pimp, at his house".
81 *egomet* = *ego* + *-met*: "I, myself".
82 *si quid*: "if at all".
83 *si quid ad eum adueniam*: "if I go see him at all" (the text may be corrupt, but probably Epidicus means that, if he has to bring Periphanes and/or Apoecides to the pimp to verify his story, the pimp will back him up).
84 *esse datum... se habere* (both infinitives in indirect discourse after *dicat*).
85 *mina, -ae* (f.): a Greek unit of money equivalent to 430g of silver.
86 *quinquaginta* (indeclinable): "fifty".
87 *quippe*: "obviously".
88 *nudiustertius* = *nudius tertius*; *nudius* = *num/nunc dies* (always paired with an ordinal number): "it is now the ... day since" (because the Romans counted inclusively, *nudiustertius* means "the day before yesterday").
89 *denumero, -are, -aui, -atum*: "pay in full", "pay down".
90 *reor, reri, ratus sum*: "think", "suppose", "believe".
91 *ibi*: "then".
92 *sceleratus, -a, -um*: "criminal", "wicked".
93 *suom* = *suum*.
94 *inprudens* = *imprudens*: "unaware", "unsuspecting".
95 *adligabit* = *alligabit* < *alligo, -are, -aui, -atum*: "implicate/involve in".
96 *uorsutior* = *uersutior*, comparative form < *uersutus, -a, -um*: "clever", "ingenious".
97 *rota figularis*: "potter's wheel".
98 *paro, -are, -aui, -atum*: "prepare", "provide", "obtain".
99 *dolosus, -a, -um*: "crafty", "cunning", "deceitful".
100 *nummus, -i* (m.): "coin".
101 *conduco, - ere, -xi, -ctum*: "bring", "hire".

quae se emptam[102] simulet,[103] quae senes duo docte[104] ludificetur.[105]
eam ducet simul[106] Apoecides ad tuom[107] patrem. **Stratippocles:** ut parate![108]

Epidicus: eam permeditatam,[109] meis dolis[110] astutiisque[111] onustam[112] 375
mittam. sed nimi'[113] longum[114] loquor, diu me estis demorati.[115]
haec scitis iam ut futura sint. abeo. — **Stratippocles:** bene ambulato.[116]

Chaeribulus: nimi' doctus illic[117] ad male faciendum.[118]

Stratippocles: me equidem certo[119]
seruauit[120] consiliis suis. **Chaeribulus:** abeamus intro hinc ad me.[121]

Stratippocles: atque aliquanto[122] lubentius[123] quam aps[124] te sum   380
egressus[125] intus;[126]
uirtute atque auspicio Epidici cum praeda[127] in castra redeo. —

---

102 *emo, -ere, emi, emptum*: "buy".
103 *simulo, -are, -aui, -atum*: "pretend".
104 *docte* (adverb < *doctus, -a, -um*): "cleverly".
105 *ludificor, -ari, -atus sum*: "make fun of", "fool".
106 *simul*: "[together] with him".
107 *tuom = tuum*.
108 *ut parate*: "how well prepared [you are]", "what good planning".
109 *permeditatus, -a, -um*: "well-prepared", "well-trained".
110 *dolus, -i* (m.): "trick".
111 *astutiis < astutia, -ae* (f.): "trick", "stratagem".
112 *onustus, -a, -um*: "burdened", "laden"; translate here: "full of".
113 *nimi' = nimis*.
114 *longum* (adverb): "for [too] long".
115 *demoror, -ari, -atus sum*: "detain", "cause delay".
116 *ambulato* (second-person singular future imperative active) < *ambulo, -are, -aui, atum*.
117 *illic = ille*.
118 *nimi' doctus illic ad male faciendum*: "that guy is too good at double-dealing".
119 *certo*: "certainly".
120 *seruo, -are, -aui, -atum*: "save".
121 *ad me*: "[to] my house".
122 *aliquanto* (adverb): "by some amount", "a bit".
123 *lubentius = libentius*: "cheerfully".
124 *aps = a*.
125 *egredior, -i, egressus sum*: "come out", "go out".
126 *intus*: "within", "inside".
127 *praeda, -ae* (f.): "booty", "[war] prize".

3.3 PERIPHANES, APOECIDES, SERVOS

Scene summary: Periphanes admits in a soliloquy that he himself behaved badly when he was younger, so he shouldn't judge his son Stratippocles too harshly. Apoecides arrives with the hired lyre-player whom he believes is Acropolistis. Periphanes directs a slave to lead her into his house but instructs the slave to keep this low-class sex worker well away from the woman he believes is his virginal daughter Telestis. Apoecides raves about Epicicus's cleverness at (as he thinks) tricking the hired lyre-player into thinking she'd merely been hired for the day instead of having been bought.

Periphanes: non oris[1] caussa[2] modo homines aequom[3] fuit
sibi habere speculum[4] ubi os contemplarent[5] suom,[6]
sed qui perspicere[7] possent [cor[8] sapientiae,
igitur perspicere ut possint] cordis copiam;[9]   385
ubi id inspexissent,[10] cogitarent[11] postea[12]
uitam ut uixissent olim in adulescentia.
fuit conducibile[13] hoc quidem mea sententia.[14]
uel[15] [quasi][16] ego[met],[17] qui dudum[18] fili[19] caussa coeperam[20]
ego me excruciare[21] animi,[22] quasi quid[23] filius   390

---

1 *os, oris* (n.): "face".
2 *caussa = causa.*
3 *aequom = aequuum*: "right", "fair".
4 *speculum, -i* (n.): "mirror".
5 *contemplo, -are, -aui, -atum*: "observe", "contemplate".
6 *suom = suum.*
7 *perspicio, -ere, perspexi, perspectum*: "see through", "examine", "observe".
8 *cor, cordis* (n.): "heart" (square brackets enclose text that may not be entirely authentic).
9 *copia, -ae* (f.): "resources", "fulness".
10 *inspicio, -ere, inspexi, inspectum*: "examine", "inspect", "consider".
11 *cogito, -are, -aui, -atum*: "think", "consider", "reflect on".
12 *postea* (adverb): "afterwards".
13 *conducibilis, -e*: "wise", "advisable".
14 *meā sententiā*: "in my opinion".
15 *uel*: "or", "actually", "indeed", "even", "if you prefer".
16 *quasi* (adverb): "as if", "just as though".
17 *ego[met] = ego + -met*: "I, myself".
18 *dudum* (adverb): "a little while ago", "formerly".
19 *fili = filii.*
20 *coepio, -ere, coepi, coeptum*: "begin".
21 *excrucio, -are, -aui, -atum*: literally "crucify", but here "torture", "upset".
22 *animi* (genitive of respect).
23 *quid = aliquid*: "[with respect to] something", "in some way".

meu'[24] deliquisset[25] med[26] erga[27] aut [quasi] non pluruma[28]
malefacta mea essent solida[29] in adulescentia.
profecto[30] deliramus[31] interdum[32] senes.
sed meu'[33] sodalis[34] it[35] cum praeda[36] Apoecides.
uenire saluom[37] mercatorem[38] gaudeo.[39]   395
quid fit?[40] **Apoecides:** di deaeque te adiuuant. **Periphanes:** omen
placet.
Apoecides: quin omini omnis[41] suppetunt[42] res[43] prospere.[44]
sed tu †hanc iubes† intro[45] abduci.[46] **Periphanes:** heus![47] foras
exite huc aliquis.[48] duce[49] istam intro mulierem.
atque audin?[50] **Seruos:** quid uis? **Periphanes:** caue[51] siris[52] cum   400
filia

---

24 *meu' = meus.*
25 *delinquo, -ere, deliqui, delictum:* "fail", "do wrong".
26 *med = me.*
27 *erga:* "towards", "in relation to", "against".
28 *pluruma = plurima.*
29 *solidus, -a, -um:* "substantial", "serious".
30 *profecto* (adverb): "certainly".
31 *deliro, -are, -aui, -atum:* literally "deviate from the straight line"; translate here: "be crazy", "be out of one's wits", "be silly".
32 *interdum* (adverb): "sometimes", "now and then".
33 *meu' = meus.*
34 *sodalis, -is* (m.): "companion", "friend", "mate".
35 *it < eo, ire, iui/ii, itum.*
36 *praeda, -ae* (f.): "booty", "[war] prize".
37 *saluom = saluum.*
38 *mercator, -oris* (m.): "trader", "merchant", "buyer".
39 *uenire saluom... gaudeo* (see line 7): Periphanes is being humorous by greeting Apoecides as though he has been away on a long voyage. He addresses him as *mercator* because he's been on a shopping trip, though the audience knows that Apoecides has not been directly involved in the supposed purchase at all.
40 *quid fit:* "how goes it".
41 *omnīs = omnes.*
42 *suppeto, -ere, -iui, -itus* (+ dative): "be at hand", "be equal to", "be sufficient for", "agree with".
43 *res* (nominative plural) *< res, rei.*
44 *prospere* (adverb from *prosperus, -a, -um:* "fortunate", "favourable"). Lindsay's emendation of the manuscript tradition to *prosperae* here is less convincing than the original *prospere*.
45 *intro:* "[to the] inside", "[to the] indoors".
46 *abduco, -ere, abduxi, abductum:* "lead away".
47 *heus:* "hey!" (used to try to get someone's attention).
48 *exite... aliquis* (the singular *aliquis* is often paired with the plural imperative *exite*).
49 *duce* (the original form of the second-person singular present imperative active of *duco, -ere* (later *duc*).
50 *audin = audis + ne:* "do you hear".
51 *caueo, -ere, caui, cautum:* "guard against", "ensure that... not".
52 *siris = siueris* (perfect subjunctive second-person singular) *< sino, -ere, siui, situm:* "allow".

mea copulari⁵³ hanc neque conspicere.⁵⁴ iam tenes?⁵⁵
in aediculam⁵⁶ istanc⁵⁷ sorsum⁵⁸ concludi⁵⁹ uolo.
diuortunt⁶⁰ mores uirgini longe ac lupae.⁶¹
Apoecides: docte et sapienter dicis. num<quam> nimi'⁶² potest
pudicitiam⁶³ quisquam⁶⁴ suae seruare filiae.   405
edepol ne⁶⁵ istam * temperi⁶⁶ gnato tuo
sumu'⁶⁷ praemercati.⁶⁸ **Periphanes:** quid⁶⁹ iam? **Apoecides:** quia dixit mihi
iam dudum⁷⁰ se alius tuom⁷¹ uidisse hic filium:
hanc edepol rem⁷² apparabat.⁷³ **Periphanes:** plane hercle hoc quidem est.
Apoecides: ne⁷⁴ tu habes seruom⁷⁵ graphicum⁷⁶ et quantiuis preti,⁷⁷   410
non carust⁷⁸ auro contra.⁷⁹ ut ille fidicinam
fecit †nesciret† esse emptam tibi!⁸⁰

---

53 *copulor, -ari, copulatus sum*: "associate".
54 *conspicio, -ere, conspexi, conspectum*: "look at".
55 *teneo, -ere, tenui, tentum*: "hold", "grasp", "understand".
56 *aedicula, -ae* (f.): "[small] room", "[small] house".
57 *istanc = istam*.
58 *sorsum = seorsum* (adverb < *seorsus, -a, -um*): "separately", "apart".
59 *concludo, -ere, conclusi, conclusum*: "confine", "limit", "shut up".
60 *diuorto/diuerto, -ere, -ti, -sum*: "differ", "be dissimilar".
61 *lupa, -ae*: "female wolf"; translate here: "prostitute".
62 *nimi' = nimis*.
63 *pudicitia, -ae* (f.): "modesty", "purity".
64 *quisquam, quaequam, quicquam/quidquam*: "anyone, anything", "someone, something".
65 *ne* (interjection followed by a personal or demonstrative pronoun): "really", "indeed".
66 *temperi = tempori* (adverb): "at the right time", "in time", "seasonably".
67 *sumu' = sumus*.
68 *praemercor, -ari, -atus sum*: "buy before (+ someone in the dative)".
69 *quid*: "why".
70 *dudum*: (adverb): "a little while ago", "formerly".
71 *tuom = tuum*.
72 *hanc... rem* (referring to Stratippocles's planned purchase of the *fidicina*).
73 *apparo, -are, -aui, -atum*: "get ready".
74 *ne* (interjection followed by a personal or demonstrative pronoun): "really", "indeed".
75 *seruom = seruum*.
76 *graphicus, -a, -um*: "picture-perfect", "artistic", "clever".
77 *quantiuis preti = quanti uis preti* (genitive of price): "of whatever price you want", "priceless", "worth any price".
78 *carust = carus est*.
79 *non carust auro contra*: "he's worth his weight in gold" (*auro contra*: "when weighed against gold").
80 *ut ille fidicinam / fecit †nesciret† esse emptam tibi* (the text is corrupt but means something like "how he managed to keep the lyre-player from realizing she'd been bought for you".

ACTVS III

ita ridibundam[81] atque hilaram[82] huc adduxit simul.[83]
Periphanes: mirum hoc qui[84] potuit fieri. **Apoecides:** te pro filio
facturum dixit rem esse diuinam[85] domi, 415
quia Thebis[86] saluos[87] redierit.[88] **Periphanes:** recte[89] institit.
Apoecides: immo[90] ipsus[91] illi[92] dixit conductam esse[93] eam
quae[94] hic administraret[95] ad rem diuinam tibi.[96]
[facturum hoc dixit rem esse diuinam tibi domi][97]
ego illic[98] med[99] autem sic adsimulabam:[100] quasi 420
stolidum,[101] combardum[102] me faciebam.[103] **Periphanes:** Immo ita
decet.[104]
Apoecides: res[105] magna amici apud forum agitur,[106] ei uolo
ire aduocatus.[107] **Periphanes:** at quaeso,[108] ubi erit otium,[109]
reuortere[110] ad me extemplo.[111] **Apoecides:** continuo[112] hic ero. —

---

81 *ridibundus, -a, um*: "laughing".
82 *hilarus, -a, -um*: "light-hearted".
83 *simul*: "[together] with him".
84 *qui* (an old ablative form): "how", "why".
85 *rem... diuinam*: "religious activity", "sacrifice".
86 *Thebis* (locative).
87 *saluos = saluus*.
88 *redierit* (third-person singular perfect subjunctive active < *redeo, -ire, -iui/ii, -itum*).
89 *insisto, -ere, institi, –* : "set about", "proceed"; *recte institit*: "he handled it well", "he did the right thing".
90 *immo*: "by all means", "indeed"; "on the contrary", "by no means".
91 *ipsus = ipse*.
92 *illi* (dative, referring to the *fidicina*).
93 *conduco, -ere, -xi, -ctum*: "bring", "hire".
94 *quae = ut ea* (relative clause of purpose).
95 *administro, -are, -aui, -atum*: "administer"; translate here: "assist".
96 *tibi* (dative of reference after *administraret*).
97 [*facturum hoc dixit rem esse diuinam tibi domi*] (this line, essentially repeating line 415, probably doesn't belong here).
98 *illic*: "there".
99 *med = me*.
100 *adsimulo, -are, -aui, -atum*: "pretend".
101 *stolidus, -a, -um*: "slow", "obtuse".
102 *combardus, -a, -um*: "stupid".
103 *me faciebam*: "I made myself [look/act]".
104 *immo ita decet*: "you acted exactly as you should", "indeed that was appropriate"; translate here: "very appropriate".
105 *res, rei* (f.): "matter"; translate here: "[legal] case".
106 *ago, -ere, egi, actum*: "do", "act"; translate here: "conduct".
107 *aduocatus, -i* (m.): "advocate", "witness".
108 *quaeso*: "please".
109 *otium, -ii* (n.): "leisure", "[a] break", "spare moment".
110 *reuorto/reuerto, -ere, -ti, –sum*: "come back", "return".
111 *extemplo* (adverb): "immediately".
112 *continuo* (adverb): "immediately".

Periphanes: nihil homini amicost[113] opportuno[114] amicius:[115] 425
sine tuo labore quod uelis actumst[116] tamen.
ego si adlegassem[117] aliquem ad hoc negotium
minus hominem doctum minu'que[118] ad hanc rem callidum,[119]
os sublitum esset,[120] itaque me albis dentibus[121]
meu'[122] derideret[123] filius meritissumo.[124] 430
atque haec stultitiast[125] me illi uitio[126] uortere[127]
egomet[128] quod factitaui[129] in adulescentia,
quom[130] militabam:[131] pugnis memorandis[132] meis[133]
eradicabam[134] hominum auris,[135] quando occeperam.[136]
sed quis illic[137] est quem huc aduenientem conspicor[138] 435
suam qui undantem[139] chlamydem[140] quassando[141] facit?

---

113 *amicost = amico est.*
114 *opportunus, -a, -um:* "useful".
115 *amicius* (comparative adjective from *amicus, -a, -um*; neuter nominative singular agreeing with *nihil*).
116 *actumst = actum est.*
117 *adlegassem = adlegauissem* (first-person singular pluperfect subjunctive active < *adlego, -are, -aui, -atum:* "dispatch", "send [someone] to do a job").
118 *minu'que = minusque.*
119 *callidus, -a, -um:* "clever", "shrewd", "ingenious".
120 *os sublitum esset:* "he would have been deceived" (again, the audience would have found this irony hilarious, but Periphanes has no idea that both he and Apoecides are the ones being tricked). *alicui os sublinere* literally means "to smear someone's face", but figuratively means "to make a fool of someone", "outwit someone".
121 *albis dentibus:* literally "with white teeth"; figuratively "by laughing out loud".
122 *meu' = meus.*
123 *derideo, -ere, derisi, derisum:* "laugh [at]", "make fun [of]".
124 *meritissumo = meritissimo* (superlative adverb): "most justly", "very deservedly".
125 *stultitiast = stultitia est.*
126 *uitium, -ii* (n.): "fault", "vice", "defect".
127 *atque haec stultitiast me illi uitio uortere:* "and it's stupid for me to blame him".
128 *egomet = ego + -met:* "I, myself".
129 *factito, -are, -aui, -atum:* "do frequently", "practice".
130 *quom = cum.*
131 *milito, -are, -aui, -atum:* "serve as a soldier", perform military service", "serve in the army", "make war".
132 *memoro, -are, -aui, -atum:* "remember", "reminisce", "speak of", "mention".
133 *pugnis memorandis meis:* "because of talking about my battles", "from reminiscing about my war stories".
134 *eradico, -are, -aui, -atum:* "root out", "eradicate".
135 *auris, -is* (f.): "ear".
136 *occipio, -ere, -cepi, -ceptum:* "begin".
137 *illic = ille.*
138 *auris, -is* (f.): "ear".
139 *undo, -are, -aui, -atum:* "wave", "billow".
140 *chlamys, clamydos/is* (f.): "[Greek] cloak", "[military] cloak".
141 *quasso, -are, -aui, -atum:* "shake repeatedly", "flourish", "swagger".

3.4 MILES, PERIPHANES

Scene summary: A swaggering soldier arrives looking for Periphanes. After a comic exchange of boastful military claims, the soldier says that he wants to buy the slave woman that he hears Periphanes has just bought. He had been planning to buy her, manumit her, and make her his concubine, and now wants to buy her back from Periphanes. Periphanes agrees to sell her for sixty *minae* (ten more than he thinks he paid for her).

Miles: Caue[1] praeterbitas[2] ullas aedis[3] quin roges,[4]
senex hic ubi habitat Periphanes Platenius.
incertus tuom[5] caue ad me rettuleris[6] pedem.[7]
Periphanes: adulescens, si istunc[8] hominem quem tu quaeritas[9]   440
tibi commostrasso,[10] ecquam[11] aps[12] te inibo gratiam?[13]
Miles: uirtute belli armatus promerui[14] ut mihi
omnis mortalis agere deceat gratias.
Periphanes: non repperisti,[15] adulescens, tranquillum locum
ubi tuas uirtutes explices[16] ut postulas.[17]   445
nam strenuiori[18] deterior[19] si praedicat[20]
suas pugnas, de illius[21] illae fiunt sordidae.[22]
sed istum quem quaeris Periphanem Platenium

---

1 *caueo, -ere, caui, cautum*: "be careful".
2 *praeterbitas = praetereas < praetereo, -ire, -iui/ii, -itum*: "go by", "go past", "pass by".
3 *aedis/aedes, -is* (f.): "building", "house" (often used in the plural, as here).
4 *quin roges*: "without asking".
5 *tuom = tuum*.
6 *rettuleris* (second-person singular perfect subjunctive active) < *refero, referre, rettuli, relatum*: "carry back", "bring back".
7 *incertus tuom caue ad me rettuleris pedem*: "make sure you don't return without finding it out".
8 *istunc = istum*.
9 *quaerito, -are, -aui, -atum*: "seek", "look for".
10 *commostrasso = commonstrasso* (alternative future tense of *commo(n)stro, -are, -aui, -atum*); *si... commostrasso*: "if I show", "if I point [him] out".
11 *ecqui, ecquae/ecqua, ecquod*: "is there any", "some sort of".
12 *aps = a*.
13 *ecquam abs te inibo gratiam*: "will I put you under an obligation", "will you be grateful to me".
14 *promereo, -ere, promerui, promeritum*: "deserve", "earn".
15 *reperio, -ire, repperi, repertum*: "find".
16 *explico, -are, -aui, -atum*: "show off", "display".
17 *postulo, -are, -aui, -atum*: "claim", "require", "ask for", "want".
18 *strenuiori* (dative singular comparative adjective) < *strenuus, -a, -um*: "active", "vigorous".
19 *deterior, -ius* (nominative singular comparative adjective): "lesser", "weaker".
20 *praedico, -are, -aui, -atum*: "announce", "proclaim", "boast about".
21 *de illius* (referring to the *strenuori* of line 446): "in contrast with the other man's military achievements".
22 *sordidus, -a, -um*: "low", "humble", "pathetic".

ego sum, si quid uis.[23] **Miles:** nemp'[24] quem in adulescentia
memorant[25] apud reges armis, arte duellica   450
diuitias[26] magnas indeptum?[27] **Periphanes:** immo,[28] si audias
meas pugnas, fugias manibus dimissis[29] domum.
Miles: pol ego magis unum[30] quaero meas[31] quoi[32] praedicem[33]
quam illum qui memoret suas[34] mihi. **Periphanes:** hic non est locus;
proin[35] tu alium quaeras quoi centones[36] sarcias.[37]   455
Miles: animum aduorte[38] ut quod[39] ego ad te aduenio intellegas.
meam amicam audiui te esse mercatum.[40] **Periphanes:** attatae![41]
nunc demum scio ego hunc qui sit: quem dudum[42] Epidicus
mihi praedicauit militem. adulescens, itast[43]
ut dicis, emi.[44] **Miles:** uolo te uerbis pauculis[45]   460
si tibi molestum[46] non est. **Periphanes:** non edepol scio
molestum necne[47] sit, nisi dicis quid uelis.
Miles: mihi illam ut tramittas,[48] argentum accipias. **Periphanes:**
adest?[49]

---

23 *si quid uis*: "if you want anything".
24 *nemp' = nempe*: "really".
25 *memoro, -are, -aui, -atum*: "remember", "reminisce", "speak of", "mention".
26 *diuitiae, -arum* (f. pl.): "wealth".
27 *indipiscor, indipisci, indeptus sum*: "overtake"; translate here: "acquire".
28 *immo*: "by all means", "indeed"; "on the contrary", "by no means".
29 *manibus dimissis*: literally "with hands let loose"; translate here: "as fast as you could run".
30 *unum = quendam*: "someone".
31 *meas = meas pugnas*.
32 *quoi = cui*.
33 *praedico, -are, -aui, -atum*: "announce", "proclaim", "boast about".
34 *suas = suas pugnas*.
35 *proin* (adverb): "therefore", "so then".
36 *cento, -onis* (m.): "garment or blanket made from patchwork".
37 *sarcio, -ire, sarsi, sartum*: "patch", "mend", "restore"; *quoi centones sarcias*: literally "for whom you can mend your patchwork cloth"; translate here: "to whom you can tell your [tall] tales", "who'll listen to your story-telling".
38 *animum aduorte*: "pay attention".
39 *quod* (accusative of the inner object): "about which", "regarding which".
40 *mercor, -ari, -atus sum*: "buy".
41 *attatae* (an expression of surprise or amazement).
42 *dudum* (adverb): "a little while ago", "formerly".
43 *itast = ita est*.
44 *emo, -ere, emi, emptum*: "buy" (supply *eam* or *amicam* as the direct object).
45 *pauculus, -a, -um* (diminutive of *paucus, -a, -um*); *uolo te uerbis pauculis* (supply *conloqui*): "I want to have a few little words with you".
46 *molestus, -a, -um*: "annoying", "[a] bother".
47 *necne*: "whether... or not".
48 *tramittas = transmittas < transmitto, -ere, -misi, -missum*: "hand over" (supply *uolo* before *ut tramittas* and [*ut*] *accipias*).
49 *adest*: "is it here", "do you have [the money] with you".

Miles: nam quid⁵⁰ ego apud te uera⁵¹ parcam⁵² proloqui?
ego illam uolo hodie facere libertam⁵³ meam   465
mihi concubina⁵⁴ quae sit. **Periphanes:** te apsoluam⁵⁵ breui:⁵⁶
argenti quinquaginta⁵⁷ mihi illa empta est minis;⁵⁸
si sexaginta⁵⁹ mihi denumerantur⁶⁰ minae,
tuas possidebit⁶¹ mulier faxo⁶² ferias;⁶³
atque ita profecto⁶⁴ ut⁶⁵ eam ex hoc exoneres⁶⁶ agro.⁶⁷
Miles: estne empta mihi istis legibus?⁶⁸ **Periphanes:** habeas licet.   470
Miles: conciliauisti⁶⁹ pulchre.⁷⁰ **Periphanes:** heus!⁷¹ foras⁷² educite⁷³
quam introduxistis⁷⁴ fidicinam. atque etiam fides,⁷⁵
ei quae accessere,⁷⁶ tibi addam⁷⁷ dono⁷⁸ gratiis.⁷⁹

---

50 *quid*: "why".
51 *uerus, -a, -um*: "true".
52 *parco, -ere, peperci, parsum*: "refrain from".
53 *liberta, ae* (f.): "freedwoman", "former slave".
54 *concubina, -ae* (f.): "concubine", "common-law wife", "mistress", "girlfriend" (in Rome, concubines were free or freedwomen who lived in a marriage-like relationship with a man of usually higher status. Any children they produced were considered illegitimate; they did not enter their father's *patria potestas*, and they inherited their mother's legal status, whatever that might be).
55 *apsoluam = absoluam < absoluo, -ere, absolui, absolutum*: "free", "let [someone] off".
56 *breui* (adverb): "quickly", "soon".
57 *quinquaginta* (indeclinable): "fifty".
58 *mina, -ae* (f.): a Greek unit of money equivalent to 430g of silver.
59 *sexaginta* (indeclinable): "sixty".
60 *denumero, -are, -aui, -atum*: "pay in full", "pay down".
61 *possideo, -ere, possedi, possessum*: "be master of", "possess", "take possession of"; translate here: "occupy".
62 *faxo* (alternative form of the first-person singular future indicative active of *facio, -ere*): "I'll make [it happen]"; translate here: "I promise".
63 *feriae, -arum* (f. pl.): "religious festival", "holiday"; translate here: "leisure time".
64 *profecto* (adverb): "certainly".
65 *ita... ut* (+ subjunctive): "on condition that".
66 *exonero, -are, -aui, -atum*: "remove".
67 *ager, agri* (m.): "field"; translate here: "land" (here it refers either to "Attic land", meaning the territory around Athens where the play is supposedly set, or "my land", meaning Periphanes's property).
68 *lex, legis* (f.): "law"; translate here: "condition" (*istis legibus* is an ablative of attendant circumstances: "under those conditions").
69 *concilio, -are, -aui, -atum*: "bring together"; translate here: "buy".
70 *pulchre* (adverb): "excellently" (*conciliauisti pulchre*: "you've made a good bargain").
71 *heus*: "hey!" (used to try to get someone's attention).
72 *foras* (adverb): "out of doors".
73 *educo, -ere, eduxi, eductum*: "lead out", "bring out".
74 *introduco, -ere, -duxi, -ductum*: "lead in", "lead inside".
75 *fides, fidium* (f. pl.): "lyre".
76 *accedo, -ere, -cessi, -cessum*: "go with" (+ dative).
77 *addo, -ere, addidi, additum*: "add".
78 *dono*: "as a gift".
79 *gratiis*: "as a favour", "for nothing", "for free".

3.4a PERIPHANES, MILES, FIDICINA

Scene summary: When the soldier sees the hired lyre-player instead of Acropolistis, he tells Periphanes that it's the wrong woman, and Periphanes begins to realize that Epidicus has cheated him. The hired lyre-player tells him that she has been a freedwoman for five years and was told she was being hired to play her lyre for an old man who would be performing a religious sacrifice. She also says that she knows the real Acropolistis, who has, she says, recently been freed by Stratippocles. Periphanes expresses shame and anger at how well Epidicus had tricked him.

Periphanes: age accipe hanc sis.[1] **Miles:** quae te intemperiae[2] 475
tenent?[3]

quas tu mihi tenebras[4] trudis?[5] quin[6] tu fidicinam

produci[7] intus[8] iubes? **Periphanes:** haec ergo est fidicina.

hic alia nullast.[9] **Miles:** non mihi nugari[10] potes.

quin tu huc producis fidicinam Acropolistidem?[11]

Periphanes: haec inquamst.[12] **Miles:** non haec inquamst. non 480
nouisse[13] me

meam rere[14] amicam posse? **Periphanes:** hanc, inquam, filius

meu'[15] deperibat[16] fidicinam. **Miles:** haec non est ea.

Periphanes: quid? non est? **Miles:** non est. **Periphanes:** unde haec
igitur gentiumst?[17]

equidem hercle argentum pro hac dedi. **Miles:** stulte datum[18]

---

1 *sis = si uis*: "please", "if you please".
2 *intemperia, -ae* (f.): "insanity", "foolishness".
3 *teneo, -ere, tenui, tentum*: "hold", "possess".
4 *tenebrae, -arum* (f. pl.): "darkness", "concealment".
5 *trudo, -ere, trusi, trusum*: "thrust", "push", "drive", "force"; *quas tu mihi tenebras trudis*: "what concealment are you pushing on me"; translate here: "what trick are you playing on me".
6 *quin*: "why... not?", "why don't you...?".
7 *produco, -ere, -duxi, -ductum*: "bring out".
8 *intus*: "from within", "from inside".
9 *nullast = nulla est*.
10 *nugor, -ari, nugatus sum*: "trick [someone]", "act like a fool".
11 *Acropolistis, Acropolistidis* (f.): the name of the first lyre-player that Stratippocles had told Epidicus to buy for him while he was away on campaign. Epidicus has, as you remember, told Periphanes that she was his illegitimate daughter (see line 88).
12 *haec inquamst = haec inquam est*: "I say that this is she", "she's the one, I tell you".
13 *nosco, -ere, noui, notum*: "get to know", "know", "recognize".
14 *rere* (second-person singular present passive indicative) < *reor, reri, ratus sum*: "reckon", "think", "believe".
15 *meu' = meus*.
16 *depereo, -ire, -iui/-ii, -tum* (conjugated like *eo, ire*): "die", "be destroyed", "fall desperately in love".
17 *unde haec igitur gentiumst?*: "where in the world did she come from then?"
18 *datum = datum esse* (its accusative subject is *argentum*).

reor,[19] peccatum[20] largiter.[21] **Periphanes:** immo[22] haec east.[23]   485
nam seruom misi qui illum sectari[24] solet
meum gnatum:[25] is ipse hanc destinauit[26] fidicinam.
Miles: em[27] istic[28] homo te articulatim[29] concidit,[30] senex,
tuo' seruos.[31] **Periphanes:** quid "concidit"? **Miles:** sic suspiciost,[32]
nam pro fidicina haec cerua[33] supposita[34] est tibi.   490
senex, tibi os est sublitum[35] plane et probe.
ego illam requiram[36] iam ubi ubi[37] est. bellator, uale. —
Periphanes: eugae,[38] eugae! Epidice, frugi's,[39] pugnasti,[40] homo es,
qui me emunxisti[41] mucidum,[42] minimi preti.[43]
mercatus[44] te hodie est de lenone[45] Apoecides?   495
Fidicina: fando[46] ego istunc hominem numquam audiui ante hunc
diem
neque me quidem emere quisquam ulla pecunia
potuit: plus iam sum libera quinquennium.[47]

---

19 *reor, reri, ratus sum*: "think", "suppose", "believe".
20 *peccatum, -i* (n.): "mistake" (supply *fuisse*, the subject of which would be the purchase of the wrong *fidicina*).
21 *largiter* (adverb): "in abundance", "greatly".
22 *immo*: "by no means".
23 *east = ea est*.
24 *sector, sectari, sectatus sum*: "follow continually", "attend".
25 *gnatum = natum < natus, -i* (m.): "son".
26 *destino, -are, -aui, -atum*: "arrange the purchase of".
27 *em* (expression of surprise, in a good or bad sense): "hah!".
28 *istic* (adverb): "now", "here", "there".
29 *articulatim*: "limb from limb", "point by point", "in detail".
30 *concido, -ere, concidi, concisum*: "cut to pieces", "kill", "destroy".
31 *tuo' seruos = tuus seruus*.
32 *suspiciost = suspicio est; sic suspiciost*: "that's what I suspect".
33 *cerua, -ae* (f.): "doe", "deer".
34 *supposita = subposita < subpono, -ere, -posui, -positum*: "substitute".
35 *tibi os est sublitum*: "you've been deceived"; *alicui os sublinere* literally means "to smear someone's face", but figuratively means "to make a fool of someone", "outwit someone".
36 *requiro, -ere, requisiui, requisitum*: "require", "seek", "ask for".
37 *ubi ubi*: "wherever".
38 *eugae* (exclamation): "good", "well done" (here meant ironically: "well that's just PERFECT!").
39 *frugi's = frugi es; frugi* (indeclinable adjective): "worthy", "frugal", "virtuous" (this is an attribute often applied to slaves who thriftily save up money in their *peculia* (personal savings) in order that they might eventually buy their own freedom).
40 *pugnasti = pugnauisti < pugno, -are, -aui, -atum*: "fight".
41 *emungo, -ere, emunxi, emunctum*: "wipe/blow the nose"; "cheat".
42 *mucidus, -a, -um*: "sniveling", "snotty".
43 *minimi preti* (genitive of price after *me... mucidum*): "of little value", "worthless".
44 *mercor, -ari, -atus sum*: "buy".
45 *leno, -onis* (m.): "pimp", "brothel keeper".
46 *fando* (gerund) *< for, fari, fatus sum*: "speak", "say"; here translate *fando*: "by report".
47 *quinquennium, -ii/-i* (n.): "for five years", "a period of five years".

Periphanes: quid tibi negotist[48] meae domi igitur? **Fidicina:** audies.
conducta[49] ueni ut fidibus[50] cantarem seni,   500
dum rem diuinam[51] faceret. **Periphanes:** fateor[52] me omnium
hominum esse Athenis Atticis minimi preti.[53]
sed tu nouistin[54] fidicinam Acropolistidem?
Fidicina: tam facile quam me.[55] **Periphanes:** ubi habitat? **Fidicina:**
postquam[56] liberast[57]
ubi habitet dicere admodum[58] incerte scio.[59]   505
Periphanes: eho[60] an libera illa est? quis eam liberauerit
uolo scire, si scis. **Fidicina:** id quod audiui audies.
Stratippoclem aiunt Periphanei[61] filium
apsentem[62] curauisse[63] ut fieret libera.
Periphanes: perii[64] hercle si istaec[65] uera sunt; planissume.[66]   510
meum exenterauit[67] Epidicus marsuppium.[68]
Fidicina: haec sic audiui. numquid[69] me uis ceterum?[70]
Periphanes: malo cruciatu[71] ut pereas atque abeas cito.[72]
Fidicina: fides[73] non reddis?[74] **Periphanes:** neque fides neque tibias.[75]

---

48 *negotist = negotii est < negotium, -i/ii* (n.): "business".
49 *conduco, -ere, -xi, -ctum*: "bring", "hire".
50 *fides, fidium* (f. pl.): "lyre".
51 *rem diuinam*: "religious activity", "sacrifice".
52 *fateor, fateri, fassus sum*: "admit", "confess".
53 *minimi preti* (genitive of price): "of little value", "worthless".
54 *nouistin = nouisti+ne < nosco, -ere, noui, notum*: "get to know", "know", "recognize".
55 *tam facile quam me*: "as well as I know myself".
56 *postquam*: "after", "since".
57 *liberast = libera est < libero, -are, -aui, atum*: "set free", "emancipate".
58 *admodum* (adverb): "fully", "thoroughly".
59 *ubi habitet dicere admodum incerte scio*: "to tell [you] where she's living, I don't really know for sure"; "I'm really not sure where she's living".
60 *eho* (an exclamation of surprise, amazement, anger, or a preface to giving someone an order or request).
61 *Periphanei* (genitive).
62 *apsentem = absentem*.
63 *curo, -are, -aui, -atum*: "arrange", "see/attend to", "take care of".
64 *pereo, -ire, -iui/-ii, -itum*: "die", "be ruined", "be lost".
65 *istaec = ista*.
66 *planissume = planissime*: "totally".
67 *exentero, -are, -aui, -atum*: "disembowel"; (in the context of a purse or store of money) "empty".
68 *marsuppium, -ii* (n.): "purse", "moneybag".
69 *numquid* (a strengthened form of *num*): "surely... not?", "can it be that...?".
70 *numquid me uis ceterum*: "can I do anything else for you?".
71 *cruciatus, -us* (m.): "torture", "crucifixion".
72 *malo cruciatu ut pereas atque abeas cito*: "[I want you] to get out of here and go die on a cross".
73 *fides, -ium* (f. pl.): "lyre".
74 *reddo, -ere, reddidi, redditum*: "return", "give back".
75 *tibia, -ae* (f.): "flute", "woodwind instrument" (originally made from the tibia or shin bone of an animal).

propera[76] sis[77] fugere hinc si te di amant. **Fidicina:** abiero.[78] 515
flagitio[79] cum maiore post reddes tamen.[80] —
Periphanes: quid nunc? qui in tantis positus sum[81] sententiis[82]
eamne ego sinam[83] impune?[84] immo[85] etiam si alterum
tantum[86] perdundumst,[87] perdam potius quam[88] sinam
me impune inrisum esse,[89] habitum[90] depeculatui.[91] 520
ei![92] seic[93] data esse uerba[94] praesenti[95] palam![96]
ac me minoris[97] facio prae[98] illo, qui omnium
legum atque iurum fictor,[99] condictor[100] cluet;[101]
is etiam sese sapere[102] memorat:[103] malleum[104]
sapientiorem uidi excusso[105] manubrio.[106] 525

---

76 *properā* (second-person singular present imperative active) < *propero, -are, -aui, -atum*: "be quick", "hurry", "go quickly").
77 *sis* (second-person singular present subjunctive active) < *sum, esse*; used here to emphasize the peremptory nature of Periphanes's command and is best not translated literally (see Lindsay 1904: 58–59).
78 *abiero* (first-person singular future perfect indicative active) < *abeo, -ire, -iui/-ii, -itum*.
79 *flagitium, -ii* (n.): "shame", "scandal".
80 *flagitio cum maiore post reddes tamen*: "but you'll give it [the lyre] back with the big scandal [I'll spread around]", "but you'll give it back or I'll make trouble for you".
81 *pono, -ere, posui, positum*: "put", "place", "set".
82 *sententia, -ae* (f.): "judgment", "opinion".
83 *sino, sinere, siui, situm*: "allow".
84 *impune* (adverb): "with impunity", "without punishment".
85 *immo*: "by no means".
86 *alterum tantum*: "as much again", "as large a sum".
87 *perdundumst* = *perdundum est* < *perdo, -ere, perdidi, perditum*: "ruin", "lose".
88 *potius quam*: "rather than".
89 *inrisum* = *irrisum* < *irrideo, -ere, irrisi, irrisum*: "make fun of", "laugh at".
90 *habitum [esse]*: "to be regarded as".
91 *habitum [esse] peculatui*: "to have been held as source of plunder", "to have been cheated".
92 *ei* (exclamation): "oh".
93 *seic* = *sic*.
94 *data esse uerba*: "to have been tricked / lied to" (see note 227 in Act 1, scene 1).
95 *praesens, praesentis* (*praesenti* agrees with a missing *mihi*): "at hand", "present", "in person".
96 *palam* (adverb): "openly".
97 *minoris* (genitive of value): "of less worth", "lowlier".
98 *prae*: "in front of".
99 *fictor, -oris* (m.): "maker".
100 *condictor, -oris* (m.): "one who fixes or arranges".
101 *clueo, -ere*: "be spoken of", "hear oneself called".
102 *sapio, -ere, sapiui, –* : "to be sensible", "to be wise".
103 *memoro, -are, -aui, -atum*: "remember", "reminisce", "speak of", "mention".
104 *malleus, -ei* (m.): "hammer".
105 *excutio, -ere, excussi, excussum*: "shake out or off"; translate here: "knock off".
106 *manubrium, -ii* (n.): "handle".

ACTVS IV

4.1 PHILIPPA, PERIPHANES

Scene summary: Philippa, the mother of Telestis, arrives on stage, expressing anxiety and sadness because her daughter has been taken captive. She is looking for Periphanes, and finally sees him. They eventually recognize each other, having not seen each other for many years. Periphanes remembers his part in the affair (during which he had helped her out financially) as having been more generous than Philippa does, since she was left with a child to bring up and no husband. Periphanes tells Philippa the good news that he has their daughter Telestis safe in his house, and he calls for her to be brought outside to see her mother.

Philippa: Si quid est homini[1] miseriarum[2] quod miserescat,[3]
miser ex animost.[4]
id ego experior,[5] quoi[6] multa in unum locum confluont[7] quae
meum pectu'[8] pulsant[9]
simul: multiplex[10] aerumna[11] exercitam[12] habet,
paupertas, pauor[13] territat[14] mentem animi,   530
neque ubi meas conlocem[15] spes[16] habeo mi usquam[17] munitum[18] locum.

---

1 *homini* (dative of possession with *est*).
2 *miseria, -ae* (f.): "suffering", "misery".
3 *miseresco, -ere*: "have compassion".
4 *animost = animo est; si quid est homini miseriarum quod miserescat, miser ex animost*: "if a person suffers so much that she pities herself, she is well and truly pitiable".
5 *experior, -iri, expertus sum*: "put to the test", "experience".
6 *quoi = cui*.
7 *confluont = confluunt < confluo, -ere, -fluxi, –* : "flow together".
8 *pectu' = pectus < pectus, pectoris* (n.): "breast", "chest"; translate here: "heart".
9 *pulso, -are, -aui, -atum*: "beat", "strike", "hammer".
10 *multiplex, -plicis*: "having many folds", "having many parts".
11 *aerumna, -ae*: "distress", "hardship", "labour", "task".
12 *exerceo, -ere, -ui, -itum*: "occupy", "exercise", "disturb".
13 *pauor, -oris* (m.): "fear", "panic".
14 *territo, -are, -aui, -atum*: "intimidate", "keep in a state of fear".
15 *conlocem = collocem < colloco, -are, -aui, -atum*: "place", "position".
16 *spes* (feminine accusative plural) *< spes, spei*.
17 *usquam*: "anywhere".
18 *munitus, -a, -um*: "safe".

ita gnata[19] mea hostiumst[20] potita[21] neque ea nunc ubi sit scio.
Periphanes: quis illaec[22] est mulier timido pectore[23] peregre[24] adueniens
quae ipsa se miseratur?[25] **Philippa:** in his dictust[26] locis habitare mihi
Periphanes. **Periphanes:** me nominat haec; credo ego illi[27] hospitio[28]   535
usu'[29] uenit.
Philippa: peruelim[30] mercedem[31] dare qui monstret eum mi
hominem [aut] ubi habitet.
Periphanes: noscito[32] ego hanc, nam uideor nescio ubi[33] mi[34]
uidisse prius.
estne ea an non east[35] quam animus retur[36] meus?
Philippa: di boni! uisitaui[37] * * antidhac?[38]
Periphanes: certo[39] east * *   540
quam in Epidauro   540a
pauperculam[40] memini[41] comprimere[42]   540b
Philippa: plane hicine[43] est
qui mi in Epidauro uirgini primu'[44] pudicitiam[45] perpulit.[46]   541a

---

19 *gnata* = *nata, -ae* (f.): "daughter".
20 *hostiumst* = *hostium est*; *hostis, -is* (m.): "stranger", "foreigner".
21 *hostiumst potita*: "[she] has been captured by the enemy".
22 *illaec* = *illa*.
23 *pectore* < *pectus, pectoris* (see above).
24 *peregre* (adverb): "to/from abroad".
25 *miseror, -ari, -atus sum*: "pity", "feel sorry for".
26 *dictust* = *dictus est*.
27 *illi* (feminive dative singular, referring to Philippa).
28 *hospitium, -ii* (n.): "hospitality".
29 *usu'* = *usus*; *usu' uenit* (+ ablative): "there is need for", "it is necessary".
30 *peruolo, peruelle, peruolui* (stronger form of *uolo*).
31 *merces, mercedis* (f.): "pay", "reward".
32 *noscito, -are, -aui, -atum*: "recognize", "try to recognize".
33 *nescio ubi*: "I don't know where".
34 *mi* = *mihi*.
35 *east* = *ea est*.
36 *reor, reri, ratus sum*: "think", "suppose", "believe".
37 *uisito, -are, -aui, -atum*: "see", "go to see".
38 *antidhac* = *antehac* (adverb): "before this time", "in the past"; *uisitaui ... antidhac?*: "have I seen [this man] before?".
39 *certo*: "certainly".
40 *pauperculus, -a, -um*: "poor little" (diminutive of *pauper, pauperis*).
41 *memini, -isse*: "remember" (only the perfect tense forms exist).
42 *comprimo, -ere, -pressi, -pressum*: "press together", "restrain"; translate here: "have sex with" (from a male point of view), "sexually penetrate".
43 *hicine*: "here".
44 *primu'* = *primus*.
45 *pudicitia, -ae* (f.): "chastity", "virginity".
46 *perpello, perpellere, perpuli, perpulsum*: "compel", "constrain", "prevail upon".

ACTVS IV

Periphanes: quae meo compressu[47] peperit[48] filiam quam domi nunc habeo.

quid si[49] adeam[50] — **Philippa:** hau scio[51] an congredias[52] — **Periphanes:** si haec east. **Philippa:** sin is est homo, sicut[53] anni multi dubia[54] dant. **Periphanes:** longa dies[55] meum incertat[56] animum.

sin[57] east quam incerte autumo,[58] hanc congrediar astu.[59]   545

Philippa: muliebris[60] adhibenda[61] mihi malitia[62] nunc est.

Periphanes: compellabo.[63] **Philippa:** orationis aciem[64] contra[65] conferam.[66]

Periphanes: salua sies.[67] **Philippa:** salutem[68] accipio mihi et meis.[69]

Periphanes: quid ceterum?

Philippa: saluos[70] sis: quod credidisti[71] reddo.[72] **Periphanes:** haud accuso[73] fidem.[74]

nouin[75] ego te? **Philippa:** si ego te noui, animum inducam[76] ut tu   550
noueris.[77]

---

47 *compressus, -us* (m.): "pressing together"; translate here: "sexual intercourse" (by a man), "sexual penetration".
48 *pario, -ere, peperi, paritum/partum*: "give birth to".
49 *quid si*: "what if".
50 *adeo, -ire, -iui/-ii, -itum*: "approach".
51 *hau = haud*: "not", "not at all".
52 *congredias* (alternative second-person singular present subjunctive active < *congredior, -iri, congressus sum*: "approach").
53 *sicut*: "as", "since".
54 *dubius, -a, -um*: "uncertain".
55 *dies, diei* (f.): "day"; translate here: "period of time".
56 *incerto, -are, -aui, -atum*: "make unsure/uncertain".
57 *sin = si + -ne*.
58 *autumo, -are, –aui, -atum*: "affirm", "think/believe".
59 *astus, -us* (m.): "cunning", "cleverness".
60 *muliebris, muliebre*: "womanly", "feminine".
61 *adhibeo, -ere, adhibui, adhibitum*: "summon", "use".
62 *malitia, -ae* (f.): "malice", "artfulness", "cunning".
63 *compello, -are, -aui, -atum*: "address", "speak to".
64 *orationis aciem*: "the sharp edge of my eloquence/speech".
65 *contra*: "against [him]".
66 *confero, -ferre, -tuli, -latum*: "direct", "aim".
67 *sies = sis*.
68 *salus, salutis* (f.): "greeting", "wishes for good health".
69 *meis = meis familiaribus*: "for my family".
70 *saluos = saluus*.
71 *credo, -ere, credidi, creditum*: "believe", "trust"; translate here: "lend".
72 *quod credidisti reddo*: "I return [the greeting] that you lent me".
73 *accuso, -are, -aui, -atum*: "find fault with".
74 *fides, fidei* (f.): "faith", "trustworthiness"; translate here: "credit".
75 *nouin = noui + -ne < nosco, -ere, noui, notum*: "get to know", "know", "recognize".
76 *induco, -ere, -duxi, -ductum*: "induce", "influence".
77 *si ego te noui, animum inducam ut tu noueris*: "if I know you, I'll persuade myself that you know me".

Periphanes: ubi te uisitaui? **Philippa:** inique[78] iniuriu's.[79]

Periphanes: quid iam? **Philippa:** quia
tuae memoriae interpretari[80] me aequom[81] censes.[82] **Periphanes:** commode[83]
fabulata's.[84] **Philippa:** mira[85] memoras,[86] <Periphane.[87]>

Periphanes: em[88] istuc[89] rectius.[90]
meministin?[91] **Philippa:** memini id quod memini. **Periphanes:** at in
Epidauro — **Philippa:** ah! guttula[92]
pectus ardens mihi aspersisti.[93] **Periphanes:** uirgini pauperculae   555
tuaeque matri me leuare[94] paupertatem?[95] **Philippa:** tun[96] is es
qui per[97] uoluptatem tuam in me aerumnam[98] obseuisti[99] grauem?
Periphanes: ego sum. salue. **Philippa:** salua[100] sum quia te esse
saluom[101] sentio.[102]

Periphanes: cedo[103] manum. **Philippa:** accipe; aerumnosam[104] et
miseriarum[105] compotem[106]

---

78 *inique* (adverb < *iniquus, -a, -um*): "unjustly", "unfairly".
79 *iniuriu's* = *iniurius es*: "you're being unfair" (Plautus sometimes pairs an adjective and adverb that mean essentially the same thing).
80 *interpretor, -ari, -atus sum*: "explain", "interpret"; translate here: "assist", "jog [your memory]" (+ dative *tuae memoriae*).
81 *aequom* = *aequum*.
82 *censeo, -ere, censui, censitum*: "think", "recommend".
83 *commode* (adverb): "rightly", "appropriately", "skillfully".
84 *fabulata's* = *fabulata es* < *fabulor, -ari, -atus sum*: "speak".
85 *mirus, -a, -um*: "amazing", "surprising".
86 *memoro, -are, -aui, -atum*: "remember", "reminisce", "speak of", "mention".
87 *Periphane* (vocative).
88 *em* (expression of surprise, in a good or bad sense): "there!", "hah!".
89 *istuc* = *istud*.
90 *rectius* (comparative adverb from *rectus, -a, -um*): "more rightly".
91 *meministin* = *meministi* + *-ne* < *memini, meminisse*: "remember" (only the perfect tense forms exist).
92 *guttulā* (ablative singular) < *guttula, -ae* (f.): "little drop".
93 *aspergo, -ere, aspersi, aspersum*: "sprinkle".
94 *me leuare* (accusative-infinitive construction after *meministin* in line 554).
95 *meministin... in Epidauro... uirgini pauperculae tuaeque matri me leuare paupertam*: "do you remember that in Epidaurus I lightened the poverty of a penniless young girl and of your mother".
96 *tun* = *tu* + *-ne*.
97 *per*: "for the sake of" (+ accusative).
98 *aerumna, -ae* (f.): "distress", "hardship", "labour", "task".
99 *obsero, -ere, obseui, obsitum*: "sow", "plant", "bring".
100 *salua... saluom* (Philippa takes Periphanes's greeting *salue* literally).
101 *saluom* = *saluum*.
102 *sentio, -ire, sensi, sensum*: "perceive".
103 *cedo* (archaic singular imperative related to *do, dare*): "give".
104 *aerumnosus, -a, -um* (adjectival form of *aerumna, -a* see above).
105 *miseria, -ae* (f.): "suffering", "misery".
106 *compos, compotis*: "in possession of"; translate here: "afflicted with" (+ genitive).

mulierem retines.[107] **Periphanes:** quid est quod[108] uoltus[109] †te 560
turbatt[110] tuos?[111]

Philippa: filiam quam ex te suscepi[112] — **Periphanes:** quid eam?[113]

Philippa: eductam[114] perdidi.[115]

hostium est potita.[116] **Periphanes:** habe animum lenem et tranquillum.
tace.

domi meae[117] eccam[118] saluam et sanam. nam postquam audiui ilico[119]

e meo seruo illam esse captam, continuo[120] argentum dedi

ut emeretur.[121] ille eam rem adeo[122] sobrie[123] et frugaliter[124] 565

accurauit[125] ut — ut ad alias res est impense[126] inprobus.[127]

Philippa: fac uideam,[128] sei[129] mea,[130] sei saluam <me> uis.[131]

Periphanes: eho![132] istinc,[133] Canthara,[134]

iube Telestidem[135] huc prodire[136] filiam ante[137] aedis[138] meam,

ut suam uideat matrem. **Philippa:** remigrat[139] animus nunc demum mihi.

---

107 *retineo, -ere, retinui, retentus*: "hold"; translate here: "hold the hand of".
108 *quid est quod*: "why is that", "why".
109 *uoltus/uultus, -ūs* (m.): "face", "facial expression".
110 *quid est quod uoltus †te turbatt tuos?* should probably be emended, as Duckworth suggests, to *quid est quod uoltus turbatur tuos*: "why is your face so troubled?".
111 *tuos = tuus*.
112 *suscipio, -ere, suscepi, susceptum*: "receive", "bear [a child]".
113 *quid eam*: "what about her?".
114 *eductam = educatam < educo, -are, -aui, -atum*: "raise / bring up [a child]".
115 *perdo, -ere, perdidi, perditum*: "ruin", "lose".
116 *hostium est potita*: "[she] has been captured by the enemy".
117 *domi meae* (locative).
118 *eccam = ecce eam* (*ecce* usually means "look!", "behold", and frequently, as here, refers to someone off stage).
119 *ilico* (adverb): "immediately".
120 *continuo* (adverb): "immediately".
121 *emo, -ere, emi, emptum*: "buy".
122 *adeo*: "precisely", "exactly".
123 *sobrie* (adverb from *sobrius, -a, -um*: "sober", "sensible").
124 *frugaliter* (adverb < *frugalis, -e*: "useful", "prudent"); see note 39 in Act 3, scene 4a.
125 *accuro, -are, -aui, -atum*: "attend to", "take care of", "perform with care".
126 *impense*: "exceedingly" < *impensus, -a, -um*: "great", "ample".
127 *inprobus = improbus < improbus, -a, -um*: "wicked", "greedy", "shameless".
128 *fac uideam*: "let me see [her]".
129 *sei = si*.
130 *sei mea*: "if she is mine".
131 *sei saluam <me> uis*: "if you want me to be well".
132 *eho* (an exclamation of surprise, amazement, anger, or a preface to giving someone an order or request).
133 *istinc*: "from [in] there".
134 *Canthara, -ae*: a woman's name.
135 *Telestis, Telestidis*: the name of Periphanes's and Philippa's illegitimate daughter.
136 *prodeo, -ire, -iui, -itum*: "come out".
137 *ante* (preposition + accusative): "in front of".
138 *aedis/aedes, -is* (f.): "building", "house" (often used in the plural, as here).
139 *remigro, -are, -aui, -atum*: "move back", "return".

4.2 ACROPOLISTIS, PERIPHANES, PHILIPPA

Scene summary: Acropolistis (whom Periphanes has been made to believe is his daughter Telestis) comes out, calling Periphanes "father". Philippa says that the woman is not Telestis, and Acropolistis says she was told by Epidicus to pretend to be Telestis. Periphanes is enraged and threatens to have Epidicus executed when he finds him.

Acropolistis: quid est, pater, quod me exciuisti[1] ante aedis? 570
Periphanes: ut matrem tuam
uideas, adeas,[2] aduenienti[3] des[4] salutem[5] atque osculum.[6]
Acropolostis: quam meam matrem?[7] **Periphanes:** quae exanimata[8]
exsequitur[9] aspectum[10] tuom.[11]
Philippa: quis istaec[12] est quam tu osculum mi[13] ferre iubes?
Periphanes: tua filia.
Philippa: haecine?[14] **Periphanes:** haec. **Philippa:** egone osculum
huic dem? **Periphanes:** qur[15]
non, quae ex te nata sit?[16]
Philippa: tu homo insanis. **Periphanes:** egone? **Philippa:** tune. 575
Periphanes: qur?[17] **Philippa:** quia ego hanc quae siet[18]
neque scio neque noui[19] neque ego hanc oculis uidi ante hunc diem.

---

1 *excio, -ire, -iui, -itum*: "rouse", "send for", "summon".
2 *adeas < adeo, -ire, -iui/-ii, -itum*: "approach".
3 *aduenienti* (dative singular of the present active participle of *aduenio, -ire, -ueni, -uentum*).
4 *des < do, dare, dedi, datum*.
5 *salus, salutis* (f.): "greeting", "wishes for good health".
6 *osculum, -i* (n.): "kiss".
7 *quam meam matrem* (accusative direct object of an implied *ut... uideam, adeam* carried over from 570–571): "[so that I may come and see] which mother of mine?".
8 *exanimo, -are, -aui, -atum*: "alarm", "exhaust", "be out of breath".
9 *exsequor, -i, -exsecutus sum*: "follow", "pursue", "search for".
10 *aspectus, -ūs* (m.): "appearance", "sight", "countenance".
11 *tuom = tuum*.
12 *istaec = ista*.
13 *mi = mihi*.
14 *haecine = haec + -ne*.
15 *qur = cur*.
16 *nata sit < nascor, nasci, natus sum*: "be born"; perfect subjunctive because it's a relative clause of concession, see Allen and Greenough's *Latin Grammar* 535.e, http://dcc.dickinson.edu/grammar/latin/category-search?field_gl_section_number_value=535.
17 *qur = cur*.
18 *siet = sit*.
19 *quia ego hanc quae siet / neque scio neque noui*: literally "because I don't know this woman — who she may be — and I don't recognize [her]".

Periphanes: scio quid[20] erres:[21] quia uestitum[22] atque ornatum[23] immutabilem[24]
habet haec, *
Philippa: * aliter[25] catuli[26] longe[27] olent,[28] aliter sues.[29]
ne[30] ego me nego nosse[31] hanc quae sit. **Periphanes:** pro[32] deum 580
atque hominum fidem!
quid? ego lenocinium[33] facio qui habeam alienas[34] domi[35]
atque argentum egurgitem[36] domo prosus?[37] quid[38] tu, quae patrem
tuom[39] uocas me atque osculare, quid stas stupida? quid taces?
Acropolostis: quid[40] loquar uis? **Periphanes:** haec negat se tuam
esse matrem. **Acropolostis:** ne fuat[41]
si non uolt:[42] equidem hac inuita[43] tamen ero[44] matris[45] filia; 585
non med[46] istanc[47] cogere[48] aequom[49] est meam esse matrem si
neuolt.[50]

---

20 *quid*: "why".
21 *erro, -are, -aui, -atum*: "err", "make a mistake", "be confused" (subjunctive because it's an indirect question).
22 *uestitus, -ūs* (m.): "clothing".
23 *ornatus, -ūs* (m.): "adornment", "accessories".
24 *immutabilis, -e*: "changed", "liable to be changed" (< *immuto, -are*: "change"; not to be confused with *immutabilis* < *in* + *mutabilis*: "unchangeable").
25 *aliter... aliter* (abverb): "one way... another way".
26 *catulus, -i* (m.): "puppy".
27 *longe* (adverb): "by a long way", "far", "much".
28 *oleo, -ere, olui, —* : "smell of", "smell like".
29 *sus, suis* (m./f.): "pig".
30 *ne* (interjection followed by a personal or demonstrative pronoun): "really", "indeed".
31 *nosse = nouisse < nosco, -ere, noui, notum*: "get to know", "know", "recognize".
32 *pro*: "oh!", "by...!", "for the sake of..." (+ accusative).
33 *lenocinium, -ii* (n.): "pimping", "sex trafficking".
34 *alienus, -a, -um*: "strange", "foreign".
35 *domi* (locative).
36 *egurgito, -are, -aui, -atum*: "pour out from" (+ ablative).
37 *prosus/prorsus* (adverb): "entirely", "utterly".
38 *quid*: "why".
39 *tuom = tuum*.
40 *quid*: "what".
41 *fuat = sit*.
42 *uolt = uult*.
43 *hāc inuitā* (ablative absolute): "even if she isn't willing", "even without her agreement".
44 *ero < sum, esse, fui, futurum*.
45 *matris* (Acropolistis here is referring to her own real mother): "my mother's".
46 *med = me*.
47 *istanc = istam*.
48 *cogo, -ere, coegi, coactum*: "compel", "force".
49 *aequom = aequum*: "right", "fair".
50 *neuolt = non uult*.

Periphanes: qur[51] me igitur patrem uocabas? **Acropolistis:** tua istaec[52] culpast,[53] non mea.

non patrem ego te nominem,[54] ubi tu tuam me appelles[55] filiam?

hanc quoque etiam, si me appellet filiam, matrem uocem.

negat haec filiam me suam esse: non ergo haec mater mea est. 590

postremo[56] haec mea culpa non est: quae didici[57] dixi omnia;

Epidicus mihi fuit magister.[58] **Periphanes:** perii![59] plaustrum[60] perculi.[61]

Acropolistis: numquid[62] ego ibi, pater, peccaui? **Periphanes:** si hercle te umquam audiuero

me patrem uocare, uitam tuam ego interimam.[63] **Acropolistis:** non uoco.

ubi[64] uoles pater esse ibi[65] esto;[66] ubi noles ne fueris[67] pater. 595

Philippa: quid <si> | ob eam rem[68] hanc emisti[69] quia tuam gnatam[70] ratu's,[71]

quibu'[72] de signis agnoscebas?[73] **Periphanes:** nullis. **Philippa:** qua re[74] filiam

credidisti nostram?[75] **Periphanes:** seruos[76] Epidicus dixit mihi.

---

51 *qur = cur.*
52 *istaec = ista.*
53 *culpast = culpa est.*
54 *nomino, -are, -aui, -atum*: "name", "call".
55 *appello, -are, -aui, -atum*: "call", "name".
56 *postremo* (adverb): "finally".
57 *disco, -ere, didici, discitum*: "learn".
58 *magister, -tri* (m.): "teacher".
59 *pereo, -ire, -iui/-ii, -itum*: "die", "be ruined", "be lost".
60 *plaustrum, -tri* (n.): "wagon".
61 *percello, -ere, perculi, perculsum*: "upset"; *plaustrum perculi* (proverbial saying): "I've really messed up".
62 *numquid* (a strengthened form of *num*): "surely... not?", "can it be that...?".
63 *interimo, -ere, interimi, interemptum*: "do away with", "kill", "put an end to".
64 *ubi*: "when", "whenever".
65 *ibi*: "then".
66 *esto* (second-person singular future imperative active) < *sum, esse, fui, futurus.*
67 *fueris* (second-person singular perfect subjunctive active) < *sum, esse, fui, futurus.*
68 *quam ob rem*: "for that reason".
69 *emo, -ere, emi, emptum*: "buy".
70 *gnatam = natam < nata, -ae* (f.): "daughter".
71 *ratu's = ratus es < reor, reri, ratus sum*: "think", "suppose", "believe". Supply *esse* to make an indirect statement with *tuam gnatam esse ratu's*).
72 *quibu' = quibus.*
73 *agnosco, -ere, agnoui, agnitum*: "recognize".
74 *qua re*: "why".
75 *qua re filiam credidisti nostram* (supply *esse* to make an indirect statement).
76 *seruos = seruus.*

Philippa: quid si seruo aliter uisum est,[77] non poteras nouisse,[78] opsecro?[79]
Periphanes: quid ego,[80] qui illam ut[81] preimum[82] uidi, numquam   600
uidi postea?
Philippa: perii misera! **Periphanes:** ne fle,[83] mulier. intro abi,[84] habe animum bonum;
ego illam reperiam.[85] **Philippa:** hinc[86] Athenis[87] ciuis eam emit Atticus:
adulescentem equidem dicebant emisse. **Periphanes:** inueniam, tace.
abi[88] modo intro atque hanc asserua[89] Circam[90] Solis[91] filiam.
ego relictis rebus[92] Epidicum operam quaerendo dabo:[93]   605
si inuenio exitiabilem[94] ego illi faciam hunc ut fiat diem. —

---

77 *quid si seruo aliter uisum est*: "so if it seemed otherwise to your slave", "just because your slave made a mistake".
78 *nosco, -ere, noui, notum*: "get to know", "know", "recognize".
79 *opsecro*: "please", "for goodness' sake".
80 *quid ego*: "how could I?".
81 *ut*: "since".
82 *preimum = primum*: "for the first time".
83 *fleo, -ere, fleui, fletum*: "weep", "cry"; *ne fle*: "stop crying".
84 *abi* (second-person singular present imperative) < *abeo, -ire, -ii/iui, -itum*.
85 *reperio, -ire, repperi, repertum*: "find".
86 *hinc*: "from here".
87 *Athenis* (ablative of place from which, referring to the place where Stratippocles, the *ciuis Atticus*, is from).
88 *abi* (second-person singular present imperative) < *abeo, -ire, -ii/iui, -itum*.
89 *asseruo, -are, -aui, -atum*: "guard, "watch".
90 *Circa, -ae* (f.): "Circe" (Circe, from Greek mythology, was the daughter of the Sun. She was a witch and lover of Odysseus. It is not a compliment for Periphanes to refer to Acropolistis as "Circe").
91 *Sol, Solis* (m.): "sun".
92 *relictis rebus* (ablative absolute): "with the [other] matter left aside".
93 *operam quaerendo dabo*: "I'll give attention to seeking", "I'll start looking for".
94 *exitiabilis, -e*: "destructive", "deadly".

ACTVS V

5.1 STRATIPPOCLES, EPIDICVS, DANISTA, TELESTIS

Scene summary: Epidicus expresses terror at the punishment he knows Periphanes is planning for him, since he has seen Periphanes and Apoecides buying straps for tying him up. He begs for help in running away, but Stratippocles is unsympathetic. The moneylender arrives with Telestis, and Stratippocles goes indoors to bring out the money he owes the moneylender. While Stratippocles is indoors, Epidicus recognizes Telestis as Periphanes's illegitimate daughter, since he'd brought her some birthday gifts some years before (presumably at Periphanes's order). She is delighted to learn that she has found her father, and when Stratippocles comes outdoors and pays off the moneylender, she greets him as her brother. Stratippocles is disappointed to find that his newly acquired slave girlfriend has turned out to be his sister but Epidicus tells him to keep quiet and to make do with Acropolistis instead. Epidicus knows that his discovery of the real Telestis will turn Periphanes's rage into gratitude, and so no longer plans to run away.

Stratippocles: male[1] morigerus[2] mihi est danista,[3] quei[4] a me argentum non petit
neque illam adducit quam \<emi\> ex praeda.[5] sed eccum[6] incedit[7] Epidicus.
quid illuc est quod[8] illi caperrat[9] frons[10] seueritudine?[11]

---

1 *male* (used to negate *morigerus*).
2 *morigerus, -a, -um*: "compliant", "obliging".
3 *danista, -ae* (m.): "moneylender".
4 *quei = qui*.
5 *praeda, -ae* (f.): "booty", "[war] prize".
6 *eccum = ecce + hunc*: "look, there he is!".
7 *incedo, -ere, incessi, incessum*: "walk", "march along".
8 *quid illuc quod*: "why is it that?".
9 *caperro, -are, -aui, -atum*: "be wrinkled", "wrinkle", "furrow".
10 *frons, frontis* (m.): "forehead", "brow".
11 *seueritudo, -tudinis* (f.): "severity", "worry".

Epidicus: si undecim[12] deos praeter[13] sese secum adducat Iuppiter, 610
ita non omnes ex cruciatu[14] poterunt eximere[15] Epidicum.
Periphanem emere lora[16] uidi, ibi aderat una[17] Apoecides;
nunc homines me quaeritare[18] credo. senserunt, sciunt
sibi data esse uerba.[19] **Stratippocles:** quid agis,[20] mea
Commoditas?[21] **Epidicus:** quod[22] miser.
Stratippocles: quid est tibi? **Epidicus:** quin[23] tu mihi adornas[24] ad 615
fugam[25] uiaticum[26]
priu' quam[27] pereo? nam per urbem duo defloccati[28] senes
quaeritant me, in manibus gestant[29] copulas[30] secum simul.[31]
Stratippocles: habe bonum animum. **Epidicus:** quippe[32] ego quoi[33]
libertas in mundo[34] sitast.[35]
Stratippocles: ego te seruabo.[36] **Epidicus:** edepol me illi melius[37] si
nancti fuant.[38]

---

12 *undecim* (indeclinable; here it qualifies *deos*): "eleven".
13 *praeter*: "except", "not including".
14 *cruciatus, -us* (m.): "torture", "crucifixion".
15 *eximo, -ere, exemi, exemptum*: "extract", "release", "save".
16 *lorum, -i* (n.): "leather strap", "whip".
17 *unā* (adverbial): "at the same time", "along with him".
18 *quaerito, -are, -aui, -atum*: "seek", "search for".
19 *sibi data esse uerba*: "that they have been tricked / lied to".
20 *quid agis*: "what are you up to" (this is a standard greeting).
21 *Commoditas, -atis* (f.): "timeliness", "convenience", "benefit" (Stratippocles uses this nickname for Epidicus perhaps from affection, or more likely as a casual acknowledgment that Epidicus is a useful tool to him).
22 *quod* (replies literally to Stratippocles's greeting): "what [a miserable man would be up to]".
23 *quin*: "why... not?", "why don't you...?".
24 *adorno, -are, -aui, -atum*: "get ready", "prepare".
25 *fuga, -ae* (f.): "escape", "running away" "exile".
26 *uiaticus, -a, -um* (adjective < *uia, -ae*): "relating to a journey"; *quin tu mihi adornaas ad fugam uiaticum*: "why don't you give me what I'll need to run away".
27 *priu' quam* = *prius quam*: "before".
28 *defloccatus, -a, -um*: "bald", "shorn", "fleeced" (probably intended in the sense of "cheated").
29 *gesto, -are, -aui, -atum*: "carry".
30 *copula, -ae* (f.): "rope", "thong", "bond".
31 *simul*: "also", "at the same time".
32 *quippe*: "obviously".
33 *quoi* = *cui*.
34 *in mundo*: "in readiness" (Epidicus is being ironic here, since it is punishment, not freedom, that he actually expects).
35 *sitast* = *sita est*: "[for whom freedom] has been allowed / permitted" < *sino, -ere, siui, situm*: "allow".
36 *seruo, -are, -aui, -atum*: "guard", "keep watch over". "protect", "save".
37 *me illi melius*: "they'll guard me better" (Stratippocles used *te seruabo* to mean "I'll protect you", but Epidicus picks up on the other meaning of the word: "guard" or "keep watch over").
38 *nancti fuant* = *nancti sunt* < *nanciscor, nancisci, nanctus sum*: "get", "find", "meet with".

sed quis haec est muliercula[39] et ille grauastellus,[40] qui uenit?   620
Stratippocles: hic est danista, haec illa est autem quam [ego] emi de praeda. **Epidicus:** haecinest?[41]
Stratippocles: haec est. estne ita ut tibi dixi? aspecta[42] et contempla,[43] Epidice:
usque ab unguiculo[44] ad capillum[45] summumst[46] festiuissuma.[47]
estne consimilis[48] quasi[49] quom[50] signum[51] pictum[52] pulchre aspexeris?[53]
Epidicus: e tuis uerbis meum futurum[54] corium[55] pulchrum[56]   625
praedicas,[57]
quem[58] Apelles[59] ac Zeuxis[60] duo[61] pingent[62] pigmentis[63] ulmeis.[64]
Stratippocles: di inmortales![65] sicin[66] iussi[67] ad me ires?[68] pedibus plumbeis[69]

---

39 *muliercula, -ae* (f.): "little woman".
40 *grauastellus, -i* (m.): "little old man".
41 *haecinest = haec + -ne est*: "this is she", "this is her".
42 *aspicio, -ere, aspexi, aspectum*: "look [at]".
43 *contemplo, -are, -aui, -atum*: "gaze [at]".
44 *unguiculus, -i* (m.): "fingernail", "toenail".
45 *capilla, -ae* (f.): "hair".
46 *summumst = summum est*.
47 *festiuissumus = festiuissimus* (superlative < *festiuus, -a, -um*): "most pleasing", "prettiest".
48 *consimilis, -e*: "similar".
49 *quasi* (adverb): "as though" (followed by the subjunctive mood).
50 *quom = cum*.
51 *signum, -i* (n.): "statue", "picture".
52 *pictus, -a, -um*: "painted".
53 *aspexeris* (second-person singular perfect active subjunctive) < *aspicio, -ere, aspexi, aspectum*: "look [at]".
54 *futurum = futurum esse*: "[my skin] is going to be".
55 *corium, -ii* (n.): "skin"; "hide".
56 *pulchrum* (here Epidicus means that his skin will be "beautiful" or "pretty as a picture" in the sense that it will be marked with whip lashes).
57 *praedico, -ere, -dixi, -dictum* (this is a different verb from *praedico, -are*): "foretell", "predict".
58 *quem* (referring to a missing *me* as antecedent).
59 *Apelles, -is*: the name of a famous Greek painter.
60 *Zeuxis, is/-idis*: the name of another famous Greek painter.
61 *Apelles atque Zeuxis duo* (referring to Periphanes and Apoecides).
62 *pingo, -ere, pinxi, pictum*: "paint".
63 *pigmentum, -i* (n.): "pigment", "paint".
64 *ulmeus, -a, -um*: "made of elmwood" (referring to the elmwood rods with which Epidicus expects to be beaten).
65 *inmortales = immortales*.
66 *sicin = sic + -ne*: "in this way?".
67 *iubeo, -ere, iussi, iussum*: "order", "tell" (often followed, as here, by the subjunctive without *ut*, see Allen and Greenough's *Latin Grammar* 565a, http://dcc.dickinson.edu/grammar/latin/category-search?field_gl_section_number_value=565).
68 *ires < eo, ire, iui/ii, itum*.
69 *plumbeus, -a, -um*: "leaden", "made of lead", "slow" (*pedibus plumbeis* is an ablative of quality).

qui[70] perhibetur[71] priu'[72] uenisset quam tu aduenisti mihi.

Danista: haec edepol remorata[73] med[74] est. **Stratippocles:** siquidem[75] istius gratia

id[76] remoratu's[77] quod[78] ista uoluit, nimium aduenisti cito.[79] 630

Danista: age age,[80] apsolue[81] <me> atque argentum numera,[82] ne comites[83] morer.[84]

Stratippocles: pernumeratumst.[85] **Danista:** tene[86] cruminam:[87] huc[88] inde.[89] **Stratippocles:** sapienter[90] uenis.

opperire[91] dum ecfero[92] ad te argentum. **Danista:** matura.[93] **Stratippocles:** domist.[94] —

Epidicus: satin[95] ego oculis[96] utilitatem[97] optineo[98] sincere[99] an parum?[100]

uideon[101] ego Telestidem[102] te, Periphanei[103] filiam, 635

---

70 *qui*: "the man who" (this seems to be a reference to some proverbial story about a man with leaden feet).
71 *perhibetur*: "is said to be".
72 *priu' ...quam* = *prius... quam*.
73 *remoror, -ari, -atus sum*: "delay".
74 *med* = *me*.
75 *siquidem*: "if indeed", "accordingly".
76 *id* (referring to the task of bringing Telestis to Stratippocles's home).
77 *remoratu's* = *remoratus es* < *remoror, -ari, -atus sum*: "delay".
78 *quod*: "because".
79 *cito*: "quickly".
80 *age age*: "come on now".
81 *apsolue* = *absolue* < *absoluo, -ere, absolui, absolutum*: "pay off".
82 *numero, -are, -aui, -atum*: "count out".
83 *comes, comitis* (m.): "partner", "associate".
84 *moror, -ari, -atus sum*: "delay".
85 *pernumeratumst* = *pernumeratum est* < *pernumero, -are, -aui, -atum*: "count out", "reckon up".
86 *teneo, -ere, tenui, tentum*: "take", "hold".
87 *crumina, -ae* (f.): "pouch", "purse", "small moneybag".
88 *huc*: "in(to) here".
89 *indo, indidi, inditum*: "put into".
90 *sapienter* (adverb < *sapiens, sapientis*).
91 *opperire* (second-person singular present imperative) < *opperior, opperiri, opperitus sum*: "wait", "await".
92 *ecfero* = *effero* < *effero, efferre, extuli, elatus*: "carry out", "bring out".
93 *maturo, -are, -aui, -atum*: "ripen", "hurry", "make haste to".
94 *domist* = *domi est*: "it's in my house".
95 *satin* = *satis* + *-ne*: "enough", "sufficiently".
96 *oculis* (ablative after *utilitatem optineo*): "[do I still have the use of my] eyes".
97 *utilitas, -tatis* (f.): "use", "usefulness".
98 *optineo, -ere, optinui, optentum*: "obtain", "possess", "keep".
99 *sincere* (adverb < *sincerus, -a, -um*): "sincerely", "genuinely".
100 *parum* (adverb): "not enough", "insufficiently".
101 *uideon* = *uideo* + *-ne*.
102 *Telestidem* (accusative form of the name Telestis).
103 *Periphanei* (genitive).

ex Philippa matre natam Thebis,[104] Epidauri[105] satam?[106]

Telestis: quis tu homo es qui meum parentum nomen memoras[107] et meum?

Epidicus: non me nouisti?[108] **Telestis:** quod quidem nunc ueniat in mentem mihi.[109]

Epidicus: non meministi[110] me auream[111] ad te adferre[112] natali[113] die lunulam[114] atque anellum[115] aureolum[116] in digitum?[117] **Telestis:**   640
memini, mi[118] homo.

tune is es? **Epidicus:** ego sum, et istic[119] frater qui te mercatust[120] tuos.[121]

** alia matre, uno patre.[122]

Telestis: quid[123] pater meu'?[124] uiuost?[125] **Epidicus:** animo[126] liquido[127] et tranquillo[128] es,[129] tace.

Telestis: di me ex perdita[130] seruatam cupiunt si uera autumas.[131]

Epidicus: non habeo ullam occasionem[132] ut apud te falsa fabuler.[133]   645

---

104 *Thebis* (locative).
105 *Epidauri* (locative).
106 *sero, -ere, seui, satum*: "sow", "plant", "beget"; translate here: "conceive".
107 *memoro, -are, -aui, -atum*: "remember", "reminisce", "speak of", "mention".
108 *nouisti* < *nosco, -ere, noui, notum*: "get to know", "know", "recognize".
109 *quod quidem nunc ueniat in mentem mihi* (the negative is implied): "not that I can recall right now".
110 *memini, meminisse*: "remember" (only the perfect tense forms exist).
111 *aureus, -a, -um*: "gold", "golden".
112 *affero, afferre, attuli, allatum* (or *adfero, adferre, adtuli, adlatum*): "bring", "deliver", "use" (+ accusative).
113 *natalis, -e*: "natal", "relating to one's birth".
114 *lunula, -ae* (f.): "little moon", "moon-shaped ornament".
115 *anellus, -i* (m.): "little ring".
116 *aureolus, -a, -um*: "golden".
117 *in digitum*: "for your finger", "to wear on your finger".
118 *mi* (vocative) < *meus, -a, -um*.
119 *istic* (adverb): "now", "here", "there".
120 *mercatust* = *mercatus est* < *mercor, -ari, -atus sum*: "buy".
121 *tuos* = *tuus*.
122 *alia matre uno patre*: "same father, different mothers".
123 *quid*: "what about".
124 *meu'* = *meus*.
125 *uiuost* = *uiuus est*: "is he alive".
126 *animo* (ablative of quality; see Bennett's *New Latin Grammar* 224, http://www.thelatinlibrary.com/bennett.html#sect224).
127 *liquidus, -a, -um*: "clear", "calm".
128 *tranquillus, -a, -um*: "quiet", "calm".
129 *es* (2nd person singular present imperative active) < *sum, esse, fui, futurus*.
130 *ex perdita*: "from/after having been lost".
131 *autumo, -are, -aui, -atum*: "say", "assert".
132 *occasio, -onis* (f.): "occasion", "opportunity".
133 *fabulor, -ari, -atus sum*: "talk", "tell".

Stratippocles: accipe argentum hoc, danista. hic sunt quadraginta[134] minae.[135]

siquid erit dubium[136] immutabo.[137] **Danista:** bene fecisti, bene uale. —

Stratippocles: nunc enim tu mea es. **Telestis:** soror quidem edepol, ut tu aeque[138] scias.

salue, frater. **Stratippocles:** sanan[139] haec est? **Epidicus:** sana, si appellat suom.[140]

Stratippocles: quid? ego <quo> modo[141] huic <sum> frater factus,   650
dum intro eo atque exeo?[142]

Epidicus: quod boni est[143] id tacitus[144] taceas[145] tute[146] tecum et gaudeas.[147]

Stratippocles: perdidisti[148] et repperisti[149] me, soror. **Epidicus:** stultu's,[150] tace.

tibi quidem quod[151] ames domi praestost,[152] fidicina, | opera mea;[153]
et sororem in libertatem idem[154] opera concilio[155] mea.

Stratippocles: Epidice, fateor[156] — **Epidicus:** abi[157] intro ac iube[158]   655
huic aquam calefieri;[159]

---

134 *quadraginta* (indeclinable): "forty".
135 *mina, -ae* (f.): a Greek unit of money equivalent to 430g of silver.
136 *siquid erit dubium*: "if any [of the coins] are of doubtful integrity" (that is, if the moneylender thinks any of the coins are counterfeit).
137 *immuto, -are, -aui, -atum*: "change".
138 *aeque* (adverb): "equally".
139 *sanan = sana + -ne < sanus, -a, -um*: "sane", "healthy".
140 *si appellat suom*: "if she is calling [you] her own [brother]".
141 *<quo> modo*: "how?", "in what way?".
142 *dum intro eo atque exeo*: "while I was going in and then out of the house".
143 *quod boni est* (*boni* is genitive of the whole): "what's good", "the good [situation] that we have".
144 *tacitus, -a, -um*: "silent".
145 *taceo, -ere, tacui, tacitum*: "be silent".
146 *tute = tu + te* (emphatic form of *tu*).
147 *id tacitus taceas tute tecum et gaudeas*: "you should just be quiet about it and be happy".
148 *perdo, perdere, perdidi, perditus*: "ruin", "lose".
149 *reperio, -ire, repperi, repertum*: "find".
150 *stultu's = stultus es*.
151 *quod ames*: "that which you may love", "an object for your love".
152 *praestost = praesto est; praesto* (adverb): "at hand", "ready", "available".
153 *operā meā*: "thanks to my efforts".
154 *idem* (adverb): "likewise".
155 *concilio, -are, -aui, -atum*: "recover", "regain".
156 *fateor, fateri, fassus sum*: "admit", "confess".
157 *abi* (second-person singular present imperative) < *abeo, -ire, -ii/iui, -itum*.
158 *iubeo -ere, iussi, iussum*: "tell", "order" (here followed by the infinitive; see Bennett's *New Latin Grammar* 295, http://www.thelatinlibrary.com/bennett.html#sect295).
159 *calefieri* (present passive infinitive) < *calefacio, calefacere, calefeci, calefactum*: "make warm/hot".

cetera haec posterius[160] faxo[161] scibis[162] ubi erit otium.[163]

Stratippocles: sequere[164] hac[165] me, soror. **Epidicus:** ego ad uos Thesprionem iussero[166]

huc transire. sed memento,[167] si quid[168] saeuibit[169] senex,

suppetias[170] mihi cum sorore ferre. **Stratippocles:** facile[171] istuc[172] erit. —

Epidicus: Thesprio, exi istac[173] per hortum, adfer domum[174] auxilium   660
mihi,

magnast[175] res. minoris multo facio[176] quam dudum[177] senes.

remeabo[178] intro, ut adcurentur[179] aduenientes hospites.

eadem[180] haec intus edocebo[181] quae ego scio Stratippoclem.

non fugio, domi adesse certumst;[182] neque ille haud[183] obiciet[184] mihi

pedibus[185] sese prouocatum.[186] abeo intro, nimi'[187] longum   665
loquor. —

---

160 *posterius* (adverb): "later".
161 *faxo* (alternative form of the first-person singular future indicative active < *facio, -ere*): "I'll make [it happen]", "I promise".
162 *scibis = scies; faxo scibit:* ""I'll make sure you know", "I'll fill you in".
163 *otium, -ii* (n.): "leisure", "spare time".
164 *sequere* (second-person present imperative) < *sequor, -i, secutus sum*.
165 *hac*: "this way".
166 *iussero* (first-person singular future perfect indicative active) < *iubeo, -ere, iussi, iussum*.
167 *memento* (second-person singular imperative active) < *memini, meminisse*: "remember"; *memento... suppetias... ferre*: "remember to bring help".
168 *quid*: "in any way", "at all", "about anything".
169 *saeuibit = saeuiet* < *saeuio, -ire, saeuiui, saeuitum*: "rage", "be/act angry/violent/ferocious", "vent rage on".
170 *suppetiae, -arum* (f. pl.): "help", "aid".
171 *facile* (neuter nominative singular form of the adjective).
172 *istuc = istud*.
173 *istac = istā*: "that way".
174 *domum* (accusative of place to which): "to the house".
175 *magnast = magna est*.
176 *minoris multo facio*: "I care a lot less about".
177 *dudum*: "formerly", "before".
178 *remeo, -are, -aui, -atum*: "go/come back", "return".
179 *adcurentur = accurentur* < *accuro, -are, -aui, -atum*: "take care of", "attend to".
180 *eadem*: "at the same time", "likewise".
181 *edoceo, edocere, edocui, edoctum*: "teach/inform thoroughly".
182 *certumst = certum est mihi*: "it is determined by me", "I'm determined".
183 *neque... haud* (the two negatives strengthen each other).
184 *obicio, -ere, obieci, obiectum*: "object", "throw in the teeth of" (+ dat.).
185 *pedibus*: "by my running away".
186 *prouocatum = prouocatum esse* (indirect discourse with the accusative subject *sese*); *prouoco, -are, -aui, -atum*: "provoke".
187 *nimi' = nimis*.

5.2 PERIPHANES, APOECIDES, EPIDICVS

Scene summary: Periphanes is still enraged at Epidicus, and Apoecides is exhausted from helping him look for Epidicus, and he blames Periphanes. Epidicus calmly strolls up, and surprises Periphanes by demanding that the latter tie him up with the straps he's bought. Epidicus, with his hands bound, admits that he tricked Periphanes into paying thirty *minae* to buy Stratippocles's lyre-playing girlfriend (Acropolistis) and to pretend that she was his daughter Telestis. Epidicus also admits that he gave Stratippocles the fifty *minae* that Periphanes had meant to be given to the pimp in exchange for Acropolistis. Epidicus says Periphanes shouldn't yell at him so angrily, as though he were merely a slave, saying that he has earned his freedom and that Periphanes will understand if he goes into his house. When Periphanes sees the real Telestis, he feels badly for having been so angry at Epidicus and wants to untie him. Epidicus, milking Periphanes's gratitude and guilt as much as he can, won't let him untie the bonds until Periphanes has begged his pardon, promised him some new clothes, promised to free him, and to provide for him as his freedman. Epidicus magnanimously accepts these offers and allows Periphanes to untie him. The play ends with the troop of actors celebrating the man (Epidicus) who has won his freedom through bad behaviour, and they ask the audience for a round of applause.

Periphanes: Satine[1] illic[2] homo ludibrio[3] nos uetulos[4] decrepitos[5] duos habet?[6] **Apoecides:** immo edepol tuquidem[7] miserum med[8] habes miseris modis.
Periphanes: tace sis, modo sine[9] me hominem apisci.[10] **Apoecides:** dico ego tibi iam, ut scias:
alium tibi te comitem meliust[11] quaerere; ita, dum te sequor,

---

1 *satine = satis + -ne*: "surely...?".
2 *illic = ille*.
3 *ludibrium, ludibri/ludibrii* (n.): "mockery", "laughingstock".
4 *uetulus, -a, -um*: "elderly", "aging".
5 *decrepitus, -a, -um*: "worn out", "feeble", "decrepit", "infirm".
6 *ludibrio... habet*: "is making a laughingstock of" (+ acc.).
7 *tuquidem = tu quidem*.
8 *med = me*.
9 *sine < sino, -ere, -siui, situm*: "allow", "let".
10 *apiscor, apisci, aptus sum*: "reach", "catch".
11 *meliust = melius est*.

lassitudine[12] inuaserunt[13] misero[14] in genua flemina.[15] 670

Periphanes: quot illic homo hodie me exemplis[16] ludificatust[17] atque te,

ut[18] illic autem exenterauit[19] mihi opes argentarias![20]

Apoecides: apage[21] illum a me! nam ille quidem Volcani iratist[22] filius:

quaqua[23] tangit, omne amburit,[24] si astes,[25] aestu[26] calefacit.[27]

Epidicus: duodecim[28] dis[29] plus quam[30] in caelo deorumst[31] inmortalium[32] 675

mihi nunc auxilio[33] adiutores[34] sunt et mecum militant.[35]

quidquid ego male feci, auxilia mi[36] et suppetiae[37] sunt domi,

apolactizo[38] inimicos omnis.[39] **Periphanes:** ubi illum quaeram[40] gentium?[41]

---

12 *lassitudine* (ablative of cause) < *lassitudo, lassitudinis* (f.): "exhaustion", "weariness.
13 *inuado, -ere, inuasi, inuasum*: "take possession of".
14 *misero*: "for wretched me".
15 *flemina, -um* (n. pl.): "swelling from blood accumulating in the ankles (or, in this case, the knees)".
16 *quot... exemplis*: "in how many ways".
17 *ludificatust = ludificatus est* < *ludificor, -ari, -atus sum*: "make a mockery of", "trick".
18 *ut*: "how!" (exclamatory).
19 *exentero, -are, -aui, -atum*: "disembowel"; (in the context of a purse or store of money) "empty".
20 *opes argentarias*: "supply of money".
21 *apage*: "be off!", "let [that man] keep away".
22 *iratist = irati est*.
23 *quaqua*: "wherever", "whatever".
24 *amburo, -ere, ambussi, ambustum*: "scorch", "burn".
25 *asto, astare, astiti, -*: "wait"; "stay", "stand near".
26 *aestus, -ūs* (m.): "heat", "fire"; "rage".
27 *calefacio, -ere, calefeci, calefactum*: "make hot", "heat"; "trouble", "vex".
28 *duodecim* (indeclinable, here agreeing with *dis*): twelve.
29 *dis* (ablative of degree of difference).
30 *duodecim dis plus quam in caelo deorumst inmortalium*: "twelve gods more than the immortal gods in heaven".
31 *deorumst = deorum est*.
32 *inmortalium = immortalium*.
33 *auxilio*: "by means of their assistance".
34 *adiutor, adiutoris* (m.): "helper", "supporter".
35 *milito, -are, -aui, -atum*: "serve as a soldier", "perform military service", "serve in the army", "make war".
36 *mi = mihi*.
37 *suppetiae, -arum* (f. pl.): "help", "aid".
38 *apolactizo, -are, -aui, -atum*: "kick away", "spurn".
39 *omnis = omnes*.
40 *quaero, -ere, quaesiui, quaesitum*: "seek", "look for".
41 *ubi... gentium*: "where in the world...?".

Apoecides: dum[42] sine me quaeras, quaeras mea caussa[43] uel[44]
medio in mari.[45]
Epidicus: quid[46] me quaeris? quid laboras?[47] quid hunc[48]   680
sollicitas?[49] ecce me.
num[50] te fugi, num ab domo apsum,[51] num oculis concessi[52] tuis?
* *
nec tibi supplico.[53] uincire[54] uis? em,[55] ostendo manus;
tu habes lora,[56] ego te emere uidi:[57] quid nunc cessas?[58] conliga.[59]
Periphanes: ilicet![60] uadimonium[61] ultro[62] mihi hic facit.[63]   685
Epidicus: quin[64] conligas?
Apoecides: edepol mancupium[65] scelestum![66] **Epidicus:** te
profecto,[67] Apoecides, —
nil[68] moror mihi deprecari.[69] **Apoecides:** facile exoras,[70] Epidice.

---

42 *dum*: "provided that".
43 *mea caussa*: "for all I care".
44 *uel* (adverb): "even", "if you prefer".
45 *medio in mari*: "in the middle of the sea".
46 *quid*: "why".
47 *laboro, -are, -aui, -atum*: "labour", "take pains", "exert oneself".
48 *hunc* (refers to Apoecides).
49 *sollicito, -are, -aui, -atum*: "disturb", "worry".
50 *num* (interrogative particle, usually implying that a negative answer is expected): "surely... not?".
51 *apsum = absum*.
52 *concedo, -ere, -cessi, -cessum*: "withdraw"; "move back".
53 *supplico, -are, -aui, -atum*: "supplicate", "beg for mercy/pardon/help" (+ dative).
54 *uincio, -ire, uinxi, uinctum*: "bind", "restrain".
55 *em* (expression of surprise, in a good or bad sense): "there!", "ha!".
56 *lorum, -i* (n.): "leather strap", "whip".
57 *te emere uidi* (indirect discourse; *lora* is the implied direct object of *emere*).
58 *cedo, -ere, cessi, cessum*: "withdraw", "leave".
59 *conligo, -are, -aui, -atum*: "bind", "tie up".
60 *ilicet*: "it's no use", "it's all up".
61 *uadimonium, -ii* (n.): "bail", "surety".
62 *ultro* (adverb): "of one's own accord", "voluntarily".
63 *uadimonium... facit*: "he offers bail".
64 *quin*: "why... not?", "why don't you...?".
65 *mancupium = mancipium*: "possession", "property"; translate here: "slave".
66 *scelestus, -a, -um*: "wicked".
67 *profecto* (adverb): "certainly".
68 *nil = nihil*.
69 *nil moror mihi deprecari*: "I don't need you to intercede for me" (on *nil/nihil moror* see note 38 in Act 3, scene 2).
70 *exoro, -are, -aui, -atum*: "obtain by persuasion", "prevail".

Epidicus: ecquid agis?[71] **Periphanes:** tuon[72] arbitratu?[73] **Epidicus:** meo[74] hercle uero atque hau[75] tuo[76]
conligandae haec[77] sunt tibi[78] hodie. **Periphanes:** at non lubet,[79] non conligo.[80]
Apoecides: tragulam[81] in te inicere[82] adornat,[83] nescioquam[84] 690
fabricam[85] facit.
Epidicus: tibi moram[86] faci'[87] quom[88] ego solutus[89] asto.[90] age, inquam, conliga.
Periphanes: at mihi magi'[91] lubet solutum te rogitare. **Epidicus:** at nihil scies.
Periphanes: quid ago? **Apoecides:** quid agas? mos geratur.[92]
Epidicus: frugi[93] es tu homo, Apoecides.
Periphanes: cedo[94] manus igitur. **Epidicus:** morantur nihil.[95] atque arte[96] conliga,
nihil uero <hoc> obnoxiosse.[97] **Periphanes:** facto opere[98] 695
arbitramino.[99]

---

71 *ecquid agis*: "are you going to do anything or not?".
72 *tuon = tuo + -ne*.
73 *arbitratus, -ūs* (m.): "decision", "wish", "choice".
74 *meo = meo arbitratu*.
75 *hau = haud*.
76 *tuo = tuo arbritratu*.
77 *haec = haec manūs*.
78 *tibi* (dative of agent after passive periphrastic).
79 *lubet = libet* (impersonal verb; see Bennett 138, http://www.thelatinlibrary.com/bennett.html#sect138).
80 Supply *eas* or *tuas manūs* after *conligo*.
81 *tragula, -ae* (f.): "dart", "javelin".
82 *inicio, -ere, inieci, iniectum*: "thow at".
83 *adorno, -are, -aui, -atum*: "get ready", "prepare".
84 *nescioquam = nescio quam*.
85 *fabrica, -ae* (f.): "crafty device", "trick".
86 *mora, ae* (f.): "delay", "obstacle", "hindrance".
87 *faci' = facis*.
88 *quom = cum*.
89 *solutus, -a, -um*: "unbound", "released", "unrestrained", "at large".
90 *asto, astare, astiti, -*: "wait"; "stay", "stand near".
91 *magi' = magis*.
92 *mos geratur*: "let [his] wish be gratified", "do what he wants".
93 *frugi* (indeclinable adjective): "worthy", "frugal", "virtuous" (see note 39 in Act 3, scene 4a).
94 *cedo* (archaic singular imperative related to *do, dare*): "give".
95 *morantur nihil*: "they don't mind" (on *nil/nihil moror* see note 38 in Act 3, scene 2).
96 *arte* (adverb < *artus, -a, -um*): "tightly".
97 *nihil uero <hoc> obnoxiosse*: "and don't go easy on me", "and without any compassion" (*obnoxiosse = obnoxie*: "subject to qualification", "in a restricted manner").
98 *facto opere* (ablative absolute): "when the job has been done".
99 *arbitramino* (archaic imperative second-person singular): "give judgment".

Epidicus: bene hoc habet.[100] age nunciam[101] ex me exquire,[102] rogita quod lubet.[103]

Periphanes: qua fiducia[104] ausu's[105] primum quae emptast[106] nudiustertius[107] filiam meam dicere esse? **Epidicus:** lubuit:[108] ea fiducia.[109]

Periphanes: ain[110] tu? lubuit? **Epidicus:** aio.[111] uel[112] da pignus,[113] ni[114] ea sit filia.

Periphanes: quam negat nouisse[115] mater? **Epidicus:** ni ergo matris filia est,   700

in meum nummum, in tuom talentum pignus da.[116] **Periphanes:** enim istaec[117] captiost.[118]

sed quis east[119] mulier? **Epidicus:** tui gnati[120] amica, ut omnem rem scias.

Periphanes: dedin[121] tibi minas[122] triginta[123] ob[124] filiam? **Epidicus:** fateor[125] datas[126]

---

100 *bene hoc habet*: "that does it".
101 *nunciam = nunc + iam* (emphatic form of *nunc*).
102 *exquiro, exquirere, exquisiui, exquisitum*: "find out", "ask".
103 *lubet = libet*.
104 *qua fiducia*: "with what boldness", "with what brazen self-confidence".
105 *ausu's = ausus es < audeo, audere, ausus sum*: "dare".
106 *emptast = empta est*.
107 *nudiustertius = nudius tertius; nudius = num/nunc dies* (always paired with an ordinal number): "it is now the ... day since" (because the Romans counted inclusively, *nudiustertius* means "the day before yesterday").
108 *lubuit = libuit* (perfect tense of impersonal verb *libet*); "it pleased [me]", "I wanted to".
109 *ea fiducia*: "with that brazen self-confidence".
110 *ain = ais + -ne*: "you say [that]?".
111 *aio*: "I do say [that]".
112 *uel*: "or", "actually", "indeed", "even", "if you prefer".
113 *pignus, pignoris* (n.): "bet", "stake, "wager", "hostage"; *da pignus* prompts the following subjunctive (*sit*).
114 *ni*: "if... not".
115 *nosco, -ere, noui, notum*: "get to know", "know", "recognize".
116 *in meum nummum, in tuom talentum pignus da*: "bet me a talent (26–32.5 kg of silver) for a coin (of unknown but not high value)". We can't be sure what kind of small coin a *nummus* was (see note 142 in Act 1, scene 1) but whether it was a sestertius, a drachma, or a didrachma, this is a wildly unequal bet, with Periphanes's stake, if he loses, being between 3,000–24,000 times higher than Epidicus's).
117 *istaec = ista*.
118 *captiost = captio est; captio, captionis* (f.): "trick", "deception", "fraud".
119 *east = ea est*.
120 *gnati = nati < natus, -i*: "son".
121 *dedin = dedi + -ne*.
122 *mina, -ae* (f.): a Greek unit of money equivalent to 430g of silver.
123 *triginta* (indeclinable): "thirty".
124 *ob*: "in return for".
125 *fateor, fateri, fassus sum*: "admit", "confess".
126 *datas* (modifies *minas*).

et eo argento illam me emisse amicam fili fidicinam

pro[127] tua filia: istam ob rem[128] te tetigi[129] triginta minis. 705

Periphanes: quomodo me ludos fecisti[130] de illa conducticia[131]

fidicina! **Epidicus:** factum hercle uero et recte factum iudico.

Periphanes: quid postremo argento factum est quod dedi? **Epidicus:** dicam tibi:

neque malo homini neque benigno[132] tuo dedi Stratippocli.

Periphanes: qur[133] dare ausu's?[134] **Epidicus:** quia mi[135] lubitum est.[136] 710

Periphanes: quae haec, malum,[137] inpudentiast?[138]

Epidicus: etiam inclamitor[139] quasi seruos?[140] **Periphanes:** quom[141]

tu es liber gaudeo.

Epidicus: merui[142] ut fierem.[143] **Periphanes:** tu meruisti? **Epidicus:**

uisse[144] intro: ego faxo[145] scies

hoc ita esse.[146] **Periphanes:** quid est negoti?[147] **Epidicus:** iam ipsa res dicet tibi.

abi[148] modo intro. **Apoecides:** i,[149] illuc[150] non temerest.[151]

Periphanes: adserua[152] istum, Apoecides. —

---

127 *pro:* "instead of".
128 *istam ob rem:* "because of that", "for that reason" (this is an emendation of a corrupted line: Lindsay's text has this line as: *pro tua filia: is te †aboret† tetigi triginta minis*).
129 *tango, -ere, tetigi, tactum:* "touch"; translate here: "rob by means of a trick", "cheat [someone] out of [something (ablative)]".
130 *quomodo me ludos fecisti:* "how you fooled me!".
131 *conducticius, -a, -um:* "hired", "rented".
132 *benignus, -a, -um:* "kindly", "good", "good natured".
133 *qur = cur*.
134 *ausu's = ausus es < audeo, -ere, ausus sum:* "dare".
135 *mi = mihi*.
136 *lubitum est = libitum est < libet, -ere, -uit, libitum* (impersonal verb): "it pleases" (+ dative of person pleased).
137 *malum* (exclamation): "you no-good rascal".
138 *inpudentiast = impudentia est; quae haec... inpudentiast:* "what is this impudence".
139 *inclamito, -are, -aui, -atum:* "abuse", "scold".
140 *seruos = seruus*.
141 *quom = cum*.
142 *mereo, -ere, merui, meritum:* "deserve", "earn".
143 *fierem* (first-person singular subjunctive active) *< fio, fieri, factus sum*.
144 *uisse = uise < uiso, -ere, uisi, uisum:* "go see", "go look at", "visit".
145 *faxo* (alternative form of the first-person singular future indicative active of *facio, -ere*): "I'll make [it happen]", "I promise".
146 *hoc ita esse:* "that this is so".
147 *quid est negoti:* "what is this business", "what is all this about".
148 *abi* (2nd person singular present imperative) *< abeo, -ire, -ii/iui, -itum*.
149 *i* (singular imperative) *< eo, ire, iui, itum*.
150 *illuc:* "there, "in there".
151 *temerest = temere est; illuc non temerest:* "it's not by chance [that he's directing you to go] in there", "there must be some explanation in there".
152 *adseruo, -are, -aui, -atum:* "keep watch", "guard".

Apoecides: quid illuc, Epidice, est negoti? **Epidicus:** maxuma[153] 715
hercle iniuria
uinctus asto,[154] quoius[155] haec hodie opera[156] inuentast[157] filia.
Apoecides: ain[158] tu te illius inuenisse filiam? **Epidicus:** inueni et
domi est.
sed ut acerbum[159] est pro bene factis quom[160] mali messim[161] metas![162]
Apoecides: quamne[163] hodie per urbem uterque sumu'[164] defessi
quaerere?
Epidicus: ego sum defessus reperire,[165] uos defessi quaerere. 720
Periphanes: quid[166] isti[167] oratis opere tanto?[168] <me> meruisse[169]
intellego[170]
ut liceat[171] merito[172] huiius[173] facere.[174] cedo[175] tu ut exsoluam[176]
manus.
Epidicus: ne attigas.[177] **Periphanes:** ostende[178] uero. **Epidicus:** nolo.
Periphanes: non aequom[179] facis.[180]

---

153 *maxuma = maxima.*
154 *asto, astare, astiti, -:* "wait"; "stay", "stand near".
155 *quoius = cuius.*
156 *operā:* "by my efforts".
157 *inuentast = inuenta est < inuenio, -ire, -iui, -itum.*
158 *ain = ais + -ne:* "are you saying".
159 *acerbus, -a, -um:* "harsh", "upsetting".
160 *quom = cum.*
161 *messim* (accusative singular) *< messis, -is* (f.): "harvest", "crop".
162 *meto, -ere, messui, messum:* "reap", "harvest".
163 *quam* (relative pronoun).
164 *sumu' = sumus.*
165 *reperio, -ire, repperi, repertum:* "find".
166 *quid:* "why".
167 *isti* (dative of reference, or dative of advantage; see Bennett 188, http://www.thelatinlibrary.com/bennett.html#sect186).
168 *opere tanto:* "so much".
169 *mereo, -ere, merui, meritum:* "deserve", "earn".
170 *intellego, -ere, -exi, ectum:* "understand", "realize".
171 *licet, licuit, licitum est* (impersonal): "it is lawful", "it is permitted".
172 *merito huiius:* "according to his merits", "as he deserves".
173 *huiius = huius.*
174 *<me> meruisse intellego, ut liceat merito huiius facere:* "I realize that I can treat him as he deserves".
175 *cedo* (archaic singular imperative related to *do, dare*): "give".
176 *exsoluo, -ere, -solui, –solutum:* "untie", "release".
177 *ne attigas* (prohibitive subjunctive, equivalent to *noli/nolite* + infinitive) *< attigo, -ere, attigi, attactum:* "touch".
178 *ostendeo, -ere, ostendi,* — : "show", "stretch out".
179 *aequom = aequum.*
180 *non aequom facis:* "you're not being fair".

Epidicus: numquam hercle hodie, nisi supplicium[181] mihi das, me solui[182] sinam.[183]

Periphanes: optumum[184] atque aequissumum[185] oras. soccos,[186]   725
tunicam, pallium[187]

tibi dabo. **Epidicus:** quid deinde porro?[188] **Periphanes:** libertatem.

Epidicus: at postea?

nouo liberto[189] opus est[190] quod[191] pappet.[192] **Periphanes:** dabitur, praebebo[193] cibum.

Epidicus: numquam hercle hodie, nisi me orassis,[194] solues.

Periphanes: oro te, Epidice,

mihi ut ignoscas[195] si quid inprudens[196] culpa[197] peccaui[198] mea.

at ob eam rem[199] liber esto.[200] **Epidicus:** inuitus do hanc ueniam[201]   730
tibi,

nisi[202] necessitate cogar.[203] solue sane[204] si lubet.[205]

Grex:[206] hic is homo est qui libertatem malitia[207] inuenit sua.

plaudite[208] et ualete. lumbos[209] porgite[210] atque exsurgite.[211]

---

181 *supplicium, -ii/-i* (n.): "supplication", humble entreaty"; "punishment".
182 *solui* (present infinitive passive) < *soluo, -ere, solui, solutum*: "release", "untie".
183 *sino, -ere, -siui, situm*: "allow", "let".
184 *optumum = optimum*.
185 *aequissumum = aequissimum*
186 *soccus, -i* (m.): "low-heeled light shoe", "slipper".
187 *pallium, ii* (n.): "cloak" (technically a Greek cloak).
188 *porro* (adverb): "afterwards", "next".
189 *libertus, -i* (m.): "freedman", "freed slave".
190 *opus est* (impersonal): "there is need for"; *nouo liberto opus est quod pappet*: "a freedman needs something that he can eat".
191 *quod*: "something".
192 *pappo, -are, -aui, -atum*: "eat" (specifically eat soft foods like porridge).
193 *praebeo, -ere, praebui, praebitum*: "offer", "supply".
194 *nisi me orassis* (alternative future < *oro, -are, -aui, -atum*): "[unless] you beg me".
195 *ignosco, -ere, ignoui, ignotum*: "forgive".
196 *inprudens = imprudens*: "without knowing", "inadvertent[ly]".
197 *culpā... meā*: "because of my own fault".
198 *pecco, -are, -aui, -atum*: "make a mistake", "be wrong", "do wrong".
199 *ob eam rem*: "for this/that reason", "for this/that purpose".
200 *esto* (second-person singular future imperative active) < *sum, esse, fui, futurus*.
201 *uenia, -ae* (f.): "pardon", "forgiveness", "kindness".
202 *nisi*: "except".
203 *cogo, -ere, coegi, coactum*: "compel", "force".
204 *sane*: "certainly", "however".
205 *lubet = libet*.
206 *grex, gregis* (m.): "flock", "herd"; "troop"; translate here: "company (of actors)".
207 *malitia, -ae* (f.): "wickedness".
208 *plaudo, -ere, plausi, plausum*: "applaud", "clap".
209 *lumbus, -i* (m.): "loin".
210 *porgite = porrigite < porrigo, -ere, porrexi, porrectum*: "stretch", stretch out".
211 *exsurgo, -ere, exsurrexi, exsurrectum*: "rise", "stand up".

Translation of Plautus's *Epidicus*

[Note: for the acrostic *argumentum* (plot summary) that was added to the play perhaps around 150 CE, see page 216]

About the Translation

Any translation is a compromise between accurately reflecting the original text, and readability. On the one hand, rigid adherence to the original tends to sound stilted and unnatural, and, in the case of comedy, is probably not going to be particularly funny. On the other hand, deviating too far from the original in order to produce something that can stand alone as a piece of literature in the new language can risk losing much of the connection to the original context. There is no perfect compromise, and no perfect translation: each translation achieves certain goals, and every translation necessarily loses some aspect of the original. The translation of *Epidicus* in this volume was made with the goal of bringing a version of mid-republican Rome to life for the reader of English by retaining as many of the Roman cultural references as possible, and by emphasizing the exuberant high spirits and the hilariously improbable plot devices of the Latin play, all in a readable prose.

The translation of Latin oaths poses an interesting problem: in modern English we tend to swear by bodily functions or private body parts, but since Plautus and the other writers of *fabulae palliatae* generally avoided obscenity, most English swear words are not appropriate translations for the religious oaths *"hercle!"* or *"edepol!"* (which are somewhat mangled forms of the names of the demigods Hercules and Pollux) that appear scattered throughout the plays. Religious oaths in English, however, tend to have a stronger effect than these casual Latin oaths, while euphemistic English swear words have too mild a sound for the context of the Plautine characters. I generally chose, therefore, to translate the Latin oaths *"hercle!"* and *"edepol!"* literally, with "by Hercules!" and "by Pollux", in order to retain the flavour of ancient Rome.[1]

---

[1] To illustrate alternative translations of the Latin swear words: the first two appearances in the play of the Latin *"hercle!"* at line 115 and 136 have been translated as "On my word" and "I' faith!" (Riley 1852), as "Heavens" and "Damn it" (Duckworth: 1942), and not translated at all by De Melo (2011). Ernout's French translation (1964) is literal at line 115 (*"par Hercule"*) but at line 136 is not translated, and Scàndola's Italian translation (2001) is literal at both places (*"per Ercole"*). The first two incidences of swearing by the demigod Pollux in Latin (lines 30 and 32) have been translated as follows: "I' faith" and "By my troth" (Riley 1852), "Heavens" and "Damned [disgraceful]" (Duckworth: 1942), not translated by De Melo (2011), *"ma foi"* and *"sérieusement"* (Ernout 1964) and into Italian as the literal *"per Polluce"* by Scàndola (2001).

I have also tried to translate the insults fairly literally rather than turn them into English insults. For instance, at line 513 Periphanes angrily tells the hired lyre-player *"malo cruciatu ut pereas,"* which literally means "may you die on the bad cross", referring to crucifixion. I have translated the phrase as "go get yourself crucified!". Thomas Henry Riley in 1852 translated it in a rather Shakespearian manner as "away to perdition in the veriest torments"; Duckworth in 1942 translated this line "die a horrible death", Ernout in 1965 used *"va te faire pendre ailleurs"* ("go hang yourself somewhere else"), Scàndola in 2001 used *"Che tu abbia a crepare d'un accidente e che te ne vada alla svelta!"* ("die in an accident and get out of here fast!"), while Wolfgang de Melo in 2011 translated this line "die a painful death", all of which make Periphanes's angry sentiment clear, but lose the very Roman reference to crucifixion. I don't want to whitewash the hideous reality of Roman slavery, in which angry slave owners had the right to inflict painful disfiguring punishments and to torture slaves to death. We can't know how seriously Plautus's audience took these comments. As was discussed in the introduction to this volume, we don't know if the slaves in the audience found the crucifixion references funny or horrifying, nor do we know if crucifixion was practiced commonly enough for it to be a realistic fear for the average slave. It is clear, however, that the cross as a form of execution was familiar to them in a way that ought not to be concealed by a non-literal translation. For similar reasons I never translate the word "slave" as "servant", since the word "servant" would obscure the Roman reality of people being treated as property.

I chose to avoid too literal a translation, however, of some words and expressions that could only sound stilted if translated too closely. The verb *perdere* (meaning "lose" or "destroy") is a case in point, where literal translations would have lost the tone of the original dialogue. At line 11a, for instance, it was useful to translate the verb as "cut off" because the reference was to a thieving slave "losing" his hand very literally, as a punishment. At line 23, however, Thesprio's wish that the gods might "destroy" (*perdere*) Epidicus would have been awkward if too literally translated, hence I decided to translate it with a polytheistic version of the common English phrase "for god's sake", adding "the" and moving the apostrophe ("the gods'" instead of "god's") to humorously remind readers that we are, after all, in pagan Rome. Similarly when Epidicus cries out *"papae!"* at line 54 the context suggested "oh. my. gods" as the best way to translate Epidicus's dismay at his predicament.

Translating references to the enslaved and freed young women Acropolistis and Telestis involved a complicated juggling of the realities of sex slavery and the circumscribed social status of women in the ancient Mediterranean on the one hand, with, on the other hand, the need to reflect the casual acceptance of such exploitative relationships by the Roman audiences. In Latin the women are frequently referred to with the word *amica* (lines 368, 457, 481, 702 and 704), which I translated as "girlfriend" each time except at line 457 where it seemed appropriate to make the realities of the relationship clearer by translating it as "the slave girl I'm in love with". While the word "girlfriend" in the modern world implies a far more consensual and egalitarian relationship than that of Stratippocles and Acropolistis or Telestis, I decided that the context of the play prevented any confusion about the nature of the women's status. Similarly I translated *amor* as "love" most of the time (at lines 105, 111, and 137, though not at line 191) despite the differently configured conceptions of Roman *amor* and modern "love".

Where a Latin idiomatic phrase or joke would have sounded clumsy or just not funny if translated literally I replaced it with a different idiomatic expression or joke in English, but noted the literal translation in a footnote. This is to avoid confusing the Latin students trying to work through the Latin text with the aid of the translation, but also to remind readers with no Latin skills that they would gain much by reading the original.

For readers who have no Latin but who want to improve their understanding of the play, comparing multiple translations of the same lines (as illustrated above in note 1 on page 125) makes for a rewarding exercise. Lines 652–654 of the play, for instance, have been translated into English in the following ways (the speaker is Epidicus):

1. Simpleton, hold your tongue! Through my endeavours, there's ready for you at home, in fact, a Music-girl for you to make love to; I too, through my endeavours, have restored your sister to liberty. (Riley's 1852 translation)

2. You're a fool. Hush, now! Through my endeavours there's some one already at home for you to love — the music girl. And likewise through my endeavours your sister is regaining her liberty. (Duckworth's 1942 translation)

3. You're being silly, be quiet. You have something to love, that is the lyre girl, ready for you at home, thanks to my efforts. And I'm bringing your sister back to freedom through my efforts. (De Melo's 2011 translation)

4. [*in a fierce whisper*] Shut up, stupid! There's a perfectly good lyre-player for you, who's already living in your house thanks to me — and I've got your sister her freedom too. (Tracy's 2021 translation)

It will be noted that my translation adds stage directions (which do not appear in the Latin) to make the mood of the speaker clearer for readers (and potentially to help in a performance of the play). I also avoided too literal a translation here since I wanted to highlight the way that Stratippocles's supposed passion for first one, and then the other of the main female characters was not taken very seriously by Epidicus, Plautus, or his ancient audience.

This translation makes no attempt to turn the recited or sung passages into English meter or songs, instead focusing on bringing the characters' conversation to life in English prose and thus allowing for a closer translation. Amy Richlin's translations of three of Plautus's plays provide an excellent model for a metrical translation, though she did not translate *Epidicus* (Richlin 2005). She turns the spoken and recitative passages of three of Plautus's other plays (*Curculio, Persa,* and *Poenulus*) into loose iambic senarii or iambic pentameters, reflecting Plautus's free metrical style, and resulting in language that might be mistaken for prose by those who don't have an ear for meter (as Richlin notes, 116). Richlin brilliantly set some of Plautus's songs to the tunes of twentieth-century comic songs like "The Man on the Flying Trapeze" for the old woman Leaena's opening lines in the second scene of *Curculio* (the play was translated by Richlin under the title *Weevil*), and turned the songs in *Persa* (titled *Iran Man* in Richlin's translation) into rhymed rap. Richlin's translations are very successful at bringing to life the exuberance of Plautine comedy for readers who have a broad enough knowledge of cross-cultural and inter-generational speech and song patterns, though for readers who don't want to peruse Richlin's extensive endnotes some of the Roman context is going to be lost.

I made this translation of *Epidicus* with my undergraduate students in mind, who are not particularly familiar with American urban speech patterns, nor with mid-twentieth-century American songs, nor with reading endnotes. It is written entirely in prose, including the songs, and information that helps to understand the Roman context is added in footnotes. I hope that I have achieved an accessible text that gives readers an insight into the world of Plautus without undermining the essential comedy of the play.

The Play in English

Cast of Characters[1]

ACROPOLISTIS — a lyre-player and female slave who was Stratippocles's girlfriend till just before the action of the play begins

APOECIDES — an old man, friend of Periphanes

CHAERIBULUS — a freeborn young man, friend of Stratippocles

EPIDICUS — a male slave of Periphanes's household who is the con-man hero of the play

LYRE PLAYER — a freedwoman and professional musician

MONEYLENDER

PERIPHANES — an old man, father of Stratippocles

PHILIPPA — a poor freeborn middle-aged woman who had an illegitimate daughter (Telestis) by Periphanes

SLAVE (MALE, UNNAMED) — belonging to Periphanes's household

SOLDIER — wealthy and boastful, like most soldiers in Plautus

STRATIPPOCLES — a freeborn young man, son of Periphanes

TELESTIS — a freeborn young woman, illegitimate daughter of Philippa and Periphanes

THESPRIO — another male slave of Periphanes's household

---

1. A note on the characters' names: "Acropolistis" means "woman of the acropolis"; "Apoecides" means "settler" or "colonist"; "Chaeribulus" (from the Greek "rejoice" + "adviser") means "one who loves to give advice" (see Duckworth-Wheeler 1940: 96 who cites Ussing 1888); "Epidicus" means "disputed at law"; "Periphanes" means "notable"; "Philippa" means "lover of horses"; "Stratippocles" means "glorious cavalryman"; "Telestis" means "perfection"; "Thesprio" means "Thesprotian", that is, man from Thesprotis, in Epirus (see Richlin 2017: 72–84 for a discussion of slaves names in Roman comedy).

Setting

The play is supposed to take place in the Greek city of Athens, but the characters generally speak and act like Romans, and the "Athens" of this play looks a lot like Rome. For a plot summary of the play, see the introducton (page 1). Scene summaries (in English) can be found at the beginning of each scene in the Latin text, starting at page 35.

Lines 1–9b

ACT 1

1.1 Scene with Epidicus and Thesprio

Thesprio, a slave belonging to Periphanes, hurries on stage from the direction of the harbour (stage right), followed by Epidicus, another of Periphanes's slaves. Thesprio is lugging two travel bags and Epidicus is trying to catch up with him. The stage represents a street in front of the houses of Periphanes (stage right) and of Chaeribulus (stage left).

Epidicus: Hey, kid!

Thesprio: Who's that, grabbing me by the cloak when I'm in a hurry?

Epidicus: You know — it's your fellow[1] slave.

Thesprio: [*about to barge past Epidicus*] Well, "fellow", you're in my way.

Epidicus: Just look for a minute, Thesprio.

Thesprio: [*realizing who it is*] Oh, it's you, Epidicus, is it?

Epidicus: [*ironically*] You're using your eyes all right.

Thesprio: Hello.

Epidicus: I hope the gods are good to you. [*using a traditional greeting for someone who's returned from a trip*] I'm glad to see you safely back.

Thesprio: [*unimpressed*] OK, and what else?

Epidicus: What usually comes with the greeting: there'll be a dinner for you too.

Thesprio: [*embracing him*] I promise you –

Epidicus: [*eagerly*] What?

Thesprio: That I'll accept, if you're inviting me.

Epidicus: Anyway, how are you doing? Are you well?

Thesprio: Yes, as you can see.

---

[1] "Fellow" here, and in Thesprio's response, is an attempt to translate a Latin pun on *familiaris* and *familiariter*. Epidicus calls himself Thesprio's *familiaris* (meaning "fellow slave" but also "friend") and Thesprio responds that Epidicus is being *nimium familiariter* (meaning "too friendly" or "too familiar" — that is, invading his personal space by grabbing his cloak).

Epidicus: Good, I can see you are! You seem fatter and sleeker.

Thesprio: Yeah, thanks to this [*gesturing to his left hand*].

Epidicus: [*snorts, and gestures to Thesprio's hand*] It should have been cut off for theft long ago.[2]

Thesprio: [*grinning*] I don't sneak around stealing as much as I used to.

Epidicus: Why's that?

Thesprio: I steal openly now [*heading towards Periphanes's house*].

Epidicus: [*hurrying to keep up with Thesprio*] May the gods bring you bad luck! What enormous strides you're taking! When I saw you at the harbour I started running after you, and I could barely catch you up.

Thesprio: You're a pathetic townie.

Epidicus: [*panting*] I know what you are — a real soldier-man.

Thesprio: [*pleased*] Say it as much as you like.

Epidicus: But how are you? Have you been in good health the whole time?

Thesprio: Up and down.

Epidicus: Now, going up and down is fine for goats and such, but I don't like to see it being done to people [*he mimes having his hands tied up to a frame before a whipping*].[3]

Thesprio: [*not looking, and therefore not getting E.'s joke*] Well, what do you want me to say?

Epidicus: How'd things go?

Thesprio: Fine.

Epidicus: How's our young master?

Thesprio: Very fit — as strong as a boxer.

Epidicus: That's good news you're bringing me now you've come back, Thesprio. But where is he?

Thesprio: He's coming now.

Epidicus: But where is he? You didn't bring him in that suitcase or in that little furry handbag of yours …did you?

Thesprio: Oh for the gods' sake!

---

2 Thieves were punished by getting a hand (possibly always the left one) cut off. It is typical of Plautus that slaves joke to each other about the very real horrors that they all potentially faced.

3 *Qui uarie ualent / capreaginum hominum non placet mihi neque pantherinum genus* (literally: "those whose health is spotty, like a goaty type of man, or a leopardy type, don't appeal to me"). This is another joke about the abusive treatment slaves lived with, referring to the "spotty" or scarred skin of a slave that has been beaten with whips.

Epidicus: I want to ask you some questions. [*speaking in mock legal language*] Give your attention to the speaker; your turn to speak will follow.

Thesprio: You speak like a law-court.

Epidicus: And so I should.[4]

Thesprio: So now you're playing praetor for us?[5]

Epidicus: Why not? Can you think of anyone better suited to the praetorship?

Thesprio: But Epidicus, you're missing one thing from this praetorship of yours.

Epidicus: What?

Thesprio: You know: two lictors, with two fasces[6] — nice bundles of sticks — *for beating you with*.[7]

Epidicus: You're such a jerk! But anyway, tell me all about it!

Thesprio: What's the question?

Epidicus: Where are Stratippocles's weapons?

Thesprio: Well, by Pollux,[8] those weapons just — deserted to the enemy side.[9]

Epidicus: His weapons did?

Thesprio: They certainly did — in super quick time, too.

Epidicus: Seriously?

Thesprio: Seriously; the enemy's got them all right.

Epidicus: By Pollux, what a shameful thing!

Thesprio: Well, others have done the same before him. He'll end up getting honoured for it.

---

4 There is an untranslatable play on words here with *ius dicis* ("you speak like a lawcourt" or "you speak the law") and Epidicus's name, which in Greek (ἐπίδικος) refers to litigation. The Latin *dicis* and the Greek *-dikos* (-δικος) sound similar, though they have different meanings.

5 The urban praetor was the judge in charge of the Roman law courts.

6 "Two lictors with two fasces": lictors were officials whose job was to walk in front of magistrates to give them status and authority. Lictors carried bundles of sticks called *fasces*, which symbolized the magistrate's authority. The urban praetor had two lictors, while the ruling consul had twelve. The term "fascism" comes from the word *fasces*.

7 *For beating you with* doesn't appear in the Latin text but has been added to the translation for the sake of clarity.

8 "By Pollux!" (*pol!* or *edepol!* in Latin) was a mild Latin swear word used by men and women, referencing the name of one of a pair of semi-divine twin brothers, Castor and Pollux (or in Greek, *Polydeukes*/ Πολυδεύκης), who were brothers of Helen of Troy. Castor and Pollux were subsequently turned into the constellation Gemini (which is the Latin for "Twins"). Jocelyn argues that *"pol"* and *"edepol"* were meant to sound comically feminine when spoken by male characters (Jocelyn 2001: 277).

9 In ancient warfare it was deeply shameful for a soldier to abandon his weapons, since it meant he had run away from the enemy as fast as he could instead of fighting like a hero.

Epidicus: Huh?

Thesprio: Others have been honoured for similar deeds.[10] Mulciber,[11] if I recall correctly, made those weapons that Stratippocles had: and they just flew over to the enemy.

Epidicus: Then let that descendant of Thetis[12] lose them for all I care; the daughters of Nereus[13] will bring him other weapons. Just make sure the shield-makers have sufficient materials to work with, if he's going to give up his weapons to the enemy in every campaign.

Thesprio: Stop all this now.

Epidicus: You can stop it whenever you like.

Thesprio: Lay off questioning me!

Epidicus: [*ignoring this*] Tell me: where is Stratippocles?

Thesprio: The reason he's not here is because he was afraid to come along with me.

Epidicus: Why on earth?

Thesprio: He doesn't want his father to see him yet.

Epidicus: Why not?

Thesprio: I'll tell you: because with his war booty he bought a young slave girl who's really cute and looks like she's freeborn.

Epidicus: [*groaning*] What am I hearing from you?!

Thesprio: What I'm telling you.

Epidicus: Why did he buy her?

Thesprio: Oh, it was just a whim.

Epidicus: [*exasperated*] How many whims is that guy going to have? You know, before he left home to join the legion, he told me to go to the local pimp and buy a lyre-player that he was in love with — and so I did it.

Thesprio: [*shrugging*] Whichever way the wind blows, Epidicus, that's the way the sail will move.

Epidicus: Oh, I'm screwed! He's ruined me.

Thesprio: What are you talking about? What's wrong?

Epidicus: That new girl he bought — how much did he pay for her?

---

10 This may be a disparaging reference to the fugitives from the Battle of Cannae (216 BCE, when Hannibal destroyed a Roman army) who were thought to have been honoured undeservedly for their defeat (see Duckworth-Wheeler 1940: 125).

11 Mulciber was another name for Vulcan, the Roman blacksmith god, and god of fire generally. In Homer's *Iliad* the Greek blacksmith god Hephaestus made armor for the hero Achilles (similarly in Vergil's *Aeneid* the Roman god Vulcan made armor for the hero Aeneas).

12 Thetis was a sea nymph, and mother of the Greek hero Achilles.

13 Nereus was a sea god; his daughters, including Thetis, were sea nymphs.

Thesprio: [*prevaricating*] She... was cheap.

Epidicus: That's not an answer.

Thesprio: What then?

Epidicus: How many *minae*[14] did he pay for her?

Thesprio: This many [*crossing one index finger over the other to make an X and repeating it four times*]. Forty *minae*.[15] He borrowed this exact amount from a Theban moneylender, who lent it at an interest rate of one *sestertius*[16] per *mina* per day.

Epidicus: [*groaning*] Oh. my. gods.

Thesprio: And that moneylender came back with him, to make sure he gets his money repaid.

Epidicus: By the immortal gods! I am royally screwed!

Thesprio: What's happened? What's been going on, Epidicus?

Epidicus: I'm lost, thanks to him!

Thesprio: Thanks to who?

Epidicus: The same guy as "lost" his armour.

Thesprio: What is all this about?

Epidicus: He kept writing to me every day from the legionary camp — [*interrupting himself*] but it's best if I don't say anything. It's better for a man who's a slave to know more than he says out loud; that's just good sense.

Thesprio: By Pollux, what's making you so anxious? You're actually shaking, Epidicus! I can tell by your face that you've been getting into some trouble while I was away.

Epidicus: Lay off me!

Thesprio: [*moving away*] OK, I'm going.

Epidicus: [*grabbing Thesprio's arm*] Wait a minute, don't go!

Thesprio: Why are you trying to keep me?

Epidicus: Is he in love with that girl he bought with his war booty?

Thesprio: Need you ask? He's completely obsessed.

Epidicus: [*groaning*] I'm gonna lose the hide off my back over this.

---

14 A *mina* (plural: *minae*) was a weight of silver (about 430g), as well as a unit of currency.

15 It is impossible to convert ancient money into the modern equivalent with any accuracy. The poorest Athenian might have been able to subsist on two or three *minae* per year, while a skilled labourer might have made about six to ten *minae* per year. Forty *minae* is, therefore, a considerable sum of money.

16 The Latin text doesn't specify a *sestertius* (a small silver coin that weighed about 2.5g silver); instead the word *nummus* is used, which simply refers to some type of coin, although it usually implies a *sestertius* in Plautus. If the interest rate is indeed forty *sestertii* per day, it is an extortionate rate of interest, wildly higher than could have been charged by a real moneylender.

Thesprio: [*smirking*] He loves her more than he ever loved you!

Epidicus: [*angrily grabbing Thesprio's arm*] I hope Jupiter smites you down!

Thesprio: Let me go! [*trying to shake Epidicus off*] I mean it, now! My master ordered me not to go home. He told me to go to Chaeribulus's[17] house next door. He told me to wait there and he said he would come there himself.

Epidicus: Why?

Thesprio: I'll tell you: because he doesn't want his dad to see him or run into him, until he's paid out that money that he owes for the girl.

Epidicus: Oh, by Pollux, what a mess we're in!

Thesprio: Now stop holding onto me so I can get going.

Epidicus: When the old man hears about these goings on, our ship will be well and truly sunk!

Thesprio: What's it to me how screwed you'll be?

Epidicus: [*whimpering*] 'Cuz I don't want to die all on my own — I want you to go down with me, like the good friends we are!

Thesprio: Get out of my sight and get yourself crucified,[18] you and that delightful suggestion of yours.

Epidicus: OK, go on then, if you're in such a hurry.

Thesprio: I've never met a man I'm happier to get away from. [*exit Thesprio into Chaeribulus's house*]

Epidicus: Well, he's gone off now. [*addressing himself, possibly taking off his mask and addressing his remarks to it*] You're on your own now. You see how things are, Epidicus; unless you can help yourself by your own devices, you're screwed. Complete ruin is hanging over you. Unless you prop yourself up firmly somehow, you won't remain standing. A mountain of misfortune is going to crash down onto you. Right now I don't see how I can free myself from this predicament.

---

17 Chaeribulus, another young man, is the friend and neighbour of Stratippocles (the young master).

18 The most extreme penalty that slaves faced was the days-long agony of dying on a cross (crucifixion). Throughout the plays of Plautus, the slave characters joke casually to each other about crucifixion and other punishments. Perhaps slaves really did this as a way of dealing with the horrors they all feared, or perhaps the slave characters on stage joked like this to amuse the slave-owners in the audience, who would be the ones potentially inflicting these punishments on their own slaves.

Poor me, I managed to trick the old man[19] into thinking that he was buying his own daughter, when he actually bought the lovely lyre player[20] for his son — the one his son was in love with and told me to buy. If he's now gone and brought another girl from the army camp — I'm going to lose the skin off my back. 'Cuz when the old man finds out that he's been tricked, he'll flog my naked back with a cudgel.

OK, you'd better watch yourself. What if — oh, what a joke, that won't work. This head of mine clearly can't think straight. You're a worthless human being, Epidicus. Why do you want to talk so negatively to yourself? 'Cuz you're giving up on yourself, that's why. [*groaning*] What should I do?!! [*answering himself*] Are you asking me??? You're the one who used to give good advice to other people. I've got to hit on some scheme, somehow.

But why am I putting off meeting the young master? I'd better find out what kind of trouble we're in. Wait, here he comes himself. He's looking sad, walking along with his buddy Chaeribulus. I'll hide here, so I can quietly hear what these two are saying.

1.2 Scene with Stratippocles, Chaeribulus, and Epidicus

Two freeborn young men walk onto the stage.

Stratippocles: I've told you the whole story, Chaeribulus, and laid out the whole crappy problem that I'm having with these love affairs of mine.

Chaeribulus: You're stupider than I'd expect you to be at your age, Stratippocles, and you, a soldier! Are you actually ashamed of having bought a girl from a good family with your war booty? Who'd blame you for it?

Stratippocles: I've found that people who envy me are my enemies for that very reason. [*virtuously*] But I've never attempted to force myself on her.

Chaeribulus: And this makes you all the more honourable, in my opinion, since you're controlling yourself even in love.

---

19 "The old man" refers to Periphanes, the old master.
20 This "lovely lyre-player" is Acropolistis.

Stratippocles: [*disgustedly*] Someone who supports a friend in trouble with words alone is useless. When there's real trouble, a real friend gives real help when it's needed.

Chaeribulus: What do you want me to do for you?

Stratippocles: Give me forty *minae* of silver, so I can pay back the moneylender who I got that high-interest loan from.

Chaeribulus: I would give it to you if I had it, by Hercules![21]

Stratippocles: What's the use of your generous words if you can't back it up with practical help?

Chaeribulus: Honestly, by Pollux, I'm being harassed by debt collectors myself.

Stratippocles: [*disgustedly*] Friends like you are better dead than indebted.[22] Right now I'd pay a pretty sum to get Epidicus's help. In fact, I'll have him beaten soundly and hand him over to the miller[23] unless he gets hold of forty *minae* for me before I finish saying the last syllable of "forty *minae*" to him.

Epidicus: [*overhearing and commenting sarcastically in a quiet voice*] Everything's fine then: great promises he's making! He'll keep his word, I hope! Without any expense to me at all, my share of the feast — a feast of blows — is being provided for my shoulders. I'll go up to him.

[*speaking louder, and giving the formal greeting to someone returning from a journey — see line 7*] Is it his master Stratippocles, returning from abroad, whom Epidicus the slave greets?

Stratippocles: [*looking around*] Where is he?

Epidicus: Here. [*continuing the formal greeting*] I'm glad to see you have returned safely.

Stratippocles: I believe you, as far as that goes, as much as I'd believe myself.

Epidicus: Have you been well?

---

21 "By Hercules!" (*hercle* or *mehercle* in Latin) was commonly used by boys and men as a mild oath, referring to the most popular hero of both Greek and Latin mythology. Both men and women also swore by the divine hero Pollux ("*pol*" or "*edepol*" in Latin — see note 8 on page 131).

22 The Latin makes an alliterative joke with *furno* and *foro*, meaning something like "I'd rather friends like that were burnt in an oven (*furno*) than were thrust into the bankruptcy courts (*foro*).

23 Flourmills were powered by treadmills turned by animals or humans. It was exhausting work, and being sent to work at a mill was a dreaded punishment for slaves. Lucius, a man turned into a donkey in Apuleius *Metamorphoses* (9.11–12), gives a brutal description of such work.

Stratippocles: Well in body, but I've been sick in spirit.

Epidicus: I took care of what I was told to do. What you ordered me to do has been achieved! The girl[24] has been purchased, since you kept sending me letters about it.

Stratippocles: [*coolly*] You wasted your efforts then.

Epidicus: How so?

Stratippocles: Because I don't care about her anymore — she doesn't appeal to me.

Epidicus: What was the use of giving me so many orders and sending me letters then?

Stratippocles: [*blithely*] Oh, I used to be in love with her, but now my heart belongs to another.

Epidicus: [*shrilly*] By Hercules, it's a little upsetting when someone doesn't appreciate a favour you've done for them. All the good work I did now turns out to be bad work, just because YOU'VE changed girlfriends.

Stratippocles: [*shrugging*] I must have been out of my mind when I sent you those letters.

Epidicus: Is it fair that I get to be the scapegoat because of your stupidity?! So that MY back gets the punishment for YOUR stupidity?[25]

Stratippocles: Why are we even talking now? This guy [*pointing both of his thumbs at himself*] needs forty red hot *minae* immediately, to pay off the moneylender — and fast!

Epidicus: Just tell me this: where do you want me to get it from? Which banker do you want me to borrow from?

Stratippocles: Whichever you want. 'Cuz unless you get it from somewhere before the sun has set don't bother coming home. You'll be taking yourself to the mill!

Epidicus: You say that so casually, without any worry or anxiety, with a carefree heart. But I know those punishment slaves we have on staff:[26] I'm the one that'll feel the pain, since I'm the one that'll get the beating.

---

24 "The girl" is Acropolistis, the "lovely lyre-player" of line 90.

25 In the Latin text Epidicus makes explicit reference to religious sacrifice, referring to himself, and then his back, with two words that meant sacrificial victim (*piacularem* in line 139 and *succidaneum* in line 140).

26 "Those punishment slaves we have on staff" is a translation of the less explicit Latin *nostros*, which literally translates to "our people" or "our staff of slaves". Context makes it clear, however, that Epidicus is referring to the slaves Periphanes keeps for inflicting punishment on other slaves.

Stratippocles: What are you on about now? Do you really want to be responsible for my suicide?!!

Epidicus: Don't do that! I'll take on the danger and do whatever risky plan rather than let you kill yourself.

Stratippocles: That's better; I can praise you for that now.

Epidicus: I'll endure whatever you want me to.

Stratippocles: What're we going to do with that lyre-player?[27]

Epidicus: I'll hit upon something. I'll fix things for you somehow — I'll get you out of this somehow.

Stratippocles: [*digging an elbow into Epidicus's ribs*] You are full of contrivances. I know you.

Epidicus: There's a rich soldier from Euboea[28] who has a lot of buying power. When he finds out that you bought the lyre-player and that you've now brought over this other girl, he'll beg you to give that first girl to him, without us even having to suggest it. But where's the one you brought home with you?

Stratippocles: She'll be here soon, I promise.

Chaeribulus: What should we do now?

Stratippocles: [*to Chaeribulus*] Let's go into your house here, so we can have a good time today. [*Stratippocles and Chaeribulus go into the latter's house*].

Epidicus: You go on in. Meanwhile I'll call a senate meeting — that is, a senate meeting in my mind — to deliberate about this money matter, and especially about who's going to get my declaration of war, and where I'll get the money from. Epidicus, [*addressing himself*] be careful what you do! This situation's been thrown at you so suddenly. Now's not the time for you to be snoozing or procrastinating: get to work. [*suddenly getting an idea*] OK! I've got a definite plan to target the old man. I'll go inside and tell the young master (the old man's son) not to stroll out of doors and to make sure not to run into the old man at all. [*Epidicus follows the young men into Chaeribulus's house*]

---

27 "That lyre-player" is, of course, Acropolistis.
28 Euboea is an island off mainland Greece. This soldier may or may not be the same as the soldier from Rhodes mentioned by Epidicus in line 300, and/or the soldier who arrives on stage at line 437.

Lines 166–180

ACT 2

2.1 Scene with Apoecides and Periphanes

Apoecides and Periphanes come out from Periphanes's house together.

Apoecides: Most men feel ashamed of things that don't actually matter, but then in situations when they should feel ashamed, well, shame ups and leaves them just when they ought to be feeling the disgrace. You're exactly that kind of man. What've you got to be ashamed about, marrying a woman from a good family, though she is poor? Especially this woman, when you say she's the mother of that daughter of yours that you brought to your house.[29]

Periphanes: I have to be respectful of my son.[30]

Apoecides: Oh, for Pollux's sake! Like I believed you were "respectful" of your wife, who's now dead and buried. [*with a hearty guffaw*] You do an animal sacrifice to Orcus the god of the dead every time you happen to see her tomb, right there and then. A very appropriate thing to do, seeing as you won in the end [*elbowing Periphanes in the ribs*] — by outliving her!

Periphanes: Ugh, I was a Hercules as long as she was still around. His Sixth Labour[31] wasn't any harder than what I had to put up with.

Apoecides: But by Pollux, a dowry is good money!

Periphanes: By Pollux, it is good — except for the marriage part!

---

29 The illegitimate daughter of Periphanes and this woman (Philippa) is Telestis, but we the audience know that the young woman Periphanes has brought into his house is not actually Telestis, but is his son's former slave girlfriend, the lyre-player Acropolistis.

30 Periphanes, it seems, worries that his son Stratippocles will object to Periphanes bringing a stepmother into their household.

31 The Sixth Labour of Hercules, according to common Roman versions, was that of the belt of Hippolyta the Amazon (Duckworth-Wheeler 1940: 218). Periphanes is thus suggesting that his dead wife was belligerent and powerful like an Amazon.

2.2 Scene with Epidicus, Periphanes, and Apoecides

Epidicus comes out of Chaeribulus's house.

Epidicus: [*aside*] Shush! Be quiet, all of you, and cheer up. I've come out to report a clear sign from the gods: a bird flew by on my left side.[32] I've got a sharp knife for cutting open the old man's moneybag.[33]

But look! I see the old man himself in front of our house, along with Apoecides. They're just the lambs for slaughter — I mean, just the old men I was wanting![34] I'm now going to turn myself into a leech and suck out their blood, those so-called pillars of the senate.

[*there may be some lines missing here, in which Apoecides probably tried to persuade Periphanes that if he married off his son Stratippocles it would leave Periphanes free to remarry*]

Apoecides: ... so he can be married off right away.

Periphanes: I like that advice, since I heard that my son was obsessed with some lyre-player, which is REALLY upsetting me.[35]

Epidicus: [*aside*] By Hercules! All the gods are on my side, they're looking out for me, they love me! These guys here are showing me the way forward — they're showing me how I can get the money from them! Go on now, Epidicus [*addressing himself*], get yourself ready! Throw your cloak out of the way over your shoulder and pretend that you've been searching for the man all over the city. Act now, if you're going to act!

---

32 When Romans wanted to know if their plans were likely to turn out well, they took the auspices (also known as practicing augury). This was a form of divination that interpreted the behaviour of birds as evidence for the will of the gods or of fate. Birds seen flying by on the left were usually considered to be a favourable omen, though there were some exceptions. These exceptions seem to have become more emphasized in later antiquity, however, since the Latin word for "left" (*sinister*) ended up meaning "malicious", or "suspicious".

33 Epidicus makes several references to religious sacrifice; here the image is of Periphanes and his moneybag as the sacrificial animal. Cutting open the moneybag with a knife is the equivalent to cutting open the belly of the sacrificial animal.

34 "Lambs for the slaughter" is an attempt to translate a probable pun on the Latin word for "old men" (*uetulos*), which sounds like *uitulos* ("calves"), animals commonly used in animal sacrifice (see Gellar-Goad 2012 and Barrios-Lech 2014).

35 Periphanes says in Latin *id ego excrucior*: "it's crucifying me".

[*pretending to have just come running up, and speaking loudly so that the old men will hear him*] By the immortal gods, if only I could find Periphanes at home! I'm exhausted from looking all over the city for him. I looked into all the doctors' offices, the barbers, I went to the gymnasium and the forum, the perfume shops, the butchers' shops, and all the banking establishments. I'm completely hoarse with asking for him, and I nearly fainted from running.

Periphanes: Hey, Epidicus!

Epidicus: Who's that back there calling out "Epidicus"?

Periphanes: It's Periphanes.

Apoecides: And it's also me, Apoecides.

Epidicus: And here's me, Epidicus! But master, I've met you both at the best possible moment.

Periphanes: What's up?

Epidicus: Wait, wait [*panting after his pretended run*], let me catch my breath please.

Periphanes: Of course, take your time.

Epidicus: I'm feeling a bit faint.

Apoecides: Catch your breath.

Periphanes: Calm down and rest for a bit.

Epidicus: [*straightening up*] OK, listen: everyone from the legion has been sent home from the war in Thebes.

Apoecides: Who says so?[36]

Epidicus: I say so!

Periphanes: Do you know it for a fact?

Epidicus: Yes I do.

Periphanes: How do you know it?

Epidicus: I saw the soldiers coming through the crowded streets, carrying their weapons and leading their pack mules.

Periphanes: This is great news!

Epidicus: And the prisoners they're bringing with them! There's boys, young women, some have got two prisoners, some three, one has five. There's a traffic jam in the streets with the people trying to see their sons.

Periphanes: By Hercules, this is wonderful!

---

36 The Latin is <*quis hoc*> *scit factum*? which would literally translate to "who knows that this has happened?", and Epidicus's response is literally "I'm telling [you] that it's happened".

Epidicus: And the huge number of prostitutes — all the whores in the city — were out there dressed in their fancy clothes, each trying to find her lover. I tell you, they were on the hunt! And do you want to know how I know that? Most of them had hunting nets — well, net tunics at least — under their dresses.[37] When I get to the city gate I see that chick waiting around for him, and there were four music girls[38] with her.

Periphanes: [*increasingly anxious*] With who, Epidicus?!!

Epidicus: With that chick your son's madly, desperately in love with — has been for years — the one for whose sake he's throwing away all his (and your) credit and fortune in a hurry. So she was waiting around for him at the gate.

Periphanes: [*very upset*] The witch! Don't you get it?!

Epidicus: [*enthusiastically*] But so well dressed, wearing gold jewelry, looking so charming, so elegant, wearing the latest fashion!

Periphanes: [*distracted for a moment*] Oh? What was she wearing? Her lingerie — was it royal, or beggarly?

Epidicus: It was the Skylight style. The names women give to their fashions! [*rolling his eyes*]

Periphanes: [*ignorant of women's fashions and so misunderstanding*] What, she was dressed in a skylight?

Epidicus: What's so strange about that? Don't lots of women walk around the streets wearing entire estates?[39] And yet when it's tax time, guys claim they can't pay up, even though they seem to be able to pay the higher taxes those ladies charge.

---

37 Apparently underclothing made out of netting were worn by Roman women, or perhaps only by Roman prostitutes. Since nets were used in hunting, Plautus can make a joke about prostitutes preying on men.

38 The "music girls" (*tibicinae*) would have been slaves or very lower-class women who played the *tibia* professionally. A *tibia* was a double-reed instrument, perhaps like an oboe.

39 This is a reference to the cost of the women's clothing, and the fact that freeborn men were thought to waste their estates paying for sex workers or supporting concubines (concubines were women who had an official and potentially long-term sexual relationship with men who supported them, though they were of significantly lower status than wives).
Epidicus's comic rant about women's clothing may relate to the repeal, in 195 BCE, of the Oppian law that had restricted the value of women's adornment (see Livy 34.4–7). If so, then the play must have been produced after 195 BCE.

[*digressing into a more general scorn for women's fashion*] And what is it with the weird names women give every year to their clothes? The "little nothing" tunic, the "full-coverage" tunic, the "blue linen-esque", the "underneath", the "edge-embroidered", the "mini-slip", the "saffron-hue", the "Oscan robe", the "over-much robe", the "praying veil", the "royal", the "foreigner", the "sea-coloured" or the "feather-patterned", the "nut-brown" or the "wax-dyed" — what extreme silliness! They've even taken a name from a dog!

Periphanes: How so?

Epidicus: They call one of their outfits "the Alsatian"![40] Anyway, it's thanks to all these silly names that the men have got to sell off their property in public auctions just to pay for it all.

Apoecides: But won't you go on with what you were starting to tell us?

Epidicus: OK, so two other women began to chat together right behind me. I moved a little away from them on purpose — I was pretending not to listen to their conversation. I didn't overhear perfectly, but I didn't miss much of what they were saying.

Periphanes: I want to know what they said!

Epidicus: Then one of them said to the one the other one was walking with —

Periphanes: [*confused*] Huh?

Epidicus: Just listen, and you'll hear it. They caught sight of that woman your son's madly in love with. "How perfectly and fortunately it's turning out for her, honestly, that woman whose lover wants to set her free" says one. "Who in the world is her lover, anyway?" says the other woman to her friend. So then she (the first woman) gives his name as Stratippocles, son of Periphanes.

Periphanes: By Hercules, I'm ruined! What is this I'm hearing from you?

Epidicus: You're hearing what happened. Now when I heard them saying this I began to slow down bit by bit so they'd be closer to me, making it look as though the crush of people ahead of me was pushing me back.

Periphanes: [*nodding*] I get it.

---

40   The Latin does not, of course, refer to "Alsatian", but to "Spartan". There was a well-known dog breed called the "Spartan" (because it had originated in the Greek state of Sparta), and presumably there was also a fabric or style of women's dress that also originated in Sparta and was called "Spartan".

Epidicus: So then the other one asked the first one: "How do you know? Who told you this?" "She got a letter today" (says the first one) "from Stratippocles saying that he'd taken out a loan in Thebes from a moneylender, and that he had the money ready and was bringing it so he could free her."

Periphanes: [*groaning*] I'm completely ruined!

Epidicus: The lady claimed to have heard this from the girl herself and to have read the letter.

Periphanes: What'll I do? [*turning to Apoecides*] I'm in desperate need of advice now, Apoecides.

Apoecides: Let's find some good and speedy advice then, because I think your son will be here soon, by Hercules, if he's not here already.

Epidicus: If it weren't wrong for me to set myself up as wiser than you two, I could give you some sensible advice that you'll both like, I think.

Periphanes: Well, what's your advice, Epidicus?

Epidicus: [*looking bashful*] It's appropriate for the circumstances.

Apoecides: Why don't you just tell us?

Epidicus: [*pretending to be very modest*] It's right for you to go first, since you're so much cleverer than me, and it's my place to speak afterwards.

Periphanes: [*scornfully*] Yeah, right! Go on, tell us.

Epidicus: You'll laugh.

Apoecides: [*encouragingly*] We won't, by Pollux.

Epidicus: OK then. If you like my plan, use it. If you don't, find a better one. It's nothing to do with me, except that I want what you want, of course.

Periphanes: [*ironically*] Thanks. Now share your wisdom with us.

Epidicus: Choose a wife for your son right away, and take your revenge on the lyre-player your son wants to set free — the lyre-player that's corrupting him. Make it so she remains a slave for the rest of her life.

Apoecides: [*rubbing his hands in glee*] You've got to make this happen!

Periphanes: [*equally enthusiastic*] I'll do whatever you say, if we can just make this happen!

Epidicus: [*briskly*] OK, look. Now's the time to do it, before he arrives, since he'll be here tomorrow. He's not going to come today.

Periphanes: How do you know that?

Epidicus: [*hastily coming up with an explanation*] I know it because someone who just came from Thebes told me that your son was going to be here tomorrow morning.

Periphanes: Anyway, you were telling us what we should do.

Epidicus: I recommend the following: pretend you want to free the lyre-player for your own sake, pretend you're madly in love with her yourself.

Periphanes: How will that help me?

Epidicus: Need you ask? So you can buy her before your son gets home. You'll be able to say that you bought her in order to free her —

Periphanes: [*interrupting*] I get it!

Epidicus: When she's been purchased, you'll get her out of the city somewhere, unless you've got a different plan.

Periphanes: No, no! Your plan is very clever!

Epidicus: What do you think, Apoecides?

Apoecides: [*rubbing his hands gleefully*] What can I say, except that this deception of yours is just too clever![41]

Epidicus: So then any doubts he may have about marriage[42] will be removed, and he won't get upset at doing what you want.

Periphanes: You are a genius. I like it!

Epidicus: OK then, you need to get going soon if you're going to do it.

Periphanes: By Hercules, you're right.

Epidicus: And I've found out how you can avoid suspicion.[43]

Periphanes: Tell me!

Epidicus: I will. Listen.

Apoecides: This guy is super smart!

Epidicus: We're going to need someone to bring the money to pay for the lyre-player, since I don't want you involved, and there's no need anyway.

Periphanes: Why not?

---

41 "Too clever" is ironic, because Apoecides doesn't get how clever Epidicus's deception is; he thinks Epidicus is going to trick Stratippocles, but in fact Epidicus is going to trick Periphanes and Apoecides.

42 This marriage would be that of Stratippocles and whatever young woman Periphanes may choose for him, as mentioned at lines 190 and 267.

43 "How you can avoid suspicion": that is, how Periphanes can prevent Stratippocles from finding out that he (Periphanes) is the one to have bought Stratippocles's lyre-playing girlfriend.

Epidicus: In case the pimp guesses you're buying her to save your son —

Periphanes: [*interrupting*] Clever!

Epidicus: [*continuing his sentence*] — to keep your son away from her. It could cause problems if your son gets suspicious.

Periphanes: Who can we find to do this?

Epidicus: [*gesturing to Apoecides*] This man here will be perfect. He'll be good and careful, and he understands the laws.[44]

Periphanes: [*grinning at his friend*] You should say thank you to Epidicus for that.

Epidicus: Meanwhile I'll do my part faithfully: I'll go and meet him [*gesturing to Apoecides*] and bring the lyre-player — who'll belong to you now — here to you, and also he [*gesturing to Apoecides again*] and I will take charge of the money.

Periphanes: What's the lowest price we can buy her for?

Epidicus: For that girl? Maybe you could get her for as low as forty *minae,* but if you give me more, I'll bring any leftover back — I'm not about to cheat you.[45] Anyway, that money won't be out of your hands for even ten days.

Periphanes: Why won't it?

Epidicus: Because there's another young man that's madly in love with the woman — a very wealthy young man, a great soldier from Rhodes[46] who's captured loads of enemy combatants.[47] Very boastful man. This guy'll buy her from you, and willingly pay a big price. Just do what I say. There'll be a big profit for you.

Periphanes: [*rubbing his hands greedily*] I pray to the gods that there will!

Epidicus: Don't worry, there will be.

Apoecides: [*to Periphanes*] Why don't you go indoors and get the money? I'll head off to the forum.[48] You meet me there, Epidicus.

Epidicus: Stay there till I show up.

Apoecides: I'll wait till you come.

---

44 The laws around buying and selling slaves, that is.
45 Oh, the irony! That's exactly what Epidicus is doing.
46 It's unclear whether or not this soldier from Rhodes is the same as the soldier from Euboea mentioned at line 153.
47 The soldier's wealth is explained by the number of enemy combatants he has captured, since he would have sold them into slavery (one of the reasons why war was so profitable for successful soldiers).
48 The forum was the big open area in the middle of the city. The direction of the forum was the stage left.

Periphanes: [*to Epidicus*] You, follow me inside now.

Epidicus: Go on, count out the money. I won't keep you waiting at all.

[*exeunt Periphanes and Apoecides*]

2.3 Scene with Epidicus

Epidicus: [*laughing to himself*] I don't think there's a piece of land in all of Attica[49] that's as profitable to me as our Periphanes here. Really, I take as much money from his locked and sealed-up money chest as I like. By Pollux, though — what I'm afraid of is if the old man finds out! He'll shear me to the bone the way a poor man fleeces a rich friend.[50] But one thing bothers me: how to get hold of some hired lyre-player to show to Apoecides?[51]

[*Epidicus thinks for a bit*]

I've got it! Just this morning the old man told me to get a lyre-player for him here, to play her lyre while he does a religious sacrifice. I'll bring her here after I give her some coaching on how to deceive the old man. I'll go indoors now and get the money from that careless old man.

---

49 Remember that the play is supposedly set in Athens, which is in the region called Attica.
50 Epidicus here is making reference to the stock figure of the "parasite" (*parasitus*), who would stick close to the richer man to take what he could get. In this somewhat strange metaphor, the rods with which Epidicus would be beaten are likened to such parasites.
51 Remember that Epidicus has claimed to Periphanes and Apoecides that he'd use Periphanes's money (see lines 296–297) to buy the slave lyre-player Acropolistis, whom Epidicus has told them is still Stratippocles's girlfriend. Epidicus had, however, already bought Acropolistis a few days earlier (using Periphanes's money then too), having convinced Periphanes that she was his long-lost daughter Telestis. Epidicus now needs to find a woman who can pretend to be Acropolistis. He is therefore going to hire the services of a freelance lyre-player.

ACT 3

3.1 Scene with Stratippocles and Chaeribulus

Stratippocles: I'm eaten up by the waiting — it's torturing me! Such plausible assurances Epidicus gave me — but how are they going to turn out? It's really wearing me down. I want to know if it's going to happen or not!

Chaeribulus: Help from that source? You can get other help. I knew right away from the beginning that there'd be no help from that guy.

Stratippocles: [*burying his head in his hands*] By Hercules, I'm doomed!

Chaeribulus: You're being silly, getting so upset. By Hercules, if I could just get hold of him I'd never let that slave go unpunished for laughing at us.

Stratippocles: What do you expect HIM to give me, when your family's got so much money but you haven't got a penny yourself, and you can't help out your mate.

Chaeribulus: By Hercules, if I had any, I'd willingly offer it. But there is some hope of something, somehow, in some way, from somewhere, from someone — some good luck for you and me.[52]

Stratippocles: You total idiot!

Chaeribulus: What makes you want to turn on me?

Stratippocles: [*sarcastically*] Obviously you are babbling something at me in some way from somewhere from some source that doesn't exist! And I don't intend to listen to you. You're no more supportive than someone who hasn't even been born yet.

---

52 Remember that Chaeribulus's name can be interpreted as meaning "one who loves to give advice", and these lines illustrate how useless his advice is.

3.2 Scene with Epidicus, Stratippocles, and Chaeribulus

Epidicus has been given the money by Periphanes and has come outdoors again.

Epidicus: [*talking through the doorway to Periphanes, who is in the house*] You've done your part, now I've got to do mine. You can relax, I'll take care of it.

[*moving out of Periphanes's earshot, and patting the purse of money gleefully*]

He's well and truly lost this! Don't go hoping otherwise — this money is well and truly buried. You can trust me on this: that's how I do things, and that's how my people have always done things.[53]

By the immortal gods, what a perfect day I've been given! So easy, so much success! But am I putting off starting on my mission? I need to bring the supplies to the outpost while the signs are good![54] Just standing around like this is delaying me.

[*catching sight of the two young men*]

But what's this? I see the two friends, my master and Chaeribulus, in front of his house. [*addressing them*] What are you doing here? [*thrusting the purse at Stratippocles*] Here, take this.

Stratippocles: How much is in the bag?

Epidicus: As much as is enough and more than enough. There's extra. I brought ten *minae* more than you owe to the moneylender. Provided that I can keep you happy and obey you, I don't have to worry at all about my back.[55]

Stratippocles: Why?

Epidicus: Because I'm going to make your dad into a dad-icide.

Stratippocles: What does that mean?

---

53 Slaves in Rome were considered, by slave-owners, no longer to have parents or ancestors, so Epidicus's reference to "how my people (or "our people") have always done things" is probably a humorous reference to how the class of slaves, or perhaps just the class of cunning/clever slaves like Epidicus (*serui callidi*) act.

54 "While the signs are good" is a translation of *meo auspicio*, meaning "under my own auspices". Auspices were signs from the gods that they approved (or potentially disapproved) of a person's course of action. This line is a military metaphor; Epidicus is likening himself to military personnel with an important mission.

55 That is, Epidicus doesn't need to worry about getting a beating as long as he keeps Stratippocles happy. The implication of the following lines seems to be that Epidicus needs to keep only Stratippocles happy, and needn't worry about Periphanes, because Periphanes will be well and truly undermined.

Epidicus: [*loftily*] I don't bother with common, old fashioned words. [*Stratippocles still looks confused, so Epidicus explains*] The punishment for killing parents is to be sewn into a sack, right? Well, I'm stitching him up in this purse. Get it?[56]

The brothel keeper took every bit of the money I paid for the lyre-player — you know, the one your dad thinks is his daughter. I paid down the money with my own hands. Now I've figured out a way to cheat your dad again and help you out. I persuaded the old man — gave a whole long speech in fact — about you not getting access to her when you got back.[57]

Stratippocles: Perfect!

Epidicus: But really she's at your home now, posing as your half-sister.

Stratippocles: [*nodding*] I get it!

Epidicus: Now your dad's given me Apoecides to act as adviser in this matter — he's waiting for me at the forum — supposedly to keep an eye on things.

Stratippocles: Not bad at all!

Epidicus: [*giggling*] But this super careful guy is the one who'll be tricked! Your father put the moneybag around my neck himself! [*laughing*] By the way, he's planning to get you married as soon as you get home.

Stratippocles: [*angrily*] The only way he'll persuade me to get married is if Orcus the god of the dead takes my girlfriend away first! The one I've just brought back, of course, not the other one.[58]

---

56 The Latin isn't very clear either, but it relates to the fact that in Roman law a person convicted of having killed his parent (parricide) was traditionally punished by being sewn into a sack, possibly along with various animals, and drowned. Epidicus's joke seems to be based on the idea that Periphanes getting cheated and outwitted (getting "stitched up") is like being literally stitched up in a sack.
The reference to parricide in the play may have been a response to what Plutarch tells us was the first Roman perpetrator of parricide, Lucius Hostius, just after the end of the Second Punic War (Plutarch, *Rom.* 22.4). If so, it helps to date the production of *Epidicus* to after 201 BCE. If the comic rant about women's expensive clothing at lines 226–235 is a response to the repeal of the Oppian law then the play can be dated to after 195 BCE.

57 "Not getting access to her when you got back": Epidicus refers to the fact that, thanks to his trickery, Periphanes thinks he's going to be buying Acropolistis the lyre-player in order to keep her away from his son Stratippocles.

58 More literally this line reads: "He'll only persuade me if Orcus takes away the girl I've brought home with me" (*uno persuadebit modo, si illam, quae adducta est mecum / mi adempsit Orcus*). This reference to Orcus coming to get a dead soul is distinctly Roman, rather than Greek (Jocelyn 2001: 281).

Epidicus: OK, I've set up a clever deception: I'll go to the pimp's establishment alone, and tell him to say, if I happen to bring them to see him, that he was given the money for the lyre-player — that he got fifty *minae* of silver for her.

He'll just think I'm trying to make a sneaky profit, but won't figure out what the full scam is.[59] Obviously the day before yesterday I paid down the money for that other girlfriend of yours — that one your father thinks is his daughter. *The pimp'll think I mean that lyre-player*.[60]

Then the corrupt pimp will implicate himself in the scam without realizing it, saying he got the money for the new girl that you've just brought home.

Chaeribulus: [*admiringly*] You're craftier than a — than a craft sale![61]

Epidicus: Now I'll get hold of some lyre-player that's good at lying, and that I can hire on the cheap, who'll pretend that I've bought her, and who's clever enough to fool the two old men. Apoecides will bring her to your dad.

Stratippocles: What a good plan!

Epidicus: I'll send her off well coached, full of my lies and tricks. But I've been talking too much — you've held me up a while. You now know what's going to happen. I'm off. [*exit Epidicus stage left*]

Stratippocles: Good luck!

Chaeribulus: [*admiringly*] That guy's too good at double-dealing!

Stratippocles: He's certainly saved me with his scheming.

Chaeribulus: Let's go into my house.

---

59 I added the comments within the asterisks for clarity (they don't appear in the Latin text). Epidicus is trying to achieve the following: he wants the pimp to mislead the old men by telling them that Epidicus has just paid fifty *minae* for the new lyre-player (who is actually a freedwoman whom Epidicus will hire for the day). The pimp, having previously sold the original lyre-player (Acropolistis) to Epidicus for thirty *minae*, will think that the only scam is Epidicus trying to claim he paid fifty *minae* instead of thirty. Pimps in Roman comedy are notoriously corrupt, so no doubt he would agree to this lesser scam out of fellow-feeling for a cheating slave, or in the hopes that Epidicus would return the favour in some way, perhaps by sharing the profits of his scam.

60 Again, the asterisks surround words that don't appear in the Latin text but are added here to make Epidicus's sense clearer.

61 The Latin (*uorsutior es quam rota figularis*) translates more literally to "you are more twisty than a potter's wheel".

Stratippocles: I'll be going inside a lot more cheerfully than I came out! Thanks to Epidicus's courage[62] and good luck I'm returning to the military base with the war prize in hand.[63] [*exeunt Chaeribulus and Stratippocles into the former's house*]

3.3 Scene with Periphanes, Apoecides, a Slave, and the [Hired] Lyre-Player (Who Doesn't Speak in this Scene)

Periphanes comes out of his house.

Periphanes: [*holding up a mirror and speaking philosophically*] When a man gazes at his own face, it's not just for the sake of the face itself that he should own a mirror. There are those who are able to examine the core of their wisdom, and therefore examine the resources of their hearts. When they've looked into a mirror, they then reflect on how they have lived their lives when they were young. It's a good idea to do so, in my opinion.

Indeed, I myself had been about to get very upset about my son, as though he'd done me wrong in some way. As though I hadn't done a lot of bad things myself when I was young! We old guys certainly stray from the right path once in a while.

[*seeing Apoecides arriving with the hired lyre-player*] But here's my buddy Apoecides coming with the goods. [*humorously giving a formal greeting*] Tradesman, I'm glad to see you safely back.[64] How'd it go?

Apoecides: The gods and goddesses favour you.

Periphanes: I like the omen!

Apoecides: Fortunately everything agrees with the omen. But give the order for her [*gesturing to the hired lyre-player*] to be taken indoors.

Periphanes: [*calling to his slaves indoors*] Hey, come outside, someone, and take this woman indoors. Do you hear?

---

62   The word Stratippocles uses for "courage" is *uirtus*, which is literally "manly excellence" (it's related to the Latin word for "man"). It is an interesting word for a slave-owner to apply to a slave, who is generally not supposed to have *uirtus*.

63   Stratippocles is a soldier (if a very cowardly one), hence his military metaphors. Many of the free members of Plautus's audience would have served as soldiers in Rome's constant warfare, so they would have understood the military references.

64   Periphanes is being humorous by greeting Apoecides as though he has been away on a long voyage (see line 7). He addresses him as "tradesman" because he's been on a shopping trip, though the audience knows that Apoecides has not been directly involved in the supposed purchase at all.

Slave: [*coming out*] Did you want something?

Periphanes: Make sure you don't let this woman associate with, or even look at my daughter, do you understand? I want that one [*pointing to the hired lyre-player*] kept away from my daughter. The manners and morals of freeborn girls are very different from a lowborn prostitute's.

Apoecides: You talk sensibly and wisely. You can't be too careful about a daughter's modesty. By Pollux, though — we bought that woman just in time, before your son could.

Periphanes: What do you mean?

Apoecides: Some guy told me that he'd seen your son here a while ago, and that he was already making moves towards buying her, by Pollux.

Periphanes: By Hercules, a close call indeed!

Apoecides: You sure have a wonderful, priceless slave, worth his weight in gold. [*laughing*] If you could have seen how he managed to keep the lyre-player from realizing it was you she'd been bought for! He brought her along, and she was giggling and cheerful.

Periphanes: That's impressive!

Apoecides: He said you'd be performing a sacrifice for his son, at home, because he'd arrived safely from Thebes.

Periphanes: He did exactly the right thing.

Apoecides: He told her that she'd been hired to assist you in the sacrifice.[65] I just pretended to be slow and tried to look really stupid.

Periphanes: Very appropriate.[66]

Apoecides: By the way, a friend of mine has got a big court case going on in the forum. I want to go and act as witness for him.

Periphanes: Please come back here as soon as there's a pause in the proceedings.

Apoecides: I'll come back right away [*exit Apoecides*].

Periphanes: There's nothing friendlier than a useful friend. You get things done that you want done without having to do them yourself. Now if I'd entrusted the business to some less skilled man, or to someone less clever in this sort of thing, my son would have outwitted him, and would have laughed at me mercilessly — and I'd have deserved it!

---

65 I have not translated line 419, which was probably a copying error and should be deleted.

66 Periphanes doesn't see the irony here, but the audience does, since they know that Apoecides has no idea what the real situation is.

Anyway, it's stupid to blame my son for what I myself did when I was young. When I was in the army... [*chuckling*] I used to talk the ears off anyone and everyone when I got started telling them about my war stories.

[*noticing the arrival of the soldier*] But who's that I see coming this way, making his cloak billow out behind him with his swaggering?

3.4 Scene with the Soldier and Periphanes (and an Unnamed, Non-Speaking Slave)

Soldier: [*to his slave*] Make sure you don't miss going into any house you pass, to ask where the old man Periphanes Platenius[67] lives. Don't come back until you find out.

Periphanes: [*addressing the soldier*] Young man, if I were to direct you to the man you're looking for, would you thank me?

Soldier: [*arrogantly*] I've earned the right for EVERYONE to thank me because of my excellence in war.

Periphanes: [*patronizingly*] You haven't found a quiet place, young man, to show off your military excellence the way you want to. If a weaker man boasts about his battles to a stronger man, those battles look pathetic next to the other man's. But the man you're looking for — Periphanes Platenius — that's me, if you're wanting anything.

Soldier: Really? The one they talk about who got incredibly rich when he was a young man, fighting alongside kings, because of his military prowess?

Periphanes: Yep. If you heard about my battles, you'd run off home as fast as you could go.

Soldier: By Pollux, I'm looking for someone to tell my stories to, not someone who'll tell me his.

Periphanes: This isn't the place for that. Look for someone else who'll believe your tall tales.

Soldier: Listen up, so you'll know what I've come to you for: I heard that you bought the slave girl I'm in love with.[68]

---

67 "Platenius" may be a demonym referring to Periphanes's hometown, or a comic family name meaning something like "Boastful" (see Schmidt 1902: 202). Soldiers in Plautus, who are always boastful, usually have two names, signaling their self-importance.

68 "The slave girl I'm in love with" is a translation of *amicam*, which could also be simply translated as "girlfriend".

Periphanes: [*aside*] Oh! Now I know who this guy is — he's the soldier Epidicus told me about a little while ago. [*to the soldier*] Young man, you are right; I bought her.

Soldier: I want to have a few little words with you, if it's no trouble.

Periphanes: By Pollux, I don't know if it's a trouble or not, unless you tell me what you want.

Soldier: I want you to hand that girl over to me and take the money for her.

Periphanes: Do you have the money with you?

Soldier: Why shouldn't I speak frankly with you? I was intending to make that girl my freedwoman today so she can become my live-in girlfriend.[69]

Periphanes: I'll make this quick then: I bought her for fifty *minae* of silver. If you pay me sixty *minae* in full, the woman will be yours to spend your free time with. Really — on condition that you take her out of the country.

Soldier: So she'll be mine on those conditions?

Periphanes: You can have her.

Soldier: You've made a good bargain.

Periphanes: [*calling to his slaves inside the house*] Hey! Bring out the lyre-player you took inside earlier. [*talking again to the soldier*] And her lyre that came with her, I'll include it as a gift for you, no extra charge.

3.4a Scene with Periphanes, the Soldier, and the [Hired] Lyre-Player

Some unnamed slaves bring the recently hired lyre-player out of the house, and Periphanes pushes her towards the soldier.

Periphanes: There, take her please.

Soldier: Are you crazy? What kind of trick are you trying to play on me? Why don't you tell them to bring the lyre-player out here?

Periphanes: This is the lyre-player. There isn't any other one.

---

69 The soldier intends to make her his concubine (*concubina*), which involved a pseudo-conjugal relationship, but a concubine's legal status was inferior to that a wife would have. Any children they produced would not come under their father's legal power (*patria potestas*), but would be considered illegitimate.

Soldier: [*angrily*] You can't fool me. Bring Acropolistis the lyre-player out here.

Periphanes: I'm telling you this is her.

Soldier: And I'm telling you it isn't. Do you think I can't recognize my own girlfriend?

Periphanes: I'm telling you that my son was madly in love with this lyre-player.

Soldier: This isn't the right one.

Periphanes: What! She's not?!

Soldier: Nope.

Periphanes: Where in the world did she come from then?! By Hercules, I paid good money for her!

Soldier: I guess you made a bad bargain — you majorly screwed up!

Periphanes: No, this has got to be the right girl. I sent a slave — one that's always hanging around that son of mine. That slave arranged for the purchase of this lyre-player himself.

Soldier: Hah! The guy's carved you up joint by joint, old man, that slave of yours.

Periphanes: What do you mean, "carved me up"?

Soldier: That's what I suspect, since this chick[70] has been substituted for your lyre-player. [*laughing*] Old man, you've been well and truly scammed! I'm off to go look for my girlfriend, wherever she is. [*ironically*] So long, warrior. [*exit the soldier*]

Periphanes: [*angrily*] Well this is just perfect! Epidicus, quite the thrifty, dependable guy, you are.[71] You've got me beaten. You're the guy that's wiped my snotty, worthless nose. [*addressing the hired lyre-player*] Did Apoecides buy you today from the pimp?

Hired lyre-player: I've never heard of the man before today, and certainly no one could have bought me at any price: I've been a freedwoman for more than five years.

Periphanes: What are you doing at my house then?

Hired lyre-player: Listen: I was hired to come play my lyre for an old man who was going to do a religious sacrifice.

---

70 "This chick" is a translation of the Latin *haec cerua*, literally meaning "this doe".

71 "Thrifty, dependable guy": in the Latin text Periphanes called Epidicus *frugi homo*, which was a term used by masters to describe their reliable, hard-working slaves who curried favour with their masters and saved any money they made in order to eventually buy their own freedom. It is particularly impudent of Epidicus later in the play at line 693 when he condescendingly describes Apoecides as a *frugi homo* since he is applying a slave attribute to a slave owner.

Periphanes: [*groaning*] I've got to admit that I'm the most worthless of all men in Athens, or in all of Attica[72] for that matter. [*turning to the hired lyre-player*] Hey, do you know Acropolistis the lyre-player?

Hired lyre-player: I know her as well as I know myself.

Periphanes: Where does she live?

Hired lyre-player: Since she's been freed, I'm not really sure where she's living.

Periphanes: What??!! She's been freed? Who freed her, I'd like to know?

Hired lyre-player: I'll tell you what I heard, which is that Stratippocles the son of Periphanes arranged for her to be freed while he was away.

Periphanes: By Hercules, if what you say is true, I'm completely ruined! Epidicus has gutted my bank account.

Hired lyre-player: [*smirking*] Yeah, so I heard. Do you want me for anything else?

Periphanes: [*enraged*] Get out of here and go get yourself crucified!

Hired lyre-player: Aren't you going to give me back my lyre?

Periphanes: No I'm not giving it back, nor your *tibia*[73] neither. If the gods love you, you'll get out of here fast.

Hired lyre-player: I'm going, but you'll give me back my lyre or I'll make trouble for you. [*exit the lyre-player*]

Periphanes: What'll I do now? I, who've had such a good reputation,[74] am I going to let her go without any punishment? No! I'd rather lose the same amount of money again than not get my revenge on those who've laughed at me and cheated me.

[*groaning*] Oh! I've been lied to right to my face! And I've made myself look like an idiot in front of someone[75] who's considered a maker and publisher of laws and legal statements. He even refers to himself as a clever guy. [*rolling his eyes*] I've seen a broken hammer that's cleverer than him.

---

72 "Athens, or in Attica" — remember that the play is supposed to be set in Athens, which is in the region called Attica.

73 A *tibia* was, as mentioned in note 38 above, a double reed instrument, perhaps like an oboe.

74 "I, who've had such a good reputation" is a translation of *qui in tantis positus sum sententiis*, which could also mean "I, whose name has been noted down in such important senatorial decisions" (meaning that he was the proposer of such senatorial decrees).

75 This "someone" is Periphanes's friend Apoecides.

Lines 526–540b

ACT 4

4.1 Scene with Philippa and Periphanes

Philippa, a middle-aged woman, arrives onstage; she and Periphanes don't see each other at first.

Philippa: [*weeping and wringing her hands*] If a person suffers so much that she even pities herself, then she's really pitiable. I should know: so many things are coming at me at once, breaking my heart. Trouble on top of trouble keeps me in a state of worry: poverty and fear are terrorizing me, and there's no safe place where I can pin my hopes. [*sobbing*] My daughter has been captured by the enemy, and I don't know where she may be now.

Periphanes: [*catching sight of Philippa*] Who is that foreign woman, coming along looking so fearful, who's moaning and pitying herself?

Philippa: Periphanes is said to live around here.

Periphanes: She mentioned my name. I expect she's here because she needs a place to stay.[76]

Philippa: I'd give a good reward to anyone who could point the man out to me or show me where he lives.

Periphanes: I'm trying to recognize this woman. I feel like I've seen her before somewhere. Is it the woman I think it is, or not?

Philippa: [*catching sight of Periphanes*] Oh good gods! Haven't I seen this man before?

Periphanes: It's definitely her — [*reminiscing*] it was in Epidaurus, I remember jumping the bones[77] of a penniless girl there...

---

76 Periphanes guesses that Philippa needs *hospitium* (hospitality); in the ancient Mediterranean world travellers preferred to stay with people whom they knew through inherited ties of hospitality, rather than risk the dangers of a public inn.

77 "Jumping the bones" and "banged" (line 542, below) are translations of *comprimere* and *compressus*, respectively. The Latin does not make it clear whether the young Philippa consented to sex with Periphanes, or if he raped her. It is, in fact, indicative of Roman and Greek attitudes around sex that the woman's consent to a sexual encounter is less important

Philippa: [*wringing her hands and looking anxious*] This is clearly the man who took my virginity when I was a girl in Epidaurus.

Periphanes: [*delighted*] She's the one who, after I banged her, gave birth to the daughter that I now have staying in my house. Should I go up to her?

Philippa: [*continuing to speak quietly to herself*] I don't know if you're going to approach?

Periphanes: If it even is her...

Philippa: If it is the same man... it's been many years, and that makes me doubt...

Periphanes: Such a long time ago. I'm just not sure. If it is her, as I sort of think it is, I'll deal with her craftily.

Philippa: I'll have to use my womanly wiles now.

Periphanes: I will speak to her.

Philippa: I'll use my clever speaking skills against him.

Periphanes: [*using the polite formulaic greeting*] Good health to you.

Philippa: [*responding coolly*] I accept your greetings for myself and my family.

Periphanes: [*surprised*] OK, and where's the rest of the greeting?

Philippa: I'll repay what you gave me: good health to you.

Periphanes: I wasn't questioning your credit.[78] Don't I know you?

Philippa: [*cautiously*] If I know you, I'll persuade myself that you know me.

Periphanes: Where have I seen you?

Philippa: You're being unfair.

Periphanes: How so?

Philippa: Because you think I should jog your memory.

Periphanes: [*admiringly*] Nicely said.

Philippa: You say surprising things. *[some text missing]*

Periphanes: There, that's even better! Don't you remember —

---

than the fact that she had sex outside of marriage. Periphanes seems to have given Philippa some financial support at the time (see lines 555–556) which causes him to view his actions as having been beneficial to her, but the negative consequences for her of having a child outside of marriage would have been ruinous. Whether Periphanes had raped the young Philippa or not, his marrying her now would be viewed by the ancient audience as a satisfactory resolution that Philippa must welcome.

78 Philippa and Periphanes are verbally sparring; the joke is that Philippa at first failed to give back the formulaic greeting "good health to you" until Periphanes pushed for it. She then makes it clear that she's only giving him the full greeting because he gave (or lent) it to her first. Periphanes then uses the term "credit" (Latin *fides*) to compare the exchange of greetings with the repayment of a loan.

Philippa: [*interrupting*] I remember... what I remember.

Periphanes: Back in Epidaurus I mean —

Philippa: [*suddenly overcome by emotion*] Oh! That's like a little drop of water on my parched heart.

Periphanes: — that I lessened the poverty of you and your mother, when you were just a penniless young girl?

Philippa: Are you the one who gave me such terrible hardship in return for your pleasure?

Periphanes: [*unrepentant*] I'm the one! Good day to you.

Philippa: [*courteously*] It's a good day for me since I see it's a good day for you.

Periphanes: Give me your hand.[79]

Philippa: Here [*holding out her hand*]; you're taking the hand of a woman who is full of troubles and misery.

Periphanes: Why is your face so troubled?

Philippa: The daughter I bore because of you —

Periphanes: What about her?

Philippa: I raised her, and now I've lost her. She's been captured by the enemy.

Periphanes: Don't be upset; hush now. She's safe and sound here, in my house. As soon as I heard from my slave that she'd been captured, I immediately gave him the money to buy her. He did exactly that, as sensibly and prudently as [*remembering how Epidicus tricked him with the hired lyre-player*] — as he is incredibly shameless in other matters.

Philippa: [*with desperate eagerness*] If she's really my daughter let me see her, if you value my health!

Periphanes: [*calling to a slave inside his house*] Hey! Canthara, are you in there? Tell my daughter Telestis to come out here in front of the house so she can see her mother.

Philippa: At last! My spirits are restored to me.

---

79 Periphanes asking Philippa for her hand, and her giving it to him, hints at the Roman marriage ceremony in which this was done (Maurice 2006: 42; James 2020: 114).

4.2 Scene with Acropolistis, Periphanes, and Philippa

Acropolistis, whom Periphanes thinks is his illegitimate daughter Telestis, comes out of the house.

Acropolistis: What is it, father? Why did you call me outside?

Periphanes: So you can come and see your mother, and give her a greeting and a kiss.

Acropolistis: [*stalling for time*] Come and see... which mother exactly?

Periphanes: The one who's worn herself out searching for a glimpse of you.

Philippa: Who is that girl you're telling to kiss me?

Periphanes: [*rolling his eyes*] Uh, your daughter...?

Philippa: This girl?!

Periphanes: Yes, this one!

Philippa: And I'm supposed to give her a kiss?

Periphanes: Why not, you gave birth to her!

Philippa: You're crazy.

Periphanes: I'm crazy?

Philippa: Yes, you!

Periphanes: Why?

Philippa: Because I neither know nor recognize who this girl is, and I've never laid eyes on her before today.

Periphanes: I know why you're confused. She's wearing different clothes and jewelry *[some text missing]*

Philippa: *[some text missing]* puppies smell quite different from pigs.[80] I tell you that I don't know who this girl is.

Periphanes: [*realizing he's fallen for another of Epidicus's tricks*] By the god! By honesty! Why?!! Have I gotten into sex trafficking, what with keeping strange girls in my house and completely draining my bank account of so much money? [*turning on Acropolistis*] You! Calling me your father and kissing me... Why are you standing there looking stupid? Why don't you say something?

Acropolistis: What do you want me to say?

Periphanes: She [*gesturing to Philippa*] says she's not your mother.

---

[80] "Puppies smell quite different from pigs" was probably a proverbial saying, about a mother dog's sense of smell causing her to reject a piglet given to her to pass as one of her puppies in hopes that she would nurse it.

Acropolistis: She doesn't have to be, if she doesn't want to. I'll still be my mother's daughter even if she [*gesturing to Philippa*] doesn't agree. It wouldn't be fair for me to make her be my mother if she doesn't want to be.

Periphanes: Why were you calling me "father" then?

Acropolistis: That's your fault, not mine. Shouldn't I call you "father" if you call me your daughter? And I'd call this woman "mother" if she called me "daughter". She says I'm not her daughter, though, so she's clearly not my mother. Anyway, it's not my fault. I did everything I was told to do, everything Epidicus taught me.

Periphanes: I'm ruined! I've really messed up!

Acropolistis: Surely I didn't mess up, father?

Periphanes: By Hercules, if I ever hear you calling me "father" again, I'll kill you!

Acropolistis: [*soothingly*] I won't. When you want to be "father", be one; when you don't, don't be one. [*Acropolistis goes into the house*]

Philippa: If you bought her because you thought she was your daughter, what made you think you recognized her?

Periphanes: I didn't recognize her.

Philippa: Then why did you believe she was our daughter?

Periphanes: My slave Epidicus said she was.

Philippa: Just because your slave made a mistake, shouldn't you have been smarter, for the gods' sake?

Periphanes: How could I, since I never saw her after that first time?[81]

Philippa: [*sobbing*] It's hopeless!

Periphanes: Stop crying, woman. Go indoors and try to keep up your spirits. I will find our daughter.

Philippa: An Athenian citizen from here in Athens bought her. They told me that it was a young man that bought her.

Periphanes: I'll find her. Hush now. Just go indoors and keep an eye on this Circe, daughter of the Sun.[82] [*Philippa goes into the house*] I'll deal with the other business later. First I'll focus on finding Epidicus. If I find him [*hitting his clenched right fist into his left palm menacingly*], I'll make this day his last. [*Periphanes strides off stage left, towards the forum*]

---

81 Periphanes apparently saw his daughter when she was a baby but hasn't seen her since. We know, however, that Epidicus saw her relatively recently, as he mentions at lines 639–640.

82 Circe was a sorceress in Greek mythology who lured the hero Odysseus to her bed (as told in Homer's *Odyssey*).

ACT 5

5.1 Scene with Stratippocles, Epidicus, the Moneylender, and Telestis

Stratippocles: [*annoyed*] The moneylender isn't very obliging to me. He's not coming to get his money from me, and he's not bringing the girl I bought from my war booty. But look! There's Epidicus coming. Why's his forehead all frowny with worry?

Epidicus: [*whimpering*] If Jupiter brought all the eleven other gods along with him they still couldn't save Epidicus from what's coming to him.[83] I saw Periphanes, with Apoecides, buying the leather straps.[84] I think they're looking for me now. They've figured it out, they know they were tricked.

Stratippocles: What are you up to, my useful one?

Epidicus: What someone who's completely screwed would be up to, that's what.

Stratippocles: What's the matter with you?

Epidicus: [*desperately*] Why don't you give me what I'll need to run away before I get killed? Those two old men I cheated are looking for me throughout the city, carrying leather thongs in their hands too!

Stratippocles: Cheer up!

Epidicus: [*sarcastically*] Yeah, you say that like I'm about to be set free!

Stratippocles: I'll keep you safe.

Epidicus: By Pollux, those old men will keep me even safer, if they catch me. [*seeing the moneylender and a beautiful young woman arriving from the harbour*] But who's this young woman and the little old man that are coming along?

---

83 "What's coming to him" (Latin *cruciatus*): Epidicus refers to the torture in store for slaves who have really angered their masters.

84 The leather straps were for tying up a slave before inflicting punishment.

Stratippocles: That's the moneylender, and SHE'S the one I bought with my war winnings.

Epidicus: That's her?

Stratippocles: [*sighing ecstatically*] Yes, that's her! Isn't she just as I described? Look at her, gaze at her, Epidicus! From her toes to the top of her head she's stunning. Isn't she just like a beautifully painted statue when you look at her?

Epidicus: You might as well be foretelling that my skin's going to be beautiful, since those two great artists Apelles and Zeuxis[85] are going to mark me up with elmwood rods.

Stratippocles: [*addressing the moneylender angrily*] By the immortal gods, did I tell you to take your time like this? A man with feet made of lead would have come before you got here.

Moneylender: She [*jerking a thumb at the young woman*] slowed me down, by Pollux.

Stratippocles: [*tenderly looking at her*] Well, if you went slow for her sake, because she wanted it, you went too quickly.

Moneylender: Come on, just pay up the money you owe me, so I don't hold up my associates.

Stratippocles: I've already got it set aside.

Moneylender: Take my moneybag and put it in here.

Stratippocles: You come well prepared. Wait till I bring the money out to you.

Moneylender: Be quick about it.

Stratippocles: It's in my house. [*he goes into his house.*]

Epidicus: [*staring at the young woman*] Do I still have proper use of my eyes, or not? Is it you that I see, Telestis, daughter of Periphanes? Born to her mother Philippa at Thebes, conceived at Epidaurus?

Telestis: Who are you, who mention my mother's name, and my name?

Epidicus: Don't you recognize me?

Telestis: Not that I can remember right now.

Epidicus: Don't you remember that I brought you a little gold moon pendant on your birthday, and a little gold ring for your finger?[86]

---

85 Apelles and Zeuxis were two famous Greek painters from the fourth and fifth centuries BCE respectively. Epidicus is referring to Periphanes and Apoecides, whom he knows are planning to beat him and thus make the skin of his back brightly coloured from the blows.

86 Epidicus must have been in Thebes no more than a few years before and was presumably commissioned by Periphanes to bring Telestis some birthday gifts. Romans celebrated birthdays, whereas ordinary Greeks did not (Jocelyn 2001: 283).

Telestis: [*with tears of joy*] I remember! You're the one?

Epidicus: I am! And this guy who just bought you is your brother. *[some text missing]* you've the same father, but different mothers.[87]

Telestis: [*very excited and anxious*] What about my father? Is he alive?

Epidicus: Hush, don't worry about that!

Telestis: The gods truly want to save me, if you are telling me the truth.

Epidicus: I have no reason to lie to you.

Stratippocles: [*coming out of the house*] Here, take this, moneylender. Here's forty *minae*. If you're suspicious about any of the coins, I'll exchange them.

Moneylender: That's fine. Bye! [*exit the moneylender*].

Stratippocles: [*looking lustfully at Telestis and taking her by the hand*] Now you are mine!

Telestis: [*hastily*] I'm your sister, by Pollux! Just so you know. Hello, brother!

Stratippocles: [*to Epidicus*] Is she crazy?

Epidicus: She's perfectly sane, if she's calling you her brother.

Stratippocles: What! How have I turned into her brother just by going into and then out of my house?!!

Epidicus: You can just keep quiet and be happy about what's happened.

Stratippocles: [*groaning*] You've lost me,[88] and you've found me, sister.

Epidicus: [*in a fierce whisper*] Shut up, stupid! There's a perfectly good lyre-player for you, who's already living in your house thanks to me — and I've got your sister her freedom too.

Stratippocles: Epidicus, I have to say —

---

87 Some scholars think that the original Greek play that Plautus adapted ended with a marriage between Telestis and her half-brother Stratippocles, which was considered acceptable in Greek culture. Such a marriage would have been considered incest by the Romans, however, so, according to this theory, Plautus changed the plot, and avoided concluding with a marriage. The line "you've the same father, but different mothers" suggests the title of two lost Greek comedies, known only by title, called *Homopatrioi* (Ὁμοπάτριοι), or "Having the Same Father", one by Antiphanes and the other by Menander (Katsouris 1977: 321). Speculation about this possible Greek original is less in vogue nowadays.

88 "You've lost me": in the Latin this has a double meaning. Stratippocles means both that she lost him (by the circumstances of her birth and thus not growing up with her half-brother) and that she's ruined his hopes for a sexual relationship with her by turning out to be his half-sister.

Epidicus: Go inside and order a hot bath for her. I'll fill you in later on everything else, when I have time.

Stratippocles: [*meekly obeying his slave*] Follow me, sister.

Epidicus: I'll tell Thesprio to help you. But remember, if the old man gets really angry you and your sister need to help me out.

Stratippocles: Yeah, yeah, no problem. [*Stratippocles goes into his house*]

Epidicus: [*calling into Periphanes's house*] Thesprio! Come out here, through the garden! Help me out over here. It's important.

[*talking to himself*] I'm not as worried about those old men as I was before. I'll go indoors and fill Stratippocles in on everything that's happened. I'm not going to try to run away. I'm determined to stay home, so my master won't be able to claim I provoked him by running away. In I go — I've been talking too long. [*Epidicus follows Stratippocles into the house*]

5.2 Scene with Periphanes, Apoecides, and Epidicus

Periphanes and Apoecides arrive on stage from the direction of the forum (stage left). They don't see Epidicus at first.

Periphanes: That slave of mine has really been making fools of us two old farts, hasn't he?

Apoecides: [*panting*] By Pollux, it's you that's been screwing me around with your stupid plans.

Periphanes: Oh be quiet. Just let me catch that man!

Apoecides: I'm letting you know now: find some other friend than me. I've got swelling joints in my poor knees from chasing around after you.

Periphanes: He's made fools of you and me in countless ways today. And the way he emptied my money chest!

Apoecides: Just keep him away from me! He's a son of the fire god Vulcan. Whatever he touches burns right up. If you're near him, he scorches you with his fire.

Epidicus: [*speaking out of the old men's hearing*] All the immortal gods in heaven plus another twelve are lined up in military order to help me out now.[89] No matter what I've done wrong, I've got help and support here at home. I give that [*making a kicking motion*] to all my enemies.

Periphanes: Where in the world will I find that slave?

Apoecides: So long as you look for him without involving me, for all I care you can look in the middle of the sea even.

Epidicus: [*walking up to them unconcernedly*] Why are you going to such trouble looking for me? Why are you worrying this guy [*gesturing to Apoecides*]? Here I am. I haven't run away, have I? I'm not absent without leave, am I? I'm not out of your sight, am I?

[some text missing] I'm not begging you to pardon me. Do you want to put me in bonds? Here are my hands [*holding out his hands as though ready to be handcuffed*]. You've got the leather straps, because I saw you buy them. Why are you backing away? Tie my hands.

Periphanes: [*confused*] It's no use — he's practically offering me bail!

Epidicus: Why aren't you going to bind me?

Apoecides: By Pollux, what a shameless slave you own!

Epidicus: [*teasing*] No really, Apoecides, you don't need to intercede for me.

Apoecides: [*sarcastically*] OK, you've easily persuaded me not to, Epidicus.

Epidicus: Are you going to do anything, or not?

Periphanes: What, to please you?

Epidicus: By Hercules, yes, it's not to please you that these hands of mine should be tied up today.

Periphanes: [*looking sulky*] Well, I don't feel like tying your hands.

Apoecides: [*warningly*] He's about to skewer you — he's up to some sort of trick.

Epidicus: You're wasting time, while I'm standing around, free to move around. [*doing a few impudent jumping jacks*] Go on, I say — put me under restraint.

Periphanes: [*stiffly*] I'd prefer to interrogate you while you're not under restraint.

Epidicus: Then I won't tell you anything.

Periphanes: [*hissing to Apoecides*] What should I do?

---

89 In line 610 Epidicus complained that the mere twelve Olympian gods couldn't save him; now that he has been saved (by his discovery of the real Telestis), he claims that an extra twelve

Apoecides: What should you do? Do what he wants.

Epidicus: [*patronizingly*] You're a thrifty, dependable guy, well done Apoecides![90]

Periphanes: OK, hold out your hands.

Epidicus: [*holding them out*] My hands have no objection! Tie them tightly now, have no mercy!

Periphanes: Keep your advice till I've finished! [*tying Epidicus's hands together*]

Epidicus: [*approvingly*] Nicely done. Now interrogate me. Ask me whatever you want.

Periphanes: What kind of impudence made you dare to claim that the slave-girl you bought the day before yesterday was my daughter?

Epidicus: Well, I felt like it. That's what kind of impudence made me dare to do it.

Periphanes: What are you saying? You "felt like it"?!

Epidicus: Yup. If you want we can have a bet on whether or not she's the daughter.

Periphanes: Oh come on, when the mother doesn't even recognize her?

Epidicus: I'll bet you a sestertius against sixty *minae*[91] that she's her mother's daughter.

Periphanes: [*muttering anxiously*] It's a trick, I know it is. [*aloud*] But who IS the woman?

Epidicus: [*sighing*] She's your son's girlfriend, OK?

Periphanes: Didn't I give you the thirty *minae* to buy my daughter?

Epidicus: Well, yes, I admit that you gave me the money, and that I used it to buy your son's lyre-player girlfriend instead of your daughter. So I cheated you out of thirty *minae*.

Periphanes: You made a total fool of me with that hired lyre-player, too!

Epidicus: [*smirking*] By Hercules, I did, and I was right to do so.

Periphanes: What did you do with the money[92] I gave you?

---

gods have rallied to his side, along with the standard twelve Olympian gods.

90   Epidicus here patronizingly calls Apoecides a *frugi homo*, which is what masters called their hard-working slaves who saved their money in order to eventually buy their freedom (see note 71 on page 157).

91   "I'll bet you a sestertius against sixty *minae*" is a translation of *in meum nummum, in tuom talentum pignus da*, which translated more literally means "bet me a talent (26–32.5kg of silver, or about sixty *minae*) for a coin (of unknown but not high value)".

92   "The money" is the fifty *minae* Periphanes gave Epidicus in lines 296–297.

Epidicus: Well, I'll tell you: I gave it to someone who's not a bad guy — and not a great guy either... I gave it to your son Stratippocles.

Periphanes: How DARE you?!

Epidicus: Well, I felt like it.

Periphanes: What is all this shamelessness, you worthless scum!

Epidicus: Why am I getting yelled at, just as though I were a slave?

Periphanes: [*with exaggerated sarcasm*] Oh, well, if you're a free man, I'm very happy for you!

Epidicus: I've certainly earned my freedom.

Periphanes: You? You've earned it?!

Epidicus: Go indoors: I promise you'll find out that I have.

Periphanes: What IS all this?

Epidicus: [*looking smug*] You'll find out. Just go indoors.

Apoecides: Oh go on [*gesturing towards Periphanes's house*]. There must be some explanation in there.

Periphanes: Keep watch on him, Apoecides [*goes indoors*].

Apoecides: What's going on, Epidicus?

Epidicus: [*looking hurt*] I'm standing here most unfairly, by Hercules, with my hands tied, when today, by my own efforts, I found this daughter of his.

Apoecides: [*stunned*] Are you telling me you've found his daughter?

Epidicus: I found her, and she's here in the house. But [*looking plaintive*] it's a bit much when a person gets this sort of reward [*gesturing to his tied hands*] for doing a good deed.

Apoecides: [*still incredulous*] You mean that girl we exhausted ourselves looking for in the city today?

Epidicus: Well, I exhausted myself FINDING her, you exhausted yourselves LOOKING for her.

Periphanes: [*coming out of his house but speaking to his son, and to Telestis and Philippa, who are still indoors*] Why are you pleading for him so much? I realize that I need to treat him as he deserves. [*to Epidicus*] Hold out your hands so I can untie them.

Epidicus: [*turning a shoulder coldly*] Don't you touch them.

Periphanes: Just hold them out.

Epidicus: I won't.

Periphanes: [*pleading*] Now, you're not being fair.

Epidicus: By Hercules, I'll never let you untie me today unless you beg my pardon.

Periphanes: [*eager to please*] You ask what is very reasonable and good. I'll give you some indoor shoes, a tunic, and a cloak!

Epidicus: And...?

Periphanes: [*hastily*] And your freedom.

Epidicus: And...? A newly freed slave has still got to eat.

Periphanes: Granted! I'll see you're fed.[93]

Epidicus: [*still refusing to relent*] By Hercules, you'll never untie me today unless you beg me.

Periphanes: [*meekly*] I beg you, Epidicus, to forgive me, if I unknowingly did wrong because of my own fault. Because of it, I declare you to be a free man.

Epidicus: [*grudgingly*] Well... I don't want to forgive you, except that I'm forced by necessity. [*holding out his hands condescendingly*] Untie me, however, if you want to.

All the actors in unison: [*pushing the actor who played Epidicus to the front of the stage to take a bow*] This is a man who won his freedom thanks to his bad behaviour! Give us a round of applause now, and fare well. Get up and stretch your loins!

THE END

---

[93] A former master was supposed to continue to look after his freed slaves (and the freed slaves owed them specific duties in return), but some former masters abandoned their freed slaves to fend for themselves. Epidicus is insisting on Periphanes behaving toward him as he ought.

Argumentum (Plot Summary)

The argumentum (plot summary) usually given at the beginning of the play was composed centuries after Plautus (perhaps around 150 CE). It formed an acrostic, whereby the first letter of each line spells out the title of the play. The acrostic has to be extremely concise, given that there are only eight letters in the name Epidicus.

Emit[1] fidicinam,[2] filiam credens, senex

Persuasu[3] serui, atque conductam[4]

Iterum[5] pro[6] amica ei[7] subiecit[8] filii.

Dat erili[9] argentum. eo[10] sororem destinat[11]

Inprudens[12] iuuenis. compressae[13] ac militis

Cognoscit[14] opera[15] sibi senex os sublitum[16]

(**V**t[17] ille[18] amicam, haec[19] quaerebat[20] filiam),

Sed inuenta[21] gnata[22] seruolum[23] emittit manu.[24]

Translation notes appear on the following page

1   *ēmit* (third-person perfect active indicative) < *emo, -ere, emi, emptum*: "buy".

2   *fidicina, -ae* (f.): a woman trained in playing the lyre, who was usually a slave or freedwoman and who was assumed, like all female performers, to be a sex worker.

3   *persuasus, -us* (m.): "persuasion", "inducement".

4   *conductus, -a, -um*: "hired".

5   *iterum* (adverb): "in turn", "again".

6   *pro*: "instead of", "in place of" (+ ablative).

7   *ei* (dative of reference, referring to the old man).

8   *subicio, -ere, subieci, subjectum*: "substitute" (the slave is the subject of this verb).

9   *erilis, -e* (adjective): "relating to the *erus* (master)"; here referring to the young master, or master's son, Stratippocles.

10   *eo* (ablative of means, referring to the money).

11   *destino, -are, -aui, -atum*: "intend to buy".

12   *inprudens/imprudens, inprudentis/imprudentis*: "unknowing", "oblivious".

13   *compressae*: "of a woman he'd had sex with" (< *comprimo, -ere, -essi, -essum*: "[of a male] have sexual intercourse with [someone]"; the passive, and possibly non consenting role of the woman is assumed with this verb.

14   *cognosco, -ere, cognoui, cognitum*: "find out".

15   *operā*: "thanks to the efforts of [*compressae ac militis*]".

16   *cognoscit ... sibi senex os sublitum*: "the old man finds out that he has been made a fool of"; *alicui os sublinere* literally means "to smear someone's face", but figuratively means "to make a fool of someone", "outwit someone".

17   *ut*: "as", "considering that".

18   *ille* (referring to the soldier).

19   *haec* (referring to the *compressa* mentioned above in line 5, that is, the woman with whom the old man had had a sexual encounter in the past).

20   *quaero, -ere, quaesiui, quaesitum*: "seek", "look for" (the verb is used twice, once with the subject *ille* and object *amicam*, and a second time with the subject *haec* and the object *filiam*).

21   *inuentā* (ablative feminine singular perfect passive participle) < *uenio, -ire, inueni, inuentum*: "find".

22   *gnatā* (ablative singular) < *gnata, -ae* (f.): "daughter".

23   *seruolus, -i* (m.): "young/mere/worthless slave".

24   *manu emittere aliquem*: "to set someone free", "to emancipate someone".

Acrostic Translation of the *Argumentum*

Entrapped by his trickster slave, an old man

Purchased a lyre-playing slave-girl thinking she was his daughter.

In place of the young master's girlfriend, meanwhile, the slave brings back a

Day-hire musician and gives money to the son to buy a different slave-girlfriend,

Ignorant of the fact that she's his sister. The old man's former sweetheart appears,

Crying for their lost daughter (whom a soldier hopes to buy). The old man is

Upset at being fooled, but when he realizes that he has found his daughter he's

So happy he rewards the slave with freedom.

Literal Translation of the *Argumentum*

Note: for the purposes of clarity, the names of the characters are added in parentheses, and, where needed, pronouns are replaced by proper nouns in square brackets.

Believing her to be his daughter (Telestis), an old man (Periphanes) bought a lyre-playing slave girl (Acropolistis) since he was tricked by his slave (Epidicus); the slave then substituted a freelance lyre-player for the son's girlfriend (Acropolistis). [The slave Epidicus] gives money to the young master (Stratippocles). The young man (Stratippocles) unknowingly buys his own sister (Telestis). The old man (Periphanes) finds out he's been fooled thanks to the efforts of his former sweetheart (Philippa) and a soldier, as she was seeking their daughter (Telestis) and the soldier was looking for a girlfriend (Telestis). But when his daughter (Telestis) is found, [the old man Periphanes] sets the young slave (Epidicus) free.

Works Cited

Allen, Joseph Henry, and J. B. Greenough. 1931. *Allen and Greenough's New Latin Grammar for Schools and Colleges*. Boston and London: Ginn & Company.

Anderson, William S. 1996. *Barbarian Play: Plautus' Roman Comedy*. Toronto: University of Toronto Press.

Arnott, W. Geoffrey. 2001. "Plautus' *Epidicus* and Greek Comedy", in Ulrike Auhagen (ed.). *Studien zu Plautus'* Epidicus. Tübingen: G. Narr.

Barbiero, Emilia. [forthcoming]. *Letters in Plautus: Reading Between the Lines*. Cambridge: Cambridge University Press.

Barrios-Lech, Peter. 2014. "Of Calves and (Old) Men: A Pun at *Epidicus* 187 and 666." *Mnemosyne* 67.3, 458–465, https://doi.org/10.1163/1568525x-12341323

Barrios-Lech, Peter. 2020. "The Language of Plautus", in Dorota Dutsch and George Fredric Franko (eds). *A Companion to Plautus*. Hoboken, NJ: Wiley-Blackwell, 221–235.

Bennett, Charles E. 1918. *New Latin Grammar*, http://www.thelatinlibrary.com/bennett.html.

Burton, Paul J. 2020. "Warfare and Imperialism in and Around Plautus", in Dorota Dutsch and George Fredric Franko (eds). *A Companion to Plautus*. Hoboken, NJ: Wiley-Blackwell, 301–316, https://doi.org/10.1002/9781118958018.ch20

de Melo, Wolfgang, and Titus Maccius Plautus. 2011. *Casina; The Casket Comedy; Curculio; Epidicus ; The Two Menaechmuses*. Cambridge, Mass: Harvard University Press.

de Melo, Wolfgang. 2013. "The Language of Roman Comedy", in James Clackson (ed.). *A Companion to the Latin Language*. Chichester, West Sussex: Wiley-Blackwell, 321–343, https://doi.org/10.1002/9781444343397.ch19

Donatus, Aelius, and Paul Wessner. 1962. *Commentum Terenti* 1 1. Stvtgardiae: Teubner.

Duckworth, George E., Arthur Leslie Wheeler, and Titus Maccius Plautus. 1940. *Epidicus*. Princeton: Princeton University Press.

Duckworth, George E. 1942. *The Complete Roman Drama. All the Extant Comedies of Plautus and Terence, and the Tragedies of Seneca, in a Variety of Translations*. New York: Random House.

Dutsch, Dorota M. 2008. *Feminine Discourse in Roman Comedy: On Echoes and Voices*. Oxford: Oxford University Press, https://doi.org/10.1093/acprof:oso/9780199533381.001.0001

Ernout, Alfred. 1965. *Plaute, tome III: Cistellaria, Curculio, Epidicus*. Paris: Société d'Édition "Les Belles Lettres".

Fitzgerald, William. 2019. "Slaves and Roman Comedy", in Martin T. Dinter (ed.). *The Cambridge Companion to Roman Comedy*. Cambridge: Cambridge University Press, 188–199, https://doi.org/10.1017/9780511740466.013

Gaca, Kathy L. 2011. "Chapter 4. Girls, Women, and the Significance of Sexual Violence in Ancient Warfare" in Elizabeth D. Heineman (ed.). *Sexual Violence in Conflict Zones: From the Ancient World to the Era of Human Rights*. Philadelphia: University of Pennsylvania Press, 73–88, https://doi.org/10.9783/9780812204346.73

Gellar-Goad, T. H. M. 2012. "The *Servus Callidus* and Ritual Imagery in Plautus' *Epidicus*". *The Classical Journal* 107.2, 149–164, https://doi.org/10.5184/classicalj.107.2.0149

Goldberg, Sander M. 1978. "Plautus' Epidicus and the Case of the Missing Original". *Transactions of the American Philological Association* 108: 81–91, https://doi.org/10.2307/284238

Goldberg, Sander M. 1998. "Plautus on the Palatine". *The Journal of Roman Studies* 88: 1–20, https://doi.org/10.2307/300802

Erik Gunderson. 2015. *Laughing Awry: Plautus and Tragicomedy*. Oxford: Oxford University Press, https://doi.org/10.1093/acprof:oso/9780198729303.001.0001

Halporn, James W., Martin Ostwald, and Thomas G. Rosenmeyer. 1994. *The Meters of Greek and Latin Poetry*. Indianapolis: Hackett Publishing.

Harley, Felicity. 2019. "Crucifixion in Roman Antiquity: The State of the Field." *Journal of Early Christian Studies* 27.2, 303–323, https://doi.org/10.1353/earl.2019.0022

Hodgman, Arthur Winfred. 1907. "Verb Forms in Plautus". *The Classical Quarterly* 1.1, 42–52.

Hunt, Peter. 2018. *Ancient Greek and Roman Slavery*. Hoboken, NJ: Wiley-Blackwell, https://doi.org/10.15291/misc.2751

"Italie." *L'Année épigraphique* 1971 (1974): 25–49.

James, Sharon L. 2020. "Plautus and the Marriage Plot", in Dorota Dutsch and George Fredric Franko (eds). *A Companion to Plautus*. Hoboken, NJ: Wiley-Blackwell, 109–121, https://doi.org/10.1002/9781118958018.ch7

Jocelyn, Henry David. 2001. "Gods, Cult and Cultic Language", in Ulrike Auhagen (ed.). *Studien zu Plautus' Epidicus*. Tübingen: G. Narr.

Keyes, Clinton W. 1940. "Half-Sister Marriage in New Comedy and the Epidicus". *Transactions and Proceedings of the American Philological Association* 71: 217, https://doi.org/10.2307/283124

Kocur, Mirosław. 2018. *The Power of Theater: Actors and Spectators in Ancient Rome*. Interdisciplinary Studies in Performance, Vol. 11. Frankfurt am Main: Peter Lang, https://doi.org/10.3726/978-3-653-06853-5

Lindsay, W. M. and Titus Maccius Plautus. 1903. *T. Macci Plavti: Comoediae (Tomus I)*. Oxonii: E. Typographeo Clarendoniano.

Lindsay, W. M. 1904. *The Ancient Editions of Plautus*. Oxford: J. Parker and Co.

Manuwald, Gesine. 2010. *Roman Drama: A Reader*. London: Duckworth.

Marshall, C. W. 2006. *The Stagecraft and Performance of Roman Comedy*. Cambridge, UK: Cambridge University Press.

Maurice, Lisa. 2006. "'*Epidicus Mihi Fuit Magister*': Structure and Metatheatricality in Plautus' 'Epidicus'". *Scholia: Studies in Classical Antiquity* 15: 35–52.

McCarthy, Kathleen. 2000. *Slaves, Masters, and the Art of Authority*. Princeton: Princeton University Press, https://doi.org/10.1515/9781400824700

McElduff, Siobhán. 2013. *Roman Theories of Translation: Surpassing the Source*. New York: Routledge, https://doi.org/10.4324/9780203588611

Moore, Timothy. 1998. *The Theater of Plautus*. Austin: University of Texas Press.

Moore, Timothy. 2013. "Don't Skip the Meter! Introducing Students to the Music of Roman Comedy". *The Classical Journal* 108 (2): 218–234, https://doi.org/10.5184/classicalj.108.2.0218

Omitowoju, Rosanna. 2009. *Rape and the Politics of Consent in Classical Athens*. Cambridge: Cambridge University Press.

Parker, Holt. 1989. "Crucially Funny or Tranio on the Couch: The *Servus Callidus* and Jokes about Torture". *Transactions of the American Philological Association* 119: 233–246, https://doi.org/10.2307/284273

Raven, D. S. 2001. *Latin Metre*. Bristol: Bristol Classical Press.

Richlin, Amy, and Plautus. 2005. *Rome and the Mysterious Orient: Three Plays by Plautus*. Berkeley: University of California Press.

Richlin, Amy. 2017. *Slave Theater in the Roman Republic: Plautus and Popular Comedy*. Cambridge: Cambridge University Press, https://doi.org/10.1017/9781316585467

Richlin, Amy. 2020. "Owners and Slaves in and Around Plautus", in Dorota Dutsch and George Fredric Franko (eds). *A Companion to Plautus*. Hoboken, NJ: Wiley-Blackwell, 347–359, https://doi.org/10.1002/9781118958018.ch23

Riley, Henry T. and Titus Maccius Plautus. 1852. *The Comedies of Plautus. Vol. 2*. London: Bohn.

Rosivach, Vincent J. 1998. *When A Young Man Falls in Love: The Sexual Exploitation of Women in New Comedy*. London: Routledge.

Schmidt, Karl. 1902. "Die Griechischen Personennamen Bei Plautus. I." *Hermes* 37.2: 173–211.

Sear, Frank. 2006. *Roman Theatres: An Architectural Study. Oxford Monographs on Classical Archaeology*. Oxford: Oxford University Press.

Slater, Niall. 2001. "Appearance, Reality, and the Spectre of Incest in *Epidicus*", in Ulrike Auhagen (ed.). *Studien zu Plautus' Epidicus*. Tübingen: Narr, 191–203.

Stürner, Ferdinand. 2020. "The *Servus Callidus* in Charge: Plays of Deception", in Dorota Dutsch and George Fredric Franko. *A Companion to Plautus*. Hoboken, NJ: Wiley-Blackwell, 135–149, https://doi.org/10.1002/9781118958018.ch9

Willcock, Malcolm. 1995. "Plautus and the *Epidicus*", in R. Brock, and A. J. Woodman (eds). *Papers of the Leeds International Latin Seminar, Eighth Volume, 1995: Roman Comedy, Augustan Poetry, Historiography*. Leeds: F. Cairns, 19–29.

Witzke, Serena S. 2020. "Gender and Sexuality in Plautus", in Dorota Dutsch and George Fredric Franko (eds). *A Companion to Plautus*. Hoboken, NJ: Wiley-Blackwell, 331–346, https://doi.org/10.1002/9781118958018.ch22

Index

References to notes

Actors 1
Audience 134, 153, 160

Date of the play's first production 142, 151
Debt 41, 133, 160

Fabula palliata 1
Fasces 38, 131
Freed slaves 172

Greek source of the play 2, 167

Lictors 38, 131

Marriage 12, 160–161, 167
Money 41, 133

Names in Plautus 125, 149

Other genres of Roman/Italian comedy
  Fabula togata 1

Patria potestas (paternal power) 85, 156

Praetor (Roman magistrate) 38, 131

Rape in Roman comedy 12–13, 159–160
Religion 55–56, 68, 74, 81, 137, 140, 150

Slavery 146
  Deracination 73, 150
  Punishment of slaves 48, 130, 134, 136, 137, 165
    Crucifixion 43, 134
    Jokes about punishment and torture 37, 130, 134
Stock characters 147
Swearing 119, 131, 136

Warfare 74, 131, 146, 150, 153
Women in Plautus
  Concubinage 85, 142, 156
  Passivity 174
  Sex workers 40, 58, 142, 174

References appearing in the main text

Actors 9, 16–17, 27
Audience 2–3, 5–6, 8–12, 16–17, 120
  Slaves in the audience 5–6, 17, 120
  Women in the audience 8–9, 17

Debt 4, 11, 13

Early Latin 21

Fabula palliata 1–2, 5, 12, 119
Fasces 10

Greek source of the play 2, 15

Infamia 8

Lictors 10

Marriage 2, 6–8, 12–15
Meter 24, 27–29, 122

Other genres of Roman/Italian comedy
  Atellan farce 2
  Fabula togata 11–12
  Mime 2, 9

Pater familias 7, 11
Patria potestas (paternal power) 11–12
Praetor (Roman magistrate) 9–10, 131

Rape in Roman comedy 8, 12
Religion 11, 16–17, 119, 140, 147, 150, 157
Roman theatrical productions 16–17

Slavery 1, 3–11, 16–17, 120
    Comic slave's domination of master 5–6
    Deracination 4, 10–11
    Punishment of slaves 3–5, 13–15, 120
        Crucifixion 4–5, 120
        Jokes about punishment and torture 4–5
    Sexual abuse 4, 7–8, 10
Stock characters 1, 7, 10

Swearing 11, 119

Warfare 3, 7, 10–11
Women in Plautus 6–9
    Concubinage 8, 15
    Passivity 7–8
    Played by masked male actors 9
    Sex workers 6, 7, 8, 10, 120

About the Team

Alessandra Tosi was the managing editor for this book.

Adele Kreager performed the copy-editing and proofreading.

Anna Gatti designed the cover. The cover was produced in InDesign using the Fontin font.

Luca Baffa typeset the book in InDesign and produced the paperback and hardback editions. The text font is Tex Gyre Pagella; the heading font is Californian FB. Luca produced the EPUB, AZW3, PDF, HTML, and XML editions — the conversion is performed with open source software freely available on our GitHub page (https://github.com/OpenBookPublishers).

This book need not end here...

Share

All our books — including the one you have just read — are free to access online so that students, researchers and members of the public who can't afford a printed edition will have access to the same ideas. This title will be accessed online by hundreds of readers each month across the globe: why not share the link so that someone you know is one of them?

This book and additional content is available at:

https://doi.org/10.11647/OBP.0269

Customise

Personalise your copy of this book or design new books using OBP and third-party material. Take chapters or whole books from our published list and make a special edition, a new anthology or an illuminating coursepack. Each customised edition will be produced as a paperback and a downloadable PDF.

Find out more at:

https://www.openbookpublishers.com/section/59/1

Like Open Book Publishers

Follow @OpenBookPublish

Read more at the Open Book Publishers BLOG

You may also be interested in:

Plato's *Republic*
An Introduction
Sean McAleer

https://doi.org/10.11647/OBP.0229

Virgil, *Aeneid* 11 (Pallas & Camilla), 1–224, 498–521, 532–96, 648–89, 725–835.
Latin Text, Study Aids with Vocabulary, and Commentary
Ingo Gildenhard and John Henderson

https://doi.org/10.11647/OBP.0158

Ovid, *Metamorphoses*, 3.511-733.
Latin Text with Introduction, Commentary, Glossary of Terms, Vocabulary Aid and Study Question
Ingo Gildenhard and Andrew Zissos

https://doi.org/10.11647/OBP.0073

www.ingramcontent.com/pod-product-compliance
Lightning Source LLC
Chambersburg PA
CBHW081159230426
43666CB00016B/2867